# THE
# LEADER'S
# MENTOR

# THE
# LEADER'S
# MENTOR

## Inspiration from the World's Most Effective Leaders

**Ian Jackman,**
editor

RANDOM HOUSE
REFERENCE

New York  Toronto  London  Sydney  Auckland

Library of Congress Cataloging-in-Publication Data is available.

Visit the Random House Reference Web site: www.randomwords.com

Cover design by Nora Rosansky

Text design by Tina Malaney

Text composition by North Market Street Graphics

Printed in the United States of America

ISBN: 0-375-72062-6

10   9   8   7   6   5   4   3   2   1

# CONTENTS

1   Introduction
5   Characteristics of Leadership

## Part I: What is Leadership?

11   Leadership Theories
21   Leadership: Challenge and Opportunity
31   Vision
43   Leaders and Followers
55   Leaders and Managers
61   Learning to be a Leader
73   Anyone Can be a Leader

## Part II: How Do Leaders Lead?

85    It Starts With You
97    Business Leaders
111   Military Leaders
129   Sports Leaders
145   Political Leaders
159   Revolutionary Leaders
167   Spiritual Leaders
179   Intellectual Leaders
191   Bad Leaders and Bad Leadership

## Part III: Effective Leaders: What Can They Teach Us?

205   Winston Churchill
215   George S. Patton and Dwight D. Eisenhower
227   Vince Lombardi
237   Mohandas K. Gandhi and Dr. Martin Luther King, Jr.
249   Women CEOs
261   The Soldiers of Omaha Beach
271   Rosa Parks

279   Bibliography and Sources
303   Index
313   Acknowledgments

# INTRODUCTION

Judging by the amount of published literature on the subjects, we're fascinated by leaders and leadership. Often a leadership book will comment on the sheer volume of other leadership books as the author mounts a defense as to why this particular contribution is necessary. Truth is, there are as many different leadership situations as there are leaders and each one of those situations could be turned into a book. The millions of Americans who lead in their jobs, community work, sports teams, elected offices, and so on display various skills and styles of leadership to greater or lesser effect. While each leader can contribute to the literature, there are few leaders who couldn't use a little help themselves.

Leadership is often daunting. Because every situation is different, there is no foolproof, one-size-fits-all approach to learning the ropes. Instead there are a dizzying number of competing ideas and theories which you may find contradictory. The leadership authority James McGregor Burns notes that "Leadership is one of the most observed and least understood phenomena on earth." The quest for enlightenment continues unabated.

Many leadership books (and seminars, tapes, conferences etc.) come from very high-profile leaders. Former New York City Mayor Rudolph Giuliani wrote a best-seller called *Leadership*. Countless CEOs have weighed in: Jack Welch, Larry Bossidy, Andrew Grove, Louis Gerstner. There are sports coaches writing on leadership, like Dean Smith, Mike Krzyzewski, Don Shula, and Joe Torre. Amid legions of politicians and generals are the specialists and academics who give us their seven laws, eight laws and nine laws of leadership, as well as their seventeen laws, twenty-one laws, and fifty laws. There are books extrapolated from the lives of leaders who didn't write about leadership: American icons such as Abraham Lincoln, various Civil War generals, and the Founding Fathers; Irish-born explorer Ernest Shackleton, British statesman Winston Churchill, and American General George S. Patton, for example, and also ancients like Attila the Hun and Alexander the Great who might have been surprised to see themselves held up as examples. There are even leadership books from people who don't exist: fictional characters like *The Sopranos'* Mafia boss Tony Soprano, or Captain Jean-Luc Picard of *Star Trek: The Next Generation* (who won't even enter Starfleet Academy until the year 2323).

There is one constant among nearly all these books. For

years, leadership experts have been telling us that leaders are less effective now than in the past.

> " 'Leadership' is a word on everyone's lips. The young attack it and the old grow wistful for it. Parents have lost it and police seek it. Experts claim it and artists spurn it, while scholars want it. Philosophers reconcile it (as authority) with liberty and theologians demonstrate its compatibility with conscience. If bureaucrats pretend they have it, politicians wish they did. Everybody agrees that there is less of it than there used to be." —Warren Bennis and Burt Nanus

> "After conducting fourteen formal studies and more than a thousand interviews, directly observing dozens of executives in action, I am completely convinced that most organizations today lack the leadership they need. And the shortfall is often large. I'm not talking about a deficit of 10% but of 200%, 400% or more in positions up and down the hierarchy." — John P. Kotter

While we're seeking leadership, we're also seeking to figure out exactly what makes a leader. *The Leader's Mentor* offers a guide through the maze of books and also offers pointers as you undertake the leadership learning process. First, we suggest some *characteristics of leadership*, not an exhaustive list but a starting point. The list supports the structure of the book. Just as with the other books in this series, *The Writer's Mentor* and *The Artist's Mentor*, you are encouraged to visit the books whose quoted passages take your eye.

In part two, we ask what particular types of leaders do when they lead. Leaders in business, the spiritual world, sports, politics, the military, and the realms of revolution and ideas don't all lead alike, but they share some skills and characteristics. Bad leaders provide negative role models to round out part two. In part three we have a short exploration of some famous leaders. Most were chosen because they've been so often studied and they therefore provide rich material for comparison. We can take some concrete lessons from these lives.

No leader is meant to offer a paradigm to be copied. Of course, some leaders are more admirable than others, but no scenario is likely to compare exactly to yours, because every leadership situation is different. We can't all be governor of California or Supreme Commander of NATO, but very often the real leaders are those who don't have the impressive title or the big stick that comes with a position of authority. Anyone can be a leader, and the leader can be you.

# CHARACTERISTICS OF LEADERSHIP

The following characteristics correspond to the chapters that follow. Those analyze the ideas in more detail and provide guides for further reading.

### Leadership begins with a challenge and an opportunity

Leadership doesn't take place in a vacuum. An opportunity for leadership presents itself as a challenge that you can choose to take up or ignore. It can take the form of a job, a crisis, an opportunity to volunteer at your local school, anything that looks to the future and aims to make a difference.

## Leaders have a vision

It is not enough just to order someone to do something. A person in a position of power is not automatically a leader. The president of a company may be a wholly ineffective leader but an adequate manager. What distinguishes a leader from a manager is *vision*.

The vision must be clearly articulated and understood by everyone. Occasionally, other people may project the vision onto the leader, as might be the case with an intellectual leader whose theories attract followers.

## Leaders have followers

By definition, a leader requires followers. Followers are attracted to their leaders for any number of reasons, and they can have a greater or lesser degree of influence over their leaders, but without at least one follower, direct or indirect, a person is not a leader.

## Leadership can be learned

There has been substantial debate as to whether leaders are born or made. Another debate has asked whether leaders display any particular character traits that predispose them to leadership. Leadership is taught in institutions as diverse as teachers' colleges and the armed forces, the latter of which actually stake the lives of their men and women on the notion that the academies can impart leadership skills to recruits. However, no matter how good the teaching, it's clear that the best training for a leader is to be gained from practice.

## There are as many leadership styles as there are leaders

What do leaders actually do when they are leading? How do they lead? The methods of leadership are contained within the style of the individual which will vary according to the context of their leadership. Certain styles of leadership provide pointers that you might want to try in your particular circumstances.

## Anyone can be a leader

Developing out of the notion that leadership can be learned is the idea that everyone has the capacity for leadership, even on a small scale. Leadership is not confined just to people with fancy job titles. In a company, it can come from anywhere within that company. For every citizen, there are opportunities to become a leader.

# Part I:

## What is Leadership?

# LEADERSHIP THEORIES

> "To an extent, leadership is like beauty: it's hard to define,
> but you know it when you see it."
> —Warren Bennis

> "The thug who sticks a gun in your ribs has power.
> Leadership is something else."
> —John Gardner

The subject of history used to consist largely of the study of Great Men and how they attained and wielded power. They were presidents and Founding Fathers, admirals, generals and the Kings and Queens (honorary persons) of England. In 1840, Scottish historian Thomas Carlyle gave a lecture that included this famous passage on the idea of the Great Man.

> "For, as I take it, Universal History, the history of what man has accomplished in this world, is at the bottom of the History of the Great Men who have worked here. They were the leaders of men, these great ones; the modellers, the patterns,

**and in a wide sense the creators, of whatsoever the general mass of men contrived to do or attain . . . "**

How did this reflect leadership potential? Simply put, in pre-democratic societies, you had little chance of being a leader unless you were born wealthy. Power was concentrated within a relatively small group of people. Power followed money, either into the hands of royalty and the barons of feudal times or the land-owners and industrialists of later eras. Reinforced by law, lines of authority were strictly defined and the lives of the majority were limited to service of the minority. It all used to be about the man in charge; the rest of us were after-thoughts. In the words of industrialist Andrew Carnegie,

**"Shakespeare tells us that honor passes in a path so narrow that but one goes abreast. So with every advance made by man there is always a leader and then came the millions of the multitude that follow."**

The principles of "We the people" embodied in the U.S. Constitution came to be reflected in democratic societies in which we, the people, have political control. Lines of authority still exist, of course, but individuals are free to make their own lives. Our leaders are not simply born to the task, as was most often the case before democracy, but can come from anywhere among us.

Not only has the nature of leadership changed, but so has our perception of past leaders. Historians have looked back and seen that the Great Men themselves were often riding currents they couldn't control—economic forces, technological innovation, intellectual progress, even climate change.

Everything looks a lot more complicated than we used to think.

Once power lay with the majority, the leader was still the center of attention but some interest was paid to the leader's personality and talents. In 1920, Columbia philosopher Irwin Edman acknowledged this development:

> **"A man is made, as it were, *ipso facto*, a leader, by being rich, powerful, of a socially distinguished family, or the director of a large industry, although he may have, besides, qualities of leadership that do not depend on his social position."**

"Leadership" is a much later word than "leader." Partway through the twentieth century, leadership came to be viewed as a separate entity from the individual leader and was studied in its own right. Theories of how leadership worked began to be established. "Leader" and "leadership" took on meaning beyond their original definitions. Theories looked at leadership as more than a relationship between a figure in authority and those over whom he wielded that power. Leaders had to do more than just order people around. They had to show *leadership*.

Of course, history was not divided as neatly as this account suggests. What we now consider leadership was practiced before the word itself was in usage and it isn't confined to democratic societies by any means. Jesus Christ was a leader, as were Joan of Arc, Julius Caesar, and Martin Luther. Ancient and Renaissance philosophers—Lao-tse, Plato, and Machiavelli, for instance, described aspects of leadership as we think of it in the modern sense. But it is in the second half of the twentieth century and beyond, as social, cultural, and economic circumstances have rapidly changed, that leadership theories and both scholarly and popular accounts have proliferated.

◎ ◎ ◎

There are now hundreds of theories and definitions of leadership. Certain types of theories have gained and lost popularity over time. For a while, leaders were studied to see what traits or characteristics they had that made them attractive to their followers. These *trait* theories were popular through the 1940s, then were followed by *behavioral* theories that looked at the relationship between a leader's behavior and the actions of subordinates. Later, *situational* studies proliferated. Here, context—behavior in different circumstances—is key. And, more recently, experts have looked at the *skills* that are utilized in leadership. When we look for skills that can be learned in pursuit of leadership, we've come a long way from thinking that certain people have traits that make them leaders. Leaders are made, not born, is what we're now saying.

Of course, the new ideas do not completely replace the old ones. Aspects of the former theories remain, or come back into vogue. Theories compete, definitions collide, and there is little consensus. You might want to think of leadership as a process, a series of dynamic relations whose sheer complexity a static theory cannot accommodate. In *Leadership: Theory and Practice*, Peter Northouse agrees that the picture is complex.

**"Leadership has been studied using both qualitative and quantitative methods in many contexts, including small**

W arren Bennis is a prolific and well-regarded author- ity on leadership. In *On Becoming a Leader*, he writes,

> "I once told an interviewer who asked how I became interested in leadership, that it was impossible to live through the 1930s and '40s without thinking about lead- ership. There *were* giants on the earth in those days— leaders of the stature of FDR, Churchill, and Gandhi. And there were also men who wielded enormous power in the most horrific ways—Hitler and Stalin—men who per- verted the very essence of leadership and killed millions of innocent people in the process."

groups, therapeutic groups, and large organizations. Collectively, the research findings in leadership from all these areas provide a picture of a process that is far more sophisti- cated and complex than the often simplistic view presented in some of the popular books on leadership."

Perhaps leadership is simply in the eye of the beholder. We're attracted to leaders for reasons we may not be able to quan- tify. First impressions are essential. In *Blink*, Malcolm Gladwell says we think leaders should be tall.

> "Most of us, in ways that we are not entirely aware of, auto- matically associate leadership ability with imposing physi- cal stature. We have a sense of what a leader is supposed to

look like, and that stereotype is so powerful that when someone fits it, we simply become blind to other considerations."

One consequence: studies show that someone six feet tall will
earn, on average, $5,525 more a year than someone five foot
five with the same qualifications.

Peter Northouse writes,

**"It is much like the words *democracy, love,* and *peace.*
Although each of us intuitively knows what he or she means
by such words, the words can have different meanings to different people."**

One of the most famous management and leadership theories
was created in 1960 when Douglas McGregor published *The
Human Side of Enterprise* and introduced the notion of
Theory X and Theory Y workers. Theory X workers, who
make up the majority, don't want responsibility, need to be
supervised, and are indifferent to work. Theory Y workers are
the opposite. McGregor was describing behavior he had
observed, but his theory came to be misapplied, as is the fate
of theories. Rather than a study of self-described management behavior, Theory X and Theory Y were looked upon as
styles, one being good and the other being bad. The theory
was spouted and the behavior the theory described wasn't
questioned.

For aspiring leaders, the important question to ask yourself
when you read about leadership theory is "How does this theory describe my behavior?" rather than "That theory's neat.
How can I change my behavior to comply with that theory?"
or, "How can I manage my Theory X workers?"

> "McGregor was often met with the following question: 'This is a great theory, but how do you make it work?' And McGregor would invariably respond, 'I don't know.' He knew that his thinking worked only when each individual figured out how it worked for *them*."

Theories and definitions are descriptive, not prescriptive. As McGregor argued, every situation is unique and organic. Leadership is such an important concept in explaining how the world works that scholars and writers will always be searching for *the* key that explains its secrets. Like love, leadership is likely to elude definitive description. Throughout the book, we describe characteristics of leadership. They might apply to you, but to no one else in quite the same way.

The key point is that no one leadership expert or popular account holds all the answers to successful leadership. But among them, they may make positive suggestions that make sense to you and your particular circumstances. Remember: your situation is unique. You're not Jack Welch, but something he writes may either resonate or put you off. You may extrapolate something from the leadership theories of Warren Bennis that applies to your company or organization. Or Alexander the Great's epic vision might have you dreaming. . . . *The Leader's Mentor* attempts to cover as much ground as it can to point you to useful and thought-provoking writers.

One important and popular work you should know about is James McGregor Burns's *Leadership* (1978). Burns makes stimulating reading, and he is often quoted so it pays to have some familiarity with his ideas. Burns is wistful, writing in the post-Nixon era when we'd gone beyond the point where we expected the best from our leaders to one where we weren't surprised when we got the worst. The ranks of the great leaders that Warren Bennis mentioned had only been slightly swelled in the thirty years since the end of the Second World War: de Gaulle and Nehru, Burns thought, and perhaps Kennedy and King. But in the main, leaders had been replaced by celebrities and personalities. We knew everything about our putative leaders but little about the process of leadership.

Burns writes that we had looked separately at the two parts of the process, leaders and followers, and he wants to bring the literatures together. Leadership differs from simply wielding power because it takes into account the motives of the followers as well. Leaders *engage*, but when a title-holder merely wields power, there is no engagement. So while leaders have power, power holders are not necessarily leaders. This is Burns's definition:

> **"I define leadership as leaders inducing followers to act for certain goals that represent the values and motivations— the wants and needs, the aspirations and expectations—*of both leaders and followers.*"**

For Burns, there are two types of leadership. The first is "transactional" leadership. "Such leadership occurs when one person takes the initiative in making contact with others for the purpose of an exchange of valued things," such things being goods, votes, or hospitality. Once the deal has been done, the parties have no abiding reason to stay together. Politicians who lose elections rarely retain a significant following.

"Transforming" leadership is different. "Such leadership

occurs when one or more persons *engage* with others in such a way that leaders and followers raise one another to higher levels of motivation and morality." For Burns, the best modern example of a transforming leader would be Gandhi.

Burns's description of transactional and transforming leadership takes its place among the hundreds of definitions that begin: "Leadership is . . . " Here are three eminent military men on the subject,

> **"I'll tell you what leadership is. It's persuasion, and conciliation and education and patience."** —Dwight D. Eisenhower

> **"Leadership is the art of accomplishing more than the science of management says is possible."** —Colin L. Powell

> **"Leadership is a potent combination of strategy and character. But if you must be without one, be without strategy."** —Norman Schwarzkopf

Finally, setting aside all the theories and definitions is the possibility that leadership is a *creative act* or a series of creative acts. In Marshall Frady's biography of Jesse Jackson, Jackson is quoted talking about the talents of Duke Ellington, and makes a fine case for putting down the textbook and standing back and nodding, "Yes."

> **"But somebody once asked Duke Ellington, 'How can you write so many different-sounding kinds of songs?' and he said, 'Well, I never went to college and learned I couldn't. Or learned I *shouldn't.*' Way it often is with the great creators. Real leader, once he moves and sets the pace and sends the word out, people say, 'Well, now. *That's* what time of day it is.' "**

# LEADERSHIP: CHALLENGE AND OPPORTUNITY

"You've got to believe, your people have got to believe, that
this crew is coming home. Now let's get going!"

—Gene Kranz, *Apollo 13 flight director*

"Okay, Houston, we have a problem." On April 11, 1970,
Apollo 13 was 200,000 miles from Earth on its way to
put two men on the Moon. When Commander Jim Lovell
raised the alarm to the communications officer at Mission
Control, both Lovell and NASA technicians could see from
their instruments that something was badly wrong. When
computers powered back up, after a period of crew sleep,
fifty-five hours, fifty-five minutes, and four seconds after
launch, readings showed that Apollo 13 was suffering a potentially catastrophic loss of power. Apollo 13's lead flight director was Eugene Kranz. It was his responsibility to ensure the

successful completion of the mission objectives. In an instant, Kranz's job changed, and far more radically than he understood at first. As Kranz recalled,

> "A crisis had begun. Events followed in rapid succession, escalating and complicating the problems as the crew's situation became increasingly perilous. It was fifteen minutes before we began to comprehend the full scope of the crisis. Once we understood it, we realized that there was not going to be a lunar mission. The mission had become one of survival."

Without hesitation, Eugene Kranz took control of the situation. Kranz had authority—on paper, he was in charge—and he met the challenge with outstanding leadership. In a moment of pure crisis like this, a leader is someone who steps up and answers the call, pulling people in one direction toward a clear goal, which in this case was getting the crew of Apollo 13 back home.

Leadership in these rare circumstances of extreme peril is easy to recognize. It can be found in wartime, among the soldiers who dragged their fellow GIs off the treacherous Omaha Beach on D-Day or from Winston Churchill buoying the spirits of the beleaguered British people in June 1940. These leaders are like Meriwether Lewis, described by historian Stephen Ambrose:

> "He was a good man in a crisis. If I was ever in a desperate situation—caught in a grass fire on the prairie, or sinking in a small boat in a big ocean, or the like—then I would want Meriwether Lewis for my leader. I am as one with Private Windsor, who, when about to slip off the bluff over the

> Marias River, barely managing to hold on, badly frightened, called out, 'God, God, Captain, What Shall I do?' I too would instinctively trust Lewis to know what to do."

In 1790, Abigail Adams wrote to Thomas Jefferson the often-quoted observation that "Great necessities call forth great leaders." Leadership does not take place in a vacuum. When confronted with a dangerous situation, individuals find the fortitude to take charge.

In *Leaders*, leadership experts Warren Bennis and Burt Nanus agree with Adams but ask if we need crisis to bring out the leaders among us. We should remember we're not just looking for *great* leaders. Not every leader has to be Churchill. Every country, city, and community, every school, workplace, and religious organization, and even every family needs leaders. Sometimes a situation is clear cut, as it was for Gene Kranz: lead right now or fail. But it's far more likely that a leadership opportunity will unfold itself gradually. At work, you might not even know you're developing into a leader until one day it hits you—your team's looking to you for direction, not directives. While each leadership opportunity is a challenge, some we take upon ourselves; others are thrown at us like a live grenade.

Aboard Apollo 13 were astronauts Jim Lovell, Fred Haise, and Jack Swigert. In the first fifteen minutes after the alert was raised, Mission Control struggled to make sense of what their instruments were showing. No one knew right away that there'd been an explosion in the service module's cryogenic hydrogen and oxygen tanks, which provided both electrical power and water. It was clear the craft was suffering failures in multiple systems and was losing all power and propulsion. Although exhaustive training prepared flight directors for crises, no one had ever seen anything like this in a simulation.

Jim Lovell looked out of the window and reported he could see gas escaping. Gene Kranz realized an oxygen tank was leaking, which was desperately serious. Kranz kicked himself for wasting fifteen minutes trying to figure out what was going on. But Kranz later wrote in his autobiography, "The feeling of self-reproach passed quickly; I became icy cold, my mind reached out for options as my training kicked in."

Kranz knew that if the astronauts were going to survive, Mission Control would have to get them back home. Because Kranz was in charge, that meant it was his job. Minutes ticked by with everyone was talking at once, trying to figure out what they needed to do. Kranz stood up at his console and established control. The priority was order and discipline so Kranz told everyone to cut the chatter. Only vital communications with the spacecraft were to be maintained. Kranz then assembled his team of flight directors to make a plan.

There were two routes home they could try: the first, which would abort the mission at once and turn the spacecraft around, was the shorter. The second meant traveling even further from Earth, going around the Moon to slingshot the damaged craft back home. Kranz liked the second option, which would use the Lunar Module as the rescue vehicle, even though it would take a full two days longer than the immediate abort. Some specialists wanted to abort at once and use the main engine. Kranz was concerned that the main engine, situated near the explosion, might be damaged. The longer route was safer, he felt. Kranz trusted that the specialists would fill in the details of the plan and establish custom-made procedures as they went along. Kranz put the first stage of his plan into effect, and the astronauts were moved to the Lunar Module.

After an hour and ten minutes Kranz and his White Team retreated to figure out how to staunch the loss of power. They had to keep the astronauts alive for four days, to get home using an engine designed to land on the Moon, and to perform the hazardous reentry procedure, all with dwindling power and water. Kranz divided the key tasks among three team leaders. One was responsible for reentry, one for managing the scant spacecraft resources, and the third for the Lunar Module that was the astronauts' lifeboat. Kranz made sure everyone knew their role and emphasized the need to maintain up-to-the-second data. The whole team had one feverish fifteen-minute brainstorming session that further defined the mission. Kranz finished with a pep talk.

> "Okay, listen up. When you leave this room, you must leave believing that *this crew is coming home.* I don't give a damn about the odds and I don't give a damn that we've never done anything like this before. Flight people have got to believe, your people have got to believe, that this crew is coming home. Now let's get going!"

Working with experts from NASA's contractors, Kranz's teams put the Lunar Module through an emergency refit in space. Engineers responded with brilliant ingenuity. Air in the Lunar Module had to be cleaned of poisonous carbon dioxide, so an air scrubber was fabricated using, among other things, a plastic bag, a sock, and a hose from a space suit. It was held together with duct tape, something that even working astronauts had lying around. The jerry-rigged repairs and flight plan calculations were simulated and tested, and solutions were found to every problem.

◎ ◎ ◎

Craft returning to Earth experience radio blackout as they reenter the atmosphere. The Apollo 13 astronauts were more than a minute overdue before they established contact, but they safely splashed down in the Pacific. For their efforts, the mission teams received the Presidential Medal of Freedom and were given a ticker tape parade in Chicago where Mayor Daley handed out keys to the city.

In his autobiography, Kranz gives credit to the experts who worked tirelessly to come up with fixes for problems that had never been foreseen. Kranz summed up the rescuers' achievement by using a phrase that was both the Mission Control credo and also the title of his book.

> **"All we had to work with was time and experience. The term we used was 'workaround' options, other ways of doing things, solutions to problems that weren't to be found in manuals and schematics. These three astronauts were beyond our physical reach. But not beyond the reach of human imagination, inventiveness, and a creed we all lived by: 'Failure is not an option.'"**

Michael Useem is the author of a book called *The Leadership Moment* that includes an account of Kranz's work. Useem's

Extraordinary leadership was demonstrated during the multiple crises of September 11, 2001. Thousands of individuals faced leadership moments and responded, often at the expense of their lives. Aboard hijacked United Flight 93, passengers knew from phone calls home that planes were being flown into buildings along the east coast.

Herded into the back of the plane, passengers decided to act. Tom Burnett told his wife,

"If they're going to crash the plane into the ground, we have to do something. We can't wait for the authorities. We have to do something now." Todd Beamer put down his phone as the fight to retake the plane started. The Verizon supervisor Beamer had been talking to heard him say, "Are you guys ready? Let's roll." Instead of hitting a strategic target in Washington, D.C., Flight 93 crashed in a field in Pennsylvania.

At the World Trade Center, emergency services personnel and office workers got an estimated 25,000 people out of the Twin Towers alive. When the buildings collapsed, 343 firefighters, 37 Port Authority officers, and 23 members of the New York Police Department were among those who lost their lives.

Firefighters routinely put their lives on the line to save others, and show great leadership in extreme conditions.

Firefighters are bound by conventions: officers lead their men who lead the civilians. John Salka's *First In, Last Out* explains how fire department leaders are expected to act,

> " 'First in, last out.' That sums up the leadership code of the New York Fire Department. Like most other leadership principles, it's a simple concept, but one that's difficult to live up to. Company officers are expected to be the first into every fire and the last to leave. It's part of the sacred trust that exists between officers and firefighters. 'First in, last out' emphasizes key leadership qualities like integrity, commitment, focus, and intensity."

As soon as he heard what had happened on the morning of September 11th, New York City Mayor Rudolph Giuliani headed straight for the World Trade Center, and was almost killed when the first tower collapsed. The city's disaster control center was destroyed in the attacks, and Giuliani and his team headed for a nearby fire station to establish an emergency HQ.

John Salka writes that one of Giuliani's most revered predecessors as mayor, Fiorello La Guardia, would routinely attend major fires.

"In response to critics who complained that he spent more time at fires than at City Hall, La Guardia asked, '[What] would the men think if I didn't have the guts to go where they went, especially if there was danger?' "

In a crisis, leadership can be found heading *toward* the danger. This idea is personified by emergency services personnel. Thomas Van Etten was New York's fire commissioner on September 11th.

"For many firefighters, an evacuation order means, 'Get the civilians out, get all my guys out and then I go.' . . . We will never know what decision many of our firefighters made that day, but I do know that firefighters do not abandon civilians in distress to save themselves."

phrase elegantly describes Kranz's decisive flash of resolve when his mind raced with the enormity of the task he was facing. Useem writes,

" 'I thought that as a group we were smart enough and clever enough,' [Kranz] would later say, 'to get out of any problem.' Kranz's latticework of teams and specialists served as half the leadership formula. His driving optimism and demand for accuracy among the teams and specialists added the other half."

The challenge of leadership can present itself as an opportunity you calmly contemplate and accept. Many individuals—military personnel, rescue workers, firefighters, aid workers, law enforcement, and the like—choose professions where they routinely face leadership moments. In an emergency, many "ordinary" people find it within themselves to step forward, and in leadership they draw on reserves of courage and resolution they didn't know they had.

Opportunities for leadership can present themselves at any moment in our lives. They can be wholly unexpected and unwelcome, as for the passengers of Flight 93 on 9/11. Or we can seek them out ourselves. One of the most respected leaders of the twentieth century was Mohandas Gandhi who courageously challenged himself to become a leader.

"By his early forties, Gandhi had come to feel terror at the prospect of living to old age in conventional comfort. He trembled when he imagined himself on his deathbed uttering the most tragic of all last words: 'I could have done much more with my life.' Instead, he embraced the challenge of fighting for the independence of India from British imperialism. For the next forty years, he focused all his energies on this ambitious goal. Notice that Gandhi came upon the work that provided meaning midway through his life. It is never too late to begin the quest."

# VISION

"While leaders come in every size, shape and disposition—
short, tall, neat, sloppy, young, old, male and female—every
leader I talked with shared at least one characteristic: a
concern with a guiding purpose, an overarching vision. They
are more than goal-directed. As Karl Wallenda said, 'Walking
the tightrope is living; everything else is waiting.' "

—Warren Bennis

To be an effective leader, you need to have vision. You
might find that "Follow me!" works for a while, but
sooner, rather than later, people will start asking, "where are
we going?" Vision is one of the essential elements a leader
requires. Without a vision, without a sense of direction and a
larger purpose, you might get results, but they will be based
on the exercise of power rather than a shared set of goals and
objectives.

Vision provides meaning to your goal. Let's say you're the
CEO of a company that makes toasters. Your company's function will always be to make toasters, but you want to take the

enterprise to another level. You might want to make the best toaster there has ever been, or provide the best service in the industry, or create a new way of doing business. Ideally, your vision will enhance effectiveness and bind the enterprise to its core values. If values are implicit to the vision, and the vision is genuinely pursued, and the pursuit of the vision benefits everyone involved, then you're exercising good leadership.

> **"When people talk about *effectiveness*, they are basically talking about vision and direction. Effectiveness has to do with focusing the organization's energy in a particular direction."** —Ken Blanchard

> **"The problem with most leaders today is they don't stand for anything. Leadership implies movement toward something and convictions provide that direction. If you don't stand for something, you'll fall for anything."** —Don Shula

But what is vision, or *a* vision? Simply put, vision is a concept of the future. Most often, a leader will communicate a sense of optimism about the future he or she is looking to. We all have hopes and aspirations, and we look to people to help us realize them. Here are three leadership authorities on vision and the future:

> **"Leaders have to think about the future because that is where they live. If they don't have some idea of what is going to happen next, they aren't very good leaders."** —Philip B. Crosby

> **"Vision is being able to think beyond the immediate transaction."** —Robert L. Dilenschneider

"Over the years I can't recall reading in any management or leadership books anything about the organizational function of hope. You might define hope as an optimistic sense of the future but it is also one of the most functional realities of society." —Max De Pree

For a politician it's clear that having a vision is fundamental, both to electoral success and to maintaining popular support. A vision statement reveals what a politician stands for and how he would create a shared future with his community. The same is true for other leaders as well. In her memoir, activist Betty Friedan writes about the vision of the National Women's Political Caucus in 1971.

"My vision for the NWPC was to bring together Republican women, Democratic women, old and young women, those not aligned with either party, to speak for themselves, finally, in the halls of government."

In business, vision can take on any number of forms.

"The very first day I arrived at Unisys, I did a broadcast on our in-house system. I was asked my vision for the company, and since I hadn't had a chance to prepare, I simply said what I've always believed: There are only three things that are important—customers, employees, and reputation. If you get these three things right, you will be successful. It's like a three-legged stool. If all three legs are strong, you have something solid to sit on." —Lawrence A. Weinbach

Lawrence Weinbach, chairman and CEO of Unisys since 1987, took the three-legged stool idea and ran with it. He had a pin designed with a stool motif and distributed it around the company. Eager employees made stools and gave them to Weinbach until he had about twenty in his office.

Jack Welch's 1990 vision for General Electric was described as: "Speed, Simplicity, and Self-Confidence." In 1975, six years before the first IBM personal computer became available, Microsoft founders Bill Gates and Paul Allen established a vision for themselves. "A personal computer on every desk and in every home." Establishing the vision is the core creative act with which a leader lays a cornerstone. It is something you can't delegate.

> **"Just as no great painting has ever been created by a committee, no great vision has ever emerged from the herd."** —Warren Bennis

> **"We find that our people are very motivated by big goals, whether it's providing customers with absolutely the best value or entering a new market with great success or achieving a particular milestone."** —Michael Dell

> **"Back in the early 1980s, and even more so today, I had a pretty clear idea of what Starbucks could become. I knew the look I wanted, the feel the stores convey, the pace of growth, and the connection with our people."** —Howard Schultz

In the military, while a vision might conceivably take the form of a battle objective, it is more realistically embodied in the *esprit de corps* of the unit. As we shall see, military leaders who convince their men that they care for their well-being, itself a vision projected to the men, are likely to be effective.

In sports, as in war, the primary objective might be obvious. The team wants to win the game. That can be achieved by discipline and application, but long-term success awaits the team that bonds with its coach with true purpose. The New England Patriots Super Bowl championship teams of 2002 and 2004–5 are excellent examples of finely coached and intelligent teams that executed game plans with great effectiveness. Those teams consistently set aside anything that would distract them from the ultimate prize; they had what we can call the vision of winning.

Great vision means nothing if you keep it to yourself. You need to spread it, and get others to help you spread it. How? In order for the vision to be effective, it should be simple. It should not be prescriptive, because over time the means of realizing the vision will have to change with circumstances.

> **"If you cannot describe your vision to someone in five minutes and get their interest, you have more work to do in this phase of a transformation process."** —John P. Kotter

> **"I once asked Max De Pree, retired chairman of Herman Miller and author of *Leadership as an Art*, what he thought the leader's role was in terms of vision. He said, 'You have to act like a third-grade teacher. You have to repeat the vision over and over again until people get it right! Right! Right!'"** —Ken Blanchard

Some great leaders have made great speeches to articulate and communicate their vision. When Martin Luther King, Jr.

made his "I have a dream" speech, he presented his core vision of equality with unforgettable eloquence.

> **"The leader is a team builder who empowers individuals in the organization and passionately 'lives the vision,' thereby serving as a mentor and example for those whose efforts are necessary to make the vision become reality. An outstanding example was Martin Luther King, who lived the vision ('I have a dream') and provided a model for everyone in the civil rights movement."** —Burt Nanus

> **"Sometimes leaders communicate by the most elegant and simple of symbols—Gandhi nakedly facing his enemies, Churchill issuing a defiant sign for victory, Martin Luther King, Jr., standing resolutely behind bars."** —Howard Gardner

Think about others leaders who have made visionary speeches, such as Ronald Reagan, who in June 1987 spoke at the Brandenburg Gate in West Berlin. In a powerful address he called on Soviet leader Mikhail Gorbachev to remove the Berlin Wall. "Mr. Gorbachev, open this gate!" Reagan demanded, "Mr. Gorbachev, tear down this wall!" This was not a practical political suggestion but a statement of a vision.

In his first inaugural address in March, 1933, in the midst of the Depression, Franklin Roosevelt made an impassioned rallying cry, calling on Americans for their support.

> **"So, first of all, let me assert my firm belief that the only thing we have to fear is fear itself—nameless, unreasoning, unjustified terror which paralyzes needed efforts to convert retreat into advance. In every dark hour of our national life a leadership of frankness and vigor has met with that understanding**

and support of the people themselves which is essential to victory. I am convinced that you will again give that support to leadership in these critical days."

Even in his vision statement Roosevelt spoke frankly about the distress the country was suffering. Although Roosevelt specifically said that America was *not* suffering Biblical catastrophes, using the terminology lent impressive gravity to his words. In the first hundred days of his administration, Roosevelt moved quickly to regulate business and to create government agencies to control large parts of the economy. In his inaugural address, he laid the groundwork. His concept was vague, almost mythic, but it is certainly a prime example of a vision communicated.

"[O]ur distress comes from no failure of substance. We are stricken by no plague of locusts. Compared with the perils which our forefathers conquered because they believed and were not afraid, we have still much to be thankful for. Nature still offers her bounty and human efforts have multiplied it. Plenty is at our doorstep, but a generous use of it languishes in the very sight of the supply. Primarily this is because the rulers of the exchange of mankind's goods have failed, through their own stubbornness and their own incompetence, have admitted their failure, and abdicated. Practices of the unscrupulous money changers stand indicted in the court of public opinion, rejected by the hearts and minds of men . . .

"The money changers have fled from their high seats in the temple of our civilization. We may now restore that temple to the ancient truths. The measure of the restoration lies in the extent to which we apply social values more noble than mere monetary profit.

In his autobiography *Jack: Straight from the Gut*, Jack Welch describes presenting his vision for GE for the first time soon after becoming CEO in 1981 when he made a speech in front of Wall Street analysts in the ballroom of the Pierre Hotel in New York. He worked hard on writing and rewriting the twenty-minute speech and rehearsed it for hours. The speech was a bomb.

Welch described how he wanted GE to be number one or number two in every business they were in and to be in growth markets. The company also had to commit to intangible "soft" values that would define the new culture. People in the company would be pushed and dared to try new things. Welch got little reaction in the room. "Wall Street yawned," Welch wrote. He believed in the vision; he just didn't communicate it.

**"I was sure the ideas were right. I just hadn't brought them to life. They were just words read on stage by a new face."**

Welch decided the meeting was too formal and staged. He established unscripted gatherings where management was questioned and challenged. "Intellectual food fights," as he put it. Through his long tenure as CEO, Welch remained faithful to his original vision.

> "My first meeting was a flop, but everything we did over the next 20 years, stumbling two steps forward, one back, was toward the vision that I laid out that day. We lived that hard reality of No. 1 or No. 2 and fought like mad to get that 'soft' feel into the company."

> "Happiness lies not in the mere possession of money; it lies in the joy of achievement, in the thrill of creative effort. The joy and moral stimulation of work no longer must be forgotten in the mad chase of evanescent profits. These dark days will be worth all they cost us if they teach us that our true destiny is not to be ministered unto but to minister to ourselves and to our fellow men." —Franklin Delano Roosevelt

Speeches aren't the only efficient means of getting your message across to a large number of people. Vision can also be communicated one-to-one or remotely. A writer might present a vision with a book, for example. Manifestoes of every kind, from *The Communist Manifesto* to Chairman Mao's *Little Red Book*, offer a vision.

> "The Constitution, for example, is a written description of the founding fathers' vision for the United States, setting a clear direction and defining values but not specifying how to get there." —Burt Nanus

Once your vision is established and communicated, you should demonstrate your style by working to realize the goals of the vision alongside your followers. This way, your vision is reinforced continually, and as those who pursue it go about their business, adherence to the values and aims of the vision will become measures of mutual success.

> **"The way I see it, leadership does not begin with power but rather, with a compelling vision or goal of excellence. One becomes a leader when he or she is able to communicate that vision in such a way that others feel empowered to achieve excellence. We must create organizations with a shared vision of excellence."** —Frederick W. Smith, founder, Federal Express

Not everyone can find vision for effective long-term leadership. John Maxwell's book offers advice on hitching your wagon to a star.

> **"You still don't have vision of your own, then consider hooking up with a leader whose vision resonates with you. Become his partner. That's what Walt Disney's brother, Roy, did. He was a good businessman and leader who could make things happen, but Walt provided the vision. Together they made an incredible team."**

Beware: vision isn't everything. Applying a coherent vision can improve results, but in the absence of results, vision is meaningless. Peter Burrows describes Louis V. Gerstner, Jr., who took over IBM in 1993.

> **"Asked about his vision, [Gerstner] responded famously in his first press conference: 'The last thing IBM needs right now is a vision.' He quickly set about building up IBM's lucrative**

**consulting business, which eventually turned the company into a $90-billion powerhouse—not through acquisitions, but by changing the culture from the bottom up."**

In his book, Gerstner said his initial challenge wasn't vision but execution. "IBM had file drawers full of vision statements," he writes. "The real issue was going out and making things happen every day in the marketplace." That's what he set out to do.

As we look for leadership in our daily lives, it helps to be reminded that vision and effective leadership are around us and not just confined to CEOs and presidents.

The everyday leader's everyday vision begins very close to home.

**"We have this authoritarian notion of what leadership means, so we relegate it to something that takes place in companies or military units or sports teams. But, fundamentally, leaders are visionaries. They speak for and evoke action on behalf of a compelling future. That vision of the future could be of anything—a closer family relationship, a violence-free school or a successful company. The scope of leadership can be global, but it doesn't have to be. It is always personal because it begins with you and the person you want to become."** —Rayona Sharpnack, *Institute for Women's Leadership*

**"Leaders take us to places we've never been before. But there are no freeways to the future, no paved highways to unknown, unexplored destinations. There's only wilderness."** —James M. Kouzes and Barry Z. Posner

# LEADERS AND FOLLOWERS

> "What does it mean to be a leader? The first natural law of leadership answers this fundamental question: A leader has willing followers. No leader exists without gaining the support of others. Yet this core element of what it means to be leader is typically overlooked."
>
> —Warren Blank

> "The ear of the leader must ring with the voices of the people."
>
> —James O'Toole

Once you've articulated a vision and communicated it, the task of implementation begins. Moving beyond "Follow me," your vision says, "This is where I want to go." More than likely, you won't be able to make it there alone, so you'll need help, and a plan to realize the vision. This is where followers come in.

It is axiomatic that leaders have followers. This is leadership expert Warren Blank's Natural Law number one: a leader has willing followers. Blank's Law number two is that the leader interacts with the followers—this is *leadership*. Blank writes,

"Consider how Lee Iacocca is credited with the dramatic turn-around of Chrysler, how Steve Jobs is acclaimed as the creator of Apple Computer, or how Gloria Steinem is hailed for the emergence of the women's movement. Yet all three had impact only in relationship with their followers."

The connection between leaders and followers can take any number of forms. The traditional position, the one we heard from Andrew Carnegie, is of a great man out in front and "the millions of the multitude that follow." The relationship between leaders and followers is much more complex than this outmoded picture would have us believe. We still study the "great men," like Alexander the Great. Look at them from a follower's perspective to see how they managed their constituency.

"Alexander did not conquer the Persian Empire—his army did, under his leadership. For you to be a great leader, you need great followers, zealots really. The employees come first, because it is they who will make your dream come true." — Lance B. Burke

As James McGregor Burns told us in *Leadership*, followers are demanding. There has to be something in it for them. Once the common purpose is identified, maintaining the health of the relationship between leader and followers is where the hard work of leadership takes place. If you want to be a leader, you will have responsibilities to your potential supporters. Fail in this, and you will fall short of the full potential of leadership.

> "Many persons think they have followers when they merely have subordinates, members, or constituents." —Kenneth E. Clark and Miriam B. Clark

A leader who fails to satisfy his followers is in danger of losing everything.

> "These alliances are transitory. A leader may have followers one day but they may desert him the next. This is not the same as a management hierarchy." —Warren Blank

A follower will always have some stake in the work that the leader undertakes. Whether the follower also has a say in how the enterprise is run, in the strategy and tactics that are employed to realize the vision, depends on the leader's style. Some leaders motivate with oratory, or they lead by example. Others coerce while they are leading, or they are moral leaders who convince people of their integrity and the ethical clarity of their vision. Whatever style they employ, leaders work to bind their followers to them.

In the military, intensive training reinforces leadership and followership responsibilities up and down the hierarchy. In combat, the prime focus of the men and women on the ground is on the nearest person in charge. Their orders will come from him and their lives depend to a great extent on the skill and knowledge of this one person. Even in a badly run division, if the unit commander displays qualities of leadership, his soldiers will be in good position to fight effectively.

Leadership style will still affect the relationship between leaders and followers even in a hierarchy based on lines of authority. An army commander might be prepared to listen to input from a trusted subordinate and be willing to act upon it or he might keep his own counsel. Military leaders are also responsible for the well-being of their soldiers, both in battle and in the field, where leaders must make sure their charges are as warm, dry, and well fed as possible.

In most leadership situations, when the leaders and followers are not in a life-or-death predicament, the flow of information and opinion from the leaders to the followers *and back again* is the crucial dynamic in the relationship. Having communicated the vision, the leader can't disappear from view and hope that everyone trusts him to make sure it's being implemented. A leader must maintain meaningful communications.

**"The trick is demonstrating to people, every day, where you want to take your organization." —Tom Peters and Nancy Austin**

Keeping people informed is part of the process by which a leader establishes a successful relationship with followers. To effectively realize the vision, a leader needs to have the right people in place and then encourage them to give maximum effort. Again, the leadership style will determine to a great extent how the leader goes about doing this.

**"One of leadership's key roles is to bring out the best in people. Since attitude is so crucial to performance, it is essential for leaders to understand what keeps people from choosing and maintaining an attitude that would best serve them and their organizations. More and more evidence points to self-**

image, or self-expression, as the key factor in this issue." —Ed Oakley and Doug Krug

Key concepts involved in bringing out the best in employees are *enabling* and *empowering*.

> "Enabling your associates to work at their very best is at the core of managerial leadership. Note that selection of the word *enabling* is purposeful—'making able; making it possible for'—as leadership today is so much more about creating environments where people can succeed than it is about making decisions or getting them done individually. You cannot possibly handle by yourself everything that must be done." —Peter Topping

You should make people *feel* involved; encourage them to believe they're making a positive contribution. You should also devolve authority where you can, so you're free from having to make every single decision. At the same time, you are creating leaders-in-training throughout your organization. Creating new leaders out of your followers is an essential task of leadership.

> "I can only make so many decisions and gather so much information, at the pace of today's economy. I want to make the best strategic decisions, but after that, if I have disseminated the decision-making process down to the people who are closest to the action ... then I have a thousand decision-makers working for me, and there is a better chance that we won't miss the market." —John Chambers, CEO, *Cisco*

Effective leaders pay great attention to the various aspects of communication: making sure individuals know where they stand and how they fit into the broad vision of the organization's future, if indeed they do fit. Good communication includes careful rewarding of success in the organization, and also a studied response to failure, where learning is a higher priority than laying blame.

> **"I want the people who report to me to feel that they are a meaningful part of shaping the company and shaping me as a leader."** —Alexandra Lebenthal, President, *Lebenthal and Company*

Dale E. Zand summarizes the essential point, that leaders rely on followers to help them get where they want to go, especially in today's complex business world.

> **"The heroic fantasy of one person at the head of a column of followers shouting 'charge' as they mount the battlements is outdated. Instead, leaders need to learn to use the sensing, searching, and thinking ability of all the people within the organization. Alex Trotman, CEO of Ford, calls this reducing the 'coefficient of bureaucratic drag.' Jack Welch, CEO of GE, calls this 'boundaryness.' Both recognize that to improve their organizations' adaptability in rapidly changing environment, leaders need to release knowledge and gain trust at every level in an organization."**

The responsibility owed to followers by leaders should be reciprocated. Leaders want followers who are loyal, but if the leader heads in the wrong direction, the follower needs to be able to point that out. The follower's loyalty shouldn't be unquestioning. If healthy, the organizational culture should allow followers to voice their concerns without that rebounding to their disadvantage. Clearly, this is often not the case. But leaders who simply expect to be followed are compromising their own leadership and undermining their own effectiveness.

> **"What makes a good follower? The single most important characteristic may well be a willingness to tell the truth. In a world of growing complexity, leaders are increasingly dependent on their subordinates for good information, whether the leaders want to hear it or not. Followers who tell the truth, and leaders who listen to it, are an unbeatable combination." —Warren Bennis**

Garry Wills places very high value on the responsibilities of followers.

> **"Not many of us will be leaders; and even those who are leaders must also be followers much of the time. This is the crucial role. Followers judge leaders. Only if the leaders pass that test do they have any impact. The potential followers, if their judgment is poor, have judged themselves. If the leader takes his or her followers to the goal, to great achievements, it is because the followers were capable of that kind of response. Jefferson said the American people responded to revolution in a way that led to a free republic, while the French responded to their revolution in a way that led to an imperial dictatorship. The followers were as much to blame for the latter development**

as was Napoleon. In the same way, the German people were jointly responsible for Hitler's atrocities. He was powerless to act without followers."

Good followers have it within their power to stop bad leaders and they are honor-bound to do so. Ira Chaleff writes in *The Courageous Follower*,

> "The bottom line of followership is that we are responsible for our decision to continue or not to continue following a leader. Even *in extremis*, we have the choice of supporting an anathema to our values or not. This is the Nuremberg trials principle. The fact that we are following orders absolves us from nothing."

Garry Wills introduced us to the idea that leaders are followers themselves much of the time. In fact, it can be argued that it is a mistake to consider too rigid a distinction between leaders and followers. For one thing, good leadership and good followership demand some of the same skills.

> "Perhaps the ultimate irony is that the follower who is willing to speak out shows precisely the kind of initiative that leadership is made of." —Warren Bennis

In *Organizing Genius: The Secrets of Creative Collaboration*, Warren Bennis and Patricia Ward Biederman challenge the dichotomous division into leaders and followers by introducing the concept of the Great Group: individuals who come together in creative collaboration. Great Groups include the Walt Disney studio team that made *Snow White and the Seven Dwarves*, the first animated feature film; the Manhattan Project that created the first atomic bomb; Xerox's Palo Alto Research Center (PARC); Apple Computer's innovation group; and the campaign team that helped win Bill Clinton's election in 1992.

> **"We have to recognize a new paradigm: not great leaders alone, but great leaders who exist in fertile relationship with a Great Group. In these creative alliances, the leader and the team are able to achieve something together that neither could achieve alone. The leader finds greatness in the group. And he or she helps the members find it themselves."**

Great Group leaders like J. Robert Oppenheimer, Steve Jobs, campaign strategist James Carville, and Walt Disney have in common a great eye for talent. Their followers are highly motivated, and, in most cases, allowed substantial creative leeway. Walt Disney's role in the making of *Snow White* (1937) is an interesting case. Disney had a particularly strong sense of the movie he wanted to make.

> **"Nobody had to guess at Walt's vision of the film. One evening in 1934, he gathered his artists together on an empty soundstage and, under a naked light bulb, he acted out the entire story."**

Disney repeated the performance later for a banker to secure funding for the movie. Disney then hired just the right person for every task. Driven by perfectionism, Disney rode his creative people, who were themselves perfectionists. If Disney wasn't satisfied, he'd have a minor character redrawn forty or more times until it was right. When asked what he did around the studio, Disney said he was the "busy bee," and it was the busy bee who got things done.

> **"It was said that Walt Disney could wring out the creativity from his artists' minds long after they themselves thought that their ideas had dried up."**

There were 750 artists who worked on *Snow White*. Walt Disney was notorious for not sharing credit with anyone and no one else's name appears on the movie. But the artists were willing to let Disney take the glory because they were achieving great things together. "As is so often true of Great Groups," Bennis and Biederman write, "Troupe Disney had the heady sense that it was inventing the future."

> **"The important thing to realize is that without necessarily being creative, a leader plays an indispensable role in the process of creation. As a crucial member of the field, a gatekeeper to the domain, the individual in a leadership position holds the keys for turning wild ideas into practical reality."** — Mihaly Csikszentmihalyi

> **"A leader gives to creative people license to be contrary."** —Max De Pree

The Great Groups described in *Organizing Genius* are still recognizably followers. James McGregor Burns has posited what he calls "The Leader-Follower Paradox," which also breaks down the dividing line between leaders and followers. According to Burns, people play different roles in different contexts: the sergeant is a leader but he follows his lieutenant and so on. Burns's Paradox goes on to ask, "If leadership and followership are so intertwined and fluid, how do we distinguish conceptually between leaders and followers?"

Burns writes that leaders take the initiative and establish relationships with people who have wants, both "the material wants of potential followers *and* their psychological wants for self-determination and self-development." At the same time, followers empower leaders, satisfying their need to be heard. These relationships are extremely complex and multidimensional and often interchangeable. To answer his own conundrum, Burns suggests we look beyond the construct of leaders and followers and concentrate on leadership itself and what it can achieve.

"The Burns Paradox ultimately disappears if, instead of identifying individual actors simply as leaders or simply as followers, we see the whole process as a *system* in which the function of leadership is palpable and central but the actors move in and out of leader and follower roles. At this crucial point we are no longer seeing individual leaders; rather we see *leadership* as the basic process of social change, of causation in a community, an organization, a nation—perhaps even the globe."

# LEADERS AND MANAGERS

**"We take eagles and teach them to fly in formation."**
—Wayne Calloway, *Pepsi CEO*

Every business book that mentions leadership points out that management is not leadership. Managers manage but leaders *lead* and there is a qualitative distinction. Why is so much made of this difference? Leadership is hard to define and so there are numerous competing definitions. It helps to be able to agree on what leadership is not. It is not the naked application of power, it is not the authority vested in a job title, and it is not management.

Many, perhaps even most, books on leadership are aimed at managers who aspire to leadership positions in their company. It's not that management is incompatible with leadership, but it is restricting, the literature says. Mired in detail, a manager is chained to his desk. Unfettered, leaders can roam free. On paper at least, they inhabit a place where the sky is blue, the horizon is limitless, and they can lead as far as their dreams may take them.

When viewed as strictly an either/or proposition, the leader/manager dichotomy can be useful as a diagnostic tool. If you want to lead, you'll find a lot of advice on how to reorient your management expertise to give you more of a leadership role. Acquiring leadership skills may help you progress further in your current environment. Or the process might make you rethink your priorities and open up entirely new avenues of opportunity. It's useful to ask in these cases, "Am I leading, or am I managing?" "Am I articulating a vision," (leading), "or am I expecting my reports just to do what I say?" (managing). "Am I empowering others and encouraging them to lead, or am I keeping everyone in his place?" "Is it feasible for me to be a leader in this organization?"

Next, you can redirect these questions upward. "Is my boss a leader or a manager?" "Does she have a vision for the future of our team?" "Is it important to me that my boss be a leader and not a manager?" "Do I want to work where I might be inspired and empowered by a genuine leader?"

Lastly, leading is not only an end in itself; it also helps managers manage more effectively. Organizations where leadership is practiced at all levels are able to do business with more effectiveness than where it isn't. What's more, in many of today's businesses, where the hierarchy is diffuse and less recognizable than the pyramid of yesterday, and where the pace of change is rapid and relentless, managers can't manage at all without being leaders.

◎ ◎ ◎

Of course, managers plain and simple still occupy key positions in an old-fashioned, hierarchical company structure. In this kind of company, power congregates at the top of the company and diminishes toward the bottom. The most junior employee is the one with the least important job and the least power. It is in this kind of top-down hierarchy where managers suffer when compared by leadership experts.

> "In business, as opposed to political and social life, those in charge are appointed rather than selected. Their loyalty then is for the one who appointed them, not for those whom they are assigned to lead. This means that many of us wind up being directed by someone who is inadequate to the task." — Philip B. Crosby

The culture of business now challenges the traditional pyramidal structure of the company organization. In a fast-paced environment, technology breaks down paradigms as soon as they're built. Innovation is essential and companies must be agile, ready to absorb change, and designed so that change is as much part of the company as the walls and the floors. When initiative is encouraged at all levels of a company, good ideas can come from anywhere. A rigid, top-down structure simply cannot respond fast enough to modern conditions.

If the traditional hierarchy is set aside, employees can become more like partners than subordinates. More and more companies view their workers as an asset to be cultivated. Hierarchies are broken up into teams, dispersing the power and flattening the pyramid. Personnel departments become human resources departments or simply "People."

> **"Increasingly 'employees' have to be managed as 'partners'—and it is the definition of a partnership that all partners are equal."** —Craig R. Hickman

> **"Because managerial work is increasingly a leadership task, and because leaders operate though a complex web of dependent relationships, managerial work is increasingly becoming a game of informal dependence on others instead of just formal power over others."** —John P. Kotter

In this scenario, management from the top down is replaced by team building and a dense and complex system of interrelationships, where valued colleagues proceed together toward an agreed goal. If we look at the Burns definition of leadership, we are recognizably inhabiting a world of leaders and leadership. In an idealized modern business environment, the line between leader and follower is indistinct and "manager" is almost a redundancy. Different skills and areas of expertise within an operation might be valued equally. Individuals take turns to lead as required where their skill set fits and, genuinely, everyone is a leader.

Companies teach leadership to their managers and business books outline how to effect broad attitude shifts and change their structures so that leaders can break out of the pack. By expending so much effort developing leaders out of regular folk, we're showing confidence that leaders are made, not born. This is especially the case in the military and, to a lesser extent, in the corporate world. Officer training forces a raw recruit to become a leader at the risk of his life and the lives of the men and women he will lead. And modern business managers are encouraged to learn how to lead lest they be left behind, pigeonholed as managers.

> **"Leaders—and you can take anyone from Roosevelt to Churchill to Reagan—inspire people with clear visions of how things can be done better. Some managers, on the other hand, muddle things with pointless complexity and detail. They equate (managing) with sophistication, with sounding smarter than anyone else. They inspire no one."** — Jack Welch

This is not to say that a manager has to forget everything she knows to become a leader. If a manager uses his mind and a leader his soul, as Craig R. Hickman's book title *Mind of a Manager, Soul of a Leader* suggests, there is no sense in losing your mind to find your soul.

> **"The words 'manager' and 'leader' are metaphors representing two opposite ends of a continuum. 'Manager' tends to signify the more analytical, structured, controlled, deliberate, and orderly end of the continuum, while 'leader' tends to occupy the more experimental, visionary, flexible, uncontrolled, and creative end."** —Craig R. Hickman

"A leader deals in emotions, excites camaraderie and unity, and guides vague notions into concrete actions. A manager determines, organizes, and directs programs and compromises among differing desires." —Roger J. Plachy

"To a large degree, leadership deals with the long term and management with the immediate future. Without enough good management, the planning, organizing, and controlling for results will not be sufficient." —John P. Kotter

Kotter's point is that without both leadership *and* management, nothing gets done. Leadership and management—the people and the tasks—must come together in pursuit of the common goal. Without contributions from each, success is unlikely. To work more effectively, managers need to learn how to lead. Leaders need to be reined in and focused. And to allow their leaders to thrive, forward-thinking companies need, in a strict sense of the word, to manage them.

The functions of leadership and management can be and are performed by the same person or people. As we'll see in another context, no one is *only* a leader. But it might be true that someone is *only* a manager, meaning that they lack particular skills that are associated with leadership. And at least a few of these skills can be learned.

# LEARNING TO BE
# A LEADER

> "I've been in this business 36 years. I've learned a lot—and most of it doesn't apply anymore."
> —Charles Exley, Chairman, *NCR Corporation*

> "Leaders are not made by corporate courses, any more than they are made by their college courses, but by experience."
> —Warren Bennis

If the potential for leadership exists in everyone, does it follow that we can be taught how to lead? Can leadership be rationalized into a subject that can be learned like algebra or German grammar? Many institutions rely on the assumption that leadership can be taught. The five service academies, for example, are dedicated to teaching leadership skills to young recruits. There is broad agreement that leadership *can* be learned—it's not an innate skill or set of skills that some individuals have and others do not. You may be born with one piece, like a charismatic personality, but not necessarily the whole package. However, even if we agree that leadership

A contrary view. In *One Thing You Need to Know . . .*, Marcus Buckingham writes that a healthy ego and a sense of optimism are absolute requirements for leaders.

> **"The necessity for leaders to possess optimism and ego serves to answer the age-old question: Are leaders born or are they made? They are born. A leader is born with an optimistic viewpoint or she is not. If she is not, then no amount of 'optimism training' is going to make her view the world in an overwhelmingly positive, opportunistic light."**

Buckingham says you can learn to be less pessimistic, but that isn't the same as being optimistic. In the same way, you can nurture self-confidence and self-assurance in someone,

> **"But nothing you can do will ever imbue him with the kind of powerful, claiming ego that so characterizes the best leaders. He either has it or he doesn't."**

can be learned, there is less consensus on the question of whether it can successfully be taught.

In his autobiography, Jack Welch states that any leadership style he has, he owes to his mother, Grace. "Tough and aggressive, warm and generous, she was a great judge of character," he writes. Welch credits his mother with developing his confidence and self-esteem. These qualities are recognized as keys to successful long-term leadership. Not only is it important that you have a sense of confidence and self-esteem yourself, but also that you propagate them in those around you.

Like Jack Welch, Donald Trump and John D. Rockefeller believe that elements of their style were developed in them from an early age.

> **"I was always something of a leader in my neighborhood. Much the way it is today, people either liked me a lot, or they didn't like me at all. In my own crowd I was very well liked and I tended to be the kid others followed."** —Donald Trump

> **"It takes infinite patience and courage to compel men to have confidence in you. I believe I have both of these qualities, and I also believe that they are the secret of my success. I learned to cultivate both of them when I was sixteen years of age."** —John D. Rockefeller

Any qualities of temperament we might have are probably established at an extremely young age. Aggression, for example, inasmuch as it's a quality required for leadership, cannot be instilled in us in adulthood. Other traits traditionally associated with strong leadership—ambitiousness, superior public speaking skills, ruthlessness—probably can't be learned either. But this only closes off certain leadership avenues for those of us who aren't accomplished in these areas. Indeed, learning how to get results by working with people and through conciliation are skills that will be effective in many leadership situations. These are skills that can be developed. In the process of becoming a leader, you have to work with what you have as a person, emphasizing your strengths and learning to work around what can be perceived as weaknesses.

> **"In part, leadership is passion. It is a passion for what we do, and it is a contagious passion. You cannot teach people to be passionate."** —Jay Conger

Clearly, not everyone can be Jack Welch, Donald Trump, or Norman Schwarzkopf. But if those of us who are not charismatic accept the fact that we are not charismatic (or passionate, or aggressive, or oratorically gifted, and so on) how can we learn about becoming a leader? In short, by leading. In *Leaders*, Warren Bennis and Burt Nanus make the point,

> **"Learning to be a leader is somewhat like learning to be a parent or a lover; your childhood and adolescence provide you with basic values and role models. Books can help you understand what's going on, but for those who are ready, most of the learning takes place during the experience itself."**

This idea reinforces the notion that anyone can be a leader. It is less important to have a complete portfolio of leadership skills than to identify and follow the challenge of a leadership opportunity.

It's important to believe that no matter where you stand in the organization, your voice can make a difference. You might be a parent with a child in elementary school. Perhaps you think the school could use newer books. You tell a couple of other parents and they've been thinking the library's a little shoddy themselves. Writing to everyone in the school brings forward a lot of ideas and volunteers to help. You come to the decision to refurbish the library entirely. A couple of years later, the work's done and you've run a campaign and raised tens of thousands of dollars to refit a vital part of the school. You didn't start out planning to work so hard chairing meetings, reaching out to local businesses, and delegating tasks to other parents. You've learned how to lead on the job. If you're willing to put yourself on the line, the path to leadership is open to all and we can all benefit. James M. Kouzes and Barry Z. Posner write:

> "It's a myth that only a lucky few can ever decipher the leadership code. Of all the research and folklore surrounding leadership, this one has done more harm to the development of people and more to slow the growth of countries and companies than any other."
>
> "Like parenthood, leadership will never be an exact science. But neither should it be a complete mystery to those who practice it." —Daniel Goleman

In *Leadership in Organizations*, John Storey writes that the traditional method where a teacher stands in front of a class and imparts knowledge is limited. It can pass on ideas *about* leadership—the theories of leadership—but is less successful in teaching people *how to* lead.

> "Leadership is learning. Whatever else leaders do, their primary role is to keep learning and to facilitate the learning of those around them."

The leadership literature is huge. There are innumerable theories, laws, and principles scattered among the practical guides to the tenets of leadership written by behavioral specialists, academics, and consultants. Politicians, coaches, CEOs, and military commanders all write books. Take some time to study in the subject. If you see an idea you like, take it. As John Myers points out, there is no copyright on ideas.

> **"The rules of business aren't like writing a term paper in college. Plagiarism isn't a guaranteed F or expulsion; it's a best practice. Copying successful people and their ideas, emulating them, and improving upon them is a strategy we shouldn't be embarrassed about."**—John H. Myers, President and CEO of *GE Asset Management, Inc.*

> **"Read six to twelve books a year on leadership or your field of specialization. Continuing to learn in an area where you are already an expert prevents you from becoming jaded and unteachable."**—John C. Maxwell

To succeed, leaders must be adaptable. No one schoolroom solution will fit every situation you might face. Storey writes that leadership has to be displayed in different contexts. Each time the characters may change, and with them the beliefs, values, skills, resources, circumstances, power relations, and so on. Leaders cannot restrict their thinking to either/or, they need to broaden it to both/and.

Because leadership revolves around building relationships, Robert L. Dilenschneider places the emphasis on communication.

> **"Leadership is not the charismatic, mystical talent that many presume it to be. Leadership can be *learned*, and modern leadership clearly rests on the mastery of communication."**

Rather than a succession of moments of inspiration, leadership can be looked at as a process. Education, and self-education, are key elements, as they are in a job.

> **"Leadership is, as you know, not a position but a job. It's hard and exciting and good work."** —Max De Pree

Few people are able to acclimatize themselves to a new job immediately. It takes them time to settle in. By the same token, if we learn as we lead, we'll need to work at it. Along the road we'll make mistakes. These are part of life and part of leadership, and we must learn from them to become more effective.

> **"There are no shortcuts to preparing for leadership. The accretion of layers of skill takes time. Polishing one's gifts requires the tumbling of experience and the gift of great discipline. Learning to identify the needs of followers and the special process of reaching simultaneously toward the potential of individuals and of organizations does not come easy. Failure is an unavoidable part of this preparation."** —Max De Pree

> **"Thomas Edison developed thousands of filaments that didn't work before he discovered the correct one for the**

**incandescent lamp. Abraham Lincoln lost more than a dozen elections before he finally got voted into office. Leaders do not view mistakes as failures, but rather as opportunities to learn something new."** —Lorraine R. Matusak

◎ ◎ ◎

The military believes it can create leaders, though the traditional idea of breaking down a recruit and building him back up in the Army mold has been tempered in recent years. Individuals are acceptable (the "Army of One") but only within certain parameters. Other organizations, principally businesses, do devote resources to teaching leadership. If you see people as assets to be cultivated, it pays to try to teach them how to lead.

Soon after taking over as chairman of GE, Jack Welch decided to rebuild the company's management development center at Crotonville, New York. The expensive new facilities were used by Welch to personally connect with legions of GE managers. Crotonville was a forum for exchanging ideas and a place to communicate the chairman's corporate vision. Welch spent a lot of time there, and in twenty-one years, he estimates he connected with 18,000 employees. Welch liked the results of the open exchanges so much, he implemented them across the whole company in what he called "Work-Out sessions."

The authors of *The Leadership Pipeline* recognize the value of GE's approach.

**"GE doesn't have a smarter or more inherently talented workforce than other companies. GE's leadership advantages stem from the investment they have made in growing their own**

leaders and their recognition that leadership revolves around mastering certain skills and values at each leadership level." — Ram Charan, Stephen Drotter, and James Noel

"When I stop learning something new and start talking about the past versus the future, I will go." —Jack Welch

In *Learning to Lead*, Jay Conger voices skepticism about companies' leadership training efforts.

"I am convinced that leadership training, for many organizations, is merely a quick-fix answer to say they are concerned about developing leaders, when, in reality, they feel more secure with managers. This attitude will have to disappear if we truly wish to see more leaders in organizations in the future."

Conger believes that leadership courses cannot adequately build key leadership components like a skill for inspirational speech, or motivational talent, or the ability to develop a vision. A student can be made more aware of the needs of leadership, but acquiring the skills is another matter. Greater emphasis should be placed on teaching skills where observable progress can be made, like in public speaking, and learning how to reward employees. What's more, Conger believes that many companies are afraid of leaders and prefer managers who are easier to control. They may pay lip-service to teaching leadership, but they don't want their employees to become leaders.

◎ ◎ ◎

As we gain experience in life and accrue skills and knowledge, we may seek leadership roles. We might not have the self-confidence to try something new till we're fifty. No matter. In *Learning to Lead*, Warren Bennis and Joan Goldsmith cite leaders who found their calling later in life: George Bernard Shaw, Margaret Mead, Charles Darwin, Eleanor Roosevelt, Nelson Mandela, Mohandas Gandhi, Golda Meir, Jean Piaget, and Martha Graham. "It is never too late to begin," they say. Bennis and Goldsmith have provided a workbook for acquiring leadership skills through a multi-faceted process.

> **"Developing one's self as a leader is a day-by-day, lifelong process that is built on continued self-examination, introspection, and self-searching honesty. As we pursue our goal of becoming a leader, we learn from failures, acknowledge wrong turns, and make amends when necessary. It is an ambiguous process that begins and ends with oneself. Becoming a leader is a process of self-invention, based on imagining and expressing your authenticity."** —Warren Bennis and Joan Goldsmith

Two business leaders who have undertaken a leadership journey are Japanese mogul Konosuke Matsushita (1894–1989) and Andrew Grove of Intel. James O'Toole notes that Grove has written three books in the course of his career. The first book was purely technical. In 1983, as Grove took on more management, he wrote *High Output Management* and the word "leadership" never appeared in it. Grove became CEO in 1987 and the company leapfrogged over Motorola to become the world's largest producer of semiconductors.

Andrew Grove's third book, published in 1996, was *Only the Paranoid Survive* and it was about leadership.

> "Descriptions of Matsushita early in life tell us of a hard-working but sickly young man. Nowhere are terms such as *brilliant*, *dynamic*, *visionary*, or *charismatic* used to describe him then, much less *leader*. Yet he grew to be an entrepreneur during his 20s, a business leader in his 30s and 40s and a major-league organizational transformer in his 50s. As a result, he helped his firm rebound after the horror of World War II, absorb new technology, expand globally, and renew itself again and again so as to succeed beyond anyone's dreams. He then took on additional successful careers as a writer in his 60s, a philanthropist in his 70s, and an educator in his 80s." —Bill Capodagli and Lynn Johnson

In sum, leadership can be learned, but it is difficult, if not impossible, to teach leadership in its entirety in a classroom setting. Each situation is unique; each vision and goal requires a distinct set of actions and reactions and the development of a particular set of facilitating relationships. If you grasp a leadership opportunity and forge ahead into the unknown, remember that in so doing, you are getting the best leadership education you can.

# ANYONE CAN BE A LEADER

◎ ◎ ◎

"Managers and executives are not necessarily leaders.
The real leaders in an organization may not have
titles on their doors."

—Philip B. Crosby

It has been some time since we assumed that our leaders were Great Men and the rest of us were an undifferentiated multitude following obediently behind. It's no longer generally accepted that leadership is contained in a set of character traits that some people have and others don't. We now understand that many of the skills of leadership can be learned and that leadership involves a complex set of relationships that can blur the distinctions between leaders and followers. Individuals can be faced with extraordinary leadership challenges in crisis situations and step forward boldly. The next step is to assert that anyone can be a leader.

The idea that we can all lead is the broadest and most democratic notion of leadership and the furthest removed from the idea of the Great Man with his minions. This progressive idea is also an optimistic one. If we believe that leadership can achieve great things, then placing its potential within reach of each citizen is empowering.

> "By viewing leadership as a fixed set of character traits or as linked to an exalted position, a self-fulfilling prophecy has been created that dooms the future to having a limited set of leaders. It's far healthier and more productive to start with the assumption that it's possible for anyone to lead . . . Somewhere, sometime, the leader within each of us may get the call to step forward. Ordinary people are capable of developing themselves far more than tradition has ever assumed possible." —James M. Kouzes and Barry Z. Posner

> "Leadership is a personal gift and unique in every human being. Every individual has some gift of leadership. The problem is, most do not know it and many never realize it." —Hilarie Owen

For Warren Bennis and Burt Nanus, the number one myth about leadership is that it is a rare skill. "Nothing can be further from the truth," they say.

> "While *great* leaders may be as rare as great runners, great actors or great painters, everyone has leadership potential, just as everyone has some ability at running, acting or painting. While there seems to be a dearth of great leaders today, particularly in high political office, there are literally millions

In his book *Nobody in Charge*, Harlan Cleveland studies the implications of seeing everyone as a potential leader. Specifically, he asks whether having everyone in charge means having no one in charge?

> **"When every man, and now every woman too, is entitled to earn through education an admission ticket to active citizenship, when leadership is not the province of a few hundred noblemen, a few thousand big landholders and shareholders, but is stored among an aristocracy of achievement numbering in the millions, decision making is done not by a club but by a crowd. So the core issue of executive leadership is a paradox of participation. *How do you get everybody in on the act and still get some action?*"**

Cleveland's advice for people who wish to lead in these circumstances is to become a generalist. You should cultivate an interest in everything and be responsible to people in general. Then, pick a *specialty*—law, medicine, architecture, music, something where your skill and interest lies. Over time, you can gradually add breadth, which is not the opposite of depth but its complement. You'll become a specialized professional who graduates into general leadership.

**of leadership roles throughout the country, and they are all filled, many of them more than adequately."**

As a society, we now have a broader concept of who our leaders are than hitherto. For better or worse, people are less deferential toward those in traditional positions of authority as each year passes. One result is that levels of trust in public figures like politicians are low. In a less hierarchical and more diverse society, we value a greater number of people in a variety of positions for their leadership than in the past. Respect has to be earned. We appreciate someone's skills and not their status; we value their leadership, not their authority.

In *Leaders*, Norma Riccucci writes about Dr. Helene Gayle, who was Director of the National Center for HIV/AIDS, STD, and TB Prevention, Centers for Disease Control 1995–2001, and who now directs the Bill & Melinda Gates Foundation's HIV, TB, and Reproductive Health Program. Dr. Gayle's colleague Dr. Kenneth Castro notes that, "Helene is viewed as an effective leader because she ensures that we are *collectively* working to achieve [the Center's] common goal." In other words, she empowers her colleagues. Riccucci describes how Dr. Gayle was able to develop broad coalitions and work across national and international boundaries; negotiate Washington; exercise technical skill; set a vision; develop realistic, realizable goals; embody a commitment to values; share leadership; empower staff; and take risks.

◎ ◎ ◎

If you provide leadership, it doesn't mean you drop what you're doing to become a full-time leader. It's not how you're defined.

A teacher may volunteer in a library after school and work her way into a leadership role. A retired person may provide leadership to a church group or community center. A father may coach soccer on the weekend. It's a part of your life, not all of it. This idea is a counterpart to those that create a distinction between leaders and followers. In *The Leader as Martial Artist*, Arnold Mindell says, "No one is only a leader." Leadership is one of our facets, just one of the things we do. Mindell writes that a leader might be involved as a facilitator for a group.

> **"Above all, a good facilitator realizes that the leadership position is just another role. It is a product, image, and feeling representing the group field, and it just happens to coincide, for the moment, with the facilitator's personal psychology. She understands that part of her momentary fate is to be a leader, just as other times her fate is to be a carpenter, parent, child, or disturber."**

It is helpful, then, to consider acts of leadership separately from individual leaders. Anyone can step forward and provide leadership even if they don't want to consider themselves a leader. By the same token, if you have a leadership role in one part of your life, you might be content to be a good follower in another. An example is the business executive who staffs her kids' holiday fair or who volunteers at church on Sunday.

We've discussed business leaders who recognize the need to empower employees because they can't make every decision or follow every trend themselves. Open-minded bosses spread opportunities for leadership throughout the organization. Under these conditions, leadership is not confined to particular jobs.

"The general view that leaders exist only at the top of an organization is far from reality. Often leadership is exercised more effectively by those without impressive positions or titles." —Kenneth E. Clark and Miriam B. Clark

"The equation of leadership with positional power also reveals assumptions about the nature and shape of our organizations that are fast becoming obsolete. Certainly, such a linkage fails to reflect the decentralized and organic structure of what Peter Drucker has called the knowledge organization, which is *the* dominant form in our emerging postcapitalist era. Drucker notes that 'the knowledges' that today's organizations exist to make productive are by definition widely distributed. They are to be found not only among those near the top, the 'lead horses,' but also those who constitute what in the industrial era we called the rank and file." —Sally Helgesen

In *Creating Leaderful Organizations*, Joseph A. Raelin gives examples of innovation from below.

"Microsoft's Internet applications are due as much to students and to new hires, among whom were inveterate Web surfers, as to Bill Gates. Starbucks's Frappachino came from a store manager in Los Angeles and most franchise operators, like McDonalds, will tell you that the best ideas come from franchisees in the field rather than from headquarters."

When organizations are divided into teams that are aligned flat rather in pyramids, or when top executives are receptive to innovation and input, then innovation and ideas—key features of leadership—can come from any point in the organization.

Herb Kelleher of Southwest Airlines was renowned for looking for leaders anywhere in his company.

> **"You know, Tom Landry was coach of the Cowboys, and he said, 'We hire great athletes. We teach them to play any position.' I converted that at Southwest Airlines to be: We hire great attitudes and we'll teach them any functionality that they need."**

Kelleher promoted a woman who joined Southwest as a secretary after raising her two kids. After two years, she was a director of marketing.

> **"I just knew from dealing with her that she had the capabilities. She was imaginative, she was effervescent, she was intelligent, she was pragmatic. And she did a fabulous job."**

In the *Flight of the Buffalo*, James A. Belasco and Ralph C. Stayer offer another analogy for old and new ideas about leadership. The old paradigm, they write, was the buffalo. Buffalo will follow one leader blindly, which was one of the reasons settlers found them so easy to kill. If you kill the lead buffalo, the others will stand around helplessly until they get picked off. Clearly, this is not an effective way of leading in business. The new paradigm is a flock of geese flying in "V" formation. The hardest job is in the lead, but the geese rotate that position, each taking the lead successively.

Some people are able to get things done from whatever position they happen to find themselves in. Joel Deluca writes about what he calls "political savvy," the unofficial influence going on out of sight regardless of someone's title or position.

"Political savvy is an essential leadership skill. Looking away from the glow of a company's few charismatic stars, like slipping behind a Broadway curtain, one can glimpse how much action in today's organizations occurs behind-the-scenes."

Many leadership texts provide advice for people looking to improve their leadership skills. Some are aimed at business executives; others are specifically designed for anyone who has the ambition for leadership no matter what they do. *Everyone a Leader* offers a grassroots model of leadership "that can be performed by anyone regardless of position."

The authors describe behaviors that any of us can learn rather than traits that are unattainable. "Share information" is a behavior that is more easily practiced than "openness." Approaches like this demystify leadership and encourage people to think of leading as being a manageable goal. Studying Alexander the Great doesn't mean we aspire to be him, but many people will find it difficult to apply abstracted lessons from his life to their own. *Everyone a Leader* doesn't mention taking on the Persian Empire. The leadership opportunities it describes are grounded in the modern world:

- "On a busy loading dock when a foreman switches carriers because he reads of an impending strike."
- "During a heated team meeting when one of the members takes it upon him- or herself to mediate the dispute."
- "When a harried administrative assistant volunteers to pull in extra people to get a proposal out on time."

Joseph A. Raelin's *Creating Leaderful Organizations* introduces the idea of "leaderful practice," which is not empowering followers to participate in leadership but instead, "transforms leadership from an individual property into a new paradigm that redefines leadership as a collective practice."

**"In the twenty-first century organization, we need to establish communities where everyone shares the experience of serving as a leader, not serially, but concurrently and collectively."**

Raelin has established a program that runs through self-leadership to mutual leadership that realizes his idea.

These kinds of practical applications of leadership begin on a small scale and plan for the longer term. The individuals who demonstrate leadership here haven't transformed themselves at once into "Leaders," but they have shown leadership, and they can again. Over time, they may find more leadership opportunities and decide to take them. Leadership can come from anywhere and make a difference for all of us.

**"Good citizenship is our responsibility! One aspect of good citizenship is being willing to lead when our talents are needed. Progress toward a vision for the future is achieved when people make use of the strength and knowledge they possess. I am not arguing that people in formal leadership positions should do less, but rather that all of us can and should assume the responsibility as citizen leaders to do more."** —Lorraine R. Matusak

# Part II:

## How Do Leaders Lead?

# It Starts With You

"The instrument of leadership is the self, and mastery of the art of leadership comes from mastery of the self."
—James M. Kouzes and Barry Z. Posner

In Part II, we're asking, "How do leaders lead?" We believe that every leadership situation is different and organic, meaning that leadership is subject to subtle pressures and constant changes over time. Still, it is useful to look at leaders who share some styles because of their roles. Some sports leaders—coaches—are great motivators while players may lead by example. Politicians know about vision and the importance of delivering on promises, and so on. But every leader needs to consider certain skills and tools, arising out of the leader's character, whatever the enterprise they are involved in.

Say you're a school principal. Your job involves managing

the roster of teachers and the school administration, working with the local board of education, and ensuring that the parents are involved and informed. You show leadership: your vision centers on the kids at the school and their individual development. You're inspiring people, pulling all the different groups you work with in the same direction, and you're managing all the various relationships carefully. Only you know each and every little thing that has gotten you to this leader's position: the school newsletter you started, the contacts at City Hall you made, the teachers you moved in or up or moved out.

Leadership is in these details. Columbia Business School professor and author Michael Feiner says that "Leadership is like an iceberg: ninety percent of it is hidden below the surface." The Great Men we often look to—Churchill, Napoleon, Jack Welch, Gandhi, JFK—are the great orators and visible leaders. They are operating at the tip of the iceberg.

**"Leadership is the aggregation of hundreds upon hundreds of small interactions—most of which take place out of our sight—projected across layer upon layer of relationships, day in and day out. It is these relationships that form the substance of organizational life—a fact that the Great Man myth, centered as it is on the power of the *individual*, largely fails to take into account." —Michael Feiner**

So if ninety percent of the iceberg is what you do at this level, how do you do it? Even if many leaders share skills and ideas, every leader has an individual *style* of leadership which may be an amalgam of numerous identifiable styles. Psychologist

Daniel Goleman, who has promoted the idea of "emotional intelligence," has written about research by the consulting firm Hay/McBer that looked at the styles of 3,871 executives and identified six distinct leadership styles.

> "*Coercive leaders* demand immediate compliance. *Authoritative leaders* mobilize people toward a vision. *Affiliative leaders* create emotional bonds and harmony. *Democratic leaders* build consensus through harmony. *Pacesetting leaders* expect excellence and self-direction. And *coaching leaders* develop people for the future."

But in order to lead effectively, the study indicated that one style wasn't enough.

> "The research indicates that leaders with the best results do not rely on only one leadership style, they use most of them in a given week—seamlessly and in different measure—depending on the business situation."

Michael Feiner coins the term "High-Performance Leaders" for those who understand the *how* of leadership. They work up close and personal, utilizing what Feiner calls "HTHC"—hand-to-hand combat—with which they infuse purpose and meaning into everything the team does. And returning to his iceberg metaphor, Feiner writes, "The ninety percent of it that we don't see demands incredible application, stamina, and dedication."

These demands are made of *you*. No matter how much you expect from those you are leading, you must expect more of yourself. It is very difficult to apply the tools and skills of leadership if they're not seen by followers to be coming from a solid base of good character. For example, we know that *trust* is a vital component of leadership, and establishing trust is a key skill. People respond well to *honesty*. *Integrity* and *authenticity* are also essential. They must come from within you. In establishing a leadership style and developing ways of leading, look to yourself first. What values do you hold precious? What values are important to you in leadership?

**"We are all drawn to authentic leaders. We admire them, count on them, and wonder what mysterious quality attracts us to them. Yet their secret is easy to discover: They are clear about who they are. To become leaders in our work lives, each of us needs to develop our capacity for authenticity. Only when we wake up to ourselves and act with integrity can we begin to ask the same of others."** —Warren Bennis and Joan Goldsmith

**"Effective leadership is a by-product of having and demonstrating the right attitudes. The timeless characteristics of honesty, integrity, and accountability are what inspire people to trust and follow their leader—not because that person is their boss."** —Keith Harrell, *The Attitude of Leadership*

PepsiCo CEO Wayne Calloway talked about *integrity*,

**"We're talking about the big sense of the word. Not just 'Don't cook the books,' and 'Don't steal.' Obviously we don't let you do that. The integrity I'm talking about is an openness, an honesty, a willingness to put yourself on the**

line and say, 'Here's what I think,' and not have any hidden agendas." —Wayne Calloway

**"If a leader is honest with himself, it'll be a lot easier to be honest with everybody else."** —Mike Krzyzewski

As we discussed in "Learning to be a Leader," there is not one single set of traits that leaders share. But leaders bring to bear elements of their character and of their values in order to lead. As followers, we expect our leaders to hold to certain standards. When they fall short of those standards, the leader/follower relationship can be compromised. President Jimmy Carter was asked how values shape leadership. He said that high moral and ethical standards are essential.

**"Honesty, truthfulness, integrity, unselfishness—these are always there. And whenever a leader violates these basic principles, through arrogance or through ignorance, there's a derogation of duty."**

President Carter's predecessor, Gerald Ford, replaced Richard Nixon, who had failed to maintain these principles. President Ford's responsibility was to reestablish them. Ford wrote:

**"As a new leader, you must be perceived as totally honest, dedicated to the proper goals, and possessed of the strength necessary to achieve results."**

In order to demonstrate your good character, and to persuade others of its strength, trust is an essential element of your effectiveness as a leader. Prolific leadership author and speaker John C. Maxwell places trust at the heart of leadership.

What might be seen as a less admirable leader's characteristic is *narcissism*. Psychoanalyst Michael Maccoby wrote an award-winning piece in the *Harvard Business School Review*, and, later, a book, that analyzed the strengths and weaknesses of narcissistic leaders. (He also named names: George Soros and Jack Welch are among those Maccoby calls "productive narcissists.") Narcissists are very adept at attracting followers. This is a two-way street.

"Although it is not always obvious, narcissistic leaders are quite dependent on their followers—they need affirmation, and preferably adulation. Think of Winston Churchill's wartime broadcasts or J.F.K.'s 'Ask not what your country can do for you' inaugural address. The adulation that follows from such speeches bolsters the self-confidence and conviction of the speakers. But if no one responds, the narcissist usually becomes insecure, overly shrill, and insistent—just as Ross Perot did."

"Trust is the foundation of leadership. To build trust, a leader must exemplify these qualities: competence, connection, and character."

"Trust is the glue that holds a team together. A leader forgets this at his own peril." —Col. Larry R. Donnithorne, *The West Point Way of Leadership.*

"Why would you follow somebody around a corner? Or up a hill? Or into a dark room? The reason is trust." —Colin Powell

No leadership manual will be able to give a one-size-fits-all guide to establishing trust. (Or authenticity or integrity, for that matter.) John C. Maxwell writes (his emphasis), "*Trust begins with a personal commitment to respect others, to take everyone seriously.*" He continues:

"To tell capable people how to do their job, even innocently or with the best intentions, erodes trust. Such 'advice' becomes a sign of disrespect for followers. How can I trust you if you believe you are better at my job than I am?"

◎ ◎ ◎

Effective leaders have identified personal characteristics beyond honesty, trustworthiness, and integrity they've drawn on. Elsewhere, for example, we note the intelligence, bravery, and endurance of Jackie Robinson; the obduracy of Ulysses S. Grant; the decisiveness and dependability admired by the U.S. Marines; the moral stance of Mohandas Gandhi; the courage of Rosa Parks. One writer believes leaders must have ego and optimism to be effective. Don't worry: you don't need all these to be effective. There is no one laundry list of attributes that makes a good leader.

Certain qualities that one leader may possess wouldn't fit many others. Some leaders could be described as dreamers while, in *The Real Work of Leaders*, Donald L. Laurie quotes Larry Bossidy advocating the virtue of being a realist.

> "Larry Bossidy, who spent thirty-four years at GE before join-
> ing Allied Signal, has described effective leaders as those who
> come to 'a brutal understanding of reality' before they deter-
> mine a specific strategy."

President Carter says that leaders have a duty to understand
the needs of people who depend on them: they should have
*empathy*. He was never a victim of racial discrimination himself, nor was he deprived of his human rights or ever hungry
or homeless. But he knows that "Understanding the needs and
suffering of others is a vital element for successful leadership."

A number of techniques that we'll come across spring from
a person's ability to project their *presence*. Visibility in the
workplace, also known as Management by Walking Around,
is not effective unless the leader has presence. Public speaking
similarly requires a leader to underscore his presence."
Theater director Richard Olivier derived leadership lessons
from Shakespeare's *Henry V*. Henry gives his legendary "band
of brothers" speech to his men in the early hours of the morning before the battle of Agincourt against the French.

> "Henry cannot really want to be out talking to his troops at
> three o'clock. But he does it because it is required of him. He
> exercises visible leadership. He is seen by others, and he sees
> them, thus bolstering confidence."

Of course, it helps to have William Shakespeare as your
speechwriter.

In his autobiography, General Norman Schwarzkopf
details instances when he reemphasized his already formida-
ble presence. Before the first Gulf War, Schwarzkopf called a

commanders' conference at the U.S. base in Dharhan in Saudi Arabia. "I'd worked myself up into a ferocious state . . . ," the general wrote. "I needed everyone in the room to embrace his mission and be breathing fire by the time he went out the door."

Earlier in his career, Schwarzkopf inherited a badly-run command in Vietnam. He recounted how a patrol of thirteen had gone out in broad daylight into the jungle, blown up air mattresses and fallen asleep. They were picked off and only one man got back to camp.

> **"I had to be a complete son of a bitch to get any results, which often entailed losing my temper five or six times a day. Being calm and reasonable just didn't work."**

Norman Schwarzkopf will never be accused of being timid or weak. Another very strong character, Theodore Roosevelt, discussed the danger of fear:

> **"I don't care how honest a man is, if he is timid he is no good. I don't want to see a division in our citizenship into good men who are afraid and bad men who are not at all afraid. The honest man who is afraid is of just as little use in civic life as in war."**

Somewhere between Schwarzkopf's anger and Roosevelt's absence of fear is another positive characteristic. *Aggression* is sometime cited, but it is too indiscriminate a term. Perhaps bravery would be better. Personal bravery, the courage of one's convictions, is the talent Leo Amery, a minister in the wartime governments in Britain, ascribes to Churchill. "No one ever left his cabinet without feeling a braver man," Amery said.

Leaders take it upon themselves to set an example. Brian Muirhead was the flight system manager for the *Pathfinder* project. Muirhead's leadership challenge was to send a craft to Mars, the first for twenty-one years, but to do it at a fraction of the cost and in a fraction of the time of other space programs. (It was known as a "Faster, Better, Cheaper" project.) Muirhead and his team worked with a budget that was less than that of the movie *Titanic*. He was told: take risks, but don't fail.

In the leadership book Muirhead produced after the successful conclusion of the project, he writes about *commitment*. The leader has to be the role model. "As the leader goes, so—in most cases, about most attitude and behavioral issues—goes the organization."

> "A leader who wants people to be committed—clearly an essential for any Faster, Better, Cheaper effort—had better be committed herself. But that's not enough. He or she must be *seen* by the people of the organization to be acting in ways that show commitment. That may mean coming in earlier or leaving later (or both) than the posted work hours; it may mean a willingness to roll up the sleeves and pitch in when the deadline nears."

In order to remain effective in the longer term, a leader must be *adaptable*. You subtly alter the emphasis of your style, changing approaches for different people, in order to remain flexible.

> "When I bought the [Atlanta] Braves, I didn't know what a balk or an infield fly was, but I've got the ability to inspire people. What makes me a successful sailboat racer is that I've got executive ability, I can make 11 guys work harder and longer than anybody else. And baseball players are the same way. They just want someone who really cares."—Ted Turner

Adaptability is difficult for leaders who've had great success with a particular style, or those who believe that one style is more progressive. In *Managerial Leadership*, Peter Topping writes,

> "It is commonly thought today that enlightened leaders are participative, encouraging, and focused on the development of their people. However there may be circumstances where that set of leadership practices would not be the most appropriate."

In a crisis, Topping says, a command-and-control approach might prove to be the most appropriate.

> "One of the lessons I have learned over the years is that changing your leadership practices to adapt to different situations is extraordinarily difficult. George Patton couldn't do it."

Whatever leadership style you settle on, it will be recognizably *you*. You will be able to learn new skills, and improve those that you already have, but the core will be established by your personality and character. Leaders take what they have and run with it as far as they can. Experience will build *confidence*, until you're able to trust yourself to go with your gut and display the courage you already have.

"There's a lot of gut instinct that comes into everything you do. Leadership is an art, not a science. It cannot be reduced to a piece of paper and a bunch of very simple mechanical equations that you apply to, and out the end drops the answer, and you just go out and do that. That's not what it's about. Much of it is gut feeling. Some of it is risk-taking." —Norman Schwarzkopf

"I can't help but wonder why leaders are often so hesitant to lead. I guess it takes a lot of conviction and trusting your gut to get ahead of your peers, your staff and your employees while they are still squabbling about which path to take, and set an unhesitating, unequivocal course whose rightness or wrongness will not be known for years." —Andrew Grove

# BUSINESS LEADERS

"The names of most corporate CEOs fade from
the collective memory, almost on the day they retire.
We remember only the leaders."
—James O'Toole, *Marshall School of Business, USC*

"Every day, I tried to get into the skin of every person in the
place. I wanted them to feel my presence."
—Jack Welch

Current business wisdom may hold that companies are best
served when leadership skills are spread throughout the
organization but the focus remains firmly on the man (occasionally the woman) at the top. *Fortune 500* CEOs and chairmen are the rock stars of the business world. These corporate
celebrities are extravagantly paid. *The New York Times*
reported that in 2003, at 200 large companies, the CEO took
home an average of $5.9 million in total compensation,
including salary and stock. Chief executives' moves are studied by a large and active business media and when a CEO
makes a major decision, the company's stock price will offer
an immediate opinion.

For CEOs, leadership is not part of their job, it *is* the job. CEOs are the public face of the company and they're looked to for direction and vision. Some business leaders come to personify the company, such is the strength of their leadership style.

Larry Bossidy, retired GE, Allied Signal, and Honeywell CEO and chairman, has written about individuals like Jack Welch, Sam Walton, and Southwest Airlines' Herb Kelleher who have impressed their forceful personalities onto their companies.

> **"Leaders of this ilk are powerful and influential presences because they *are* their businesses. They are intimately and intensely involved with their people and operations."**

These CEOs have good leadership skills—they're good communicators and are highly visible around their companies. There is also real substance to what the leaders are doing. Larry Bossidy writes, "There's an enormous difference between leading an organization and presiding over it." For Bossidy, the difference lies in *execution*. These leaders are "doing things leaders should be doing in the first place."

> **"Don't make the mistake of thinking you can lead with your feet up on the desk. If you're responsible for sales and marketing, you should be in the field talking to customers, not just managing the sales force from your office. If you're the head of R&D, you should be visible in the lab to see what's happening. If you're in charge of human resources, you should be on the factory floor to determine what's on the mind of your employees." —Larry Bossidy**

> **"Personal leadership is about visibility—with all members of the institution. Great CEOs roll up their sleeves and tackle**

**problems personally. They don't hide behind staff. They never simply preside over the work of others. They are visible every day with customers, suppliers, and business partners."**
—Louis Gerstner

Bossidy, Louis Gerstner of IBM, and many other CEOs have written books describing how they lead their companies. GE's Jack Welch reportedly received $7.1 million to write *Jack: Straight From the Gut*, which was published days after Welch's retirement in September 2001. Welch has also been the subject of numerous books, and his quotes and sayings often crop up in business literature. Another frequently quoted leader is Southwest Airlines' Herb Kelleher.

Herb Kelleher was a founder of Southwest Airlines who stepped down as CEO and president in 2001 but remained chairman. Kelleher talked many times about putting people first, not just the customer but the airline's employees.

**"A financial analyst once asked me if I was afraid of losing control of our organization. I told him I've never had control and I never wanted it. If you create an environment where people only participate, you don't need control. They know what needs to be done, and they do it."**

Kelleher said he wanted to hire people with a sense of humor—not a requirement everywhere in business. They should also demonstrate heart. As reported in *Values-Based Leadership*, when a Southwest employee's young son was fighting leukemia, 3,000 employees, out of a workforce of 5,000, sent cards.

Kelleher's Southwest has enjoyed great success. The company notes that money invested in Southwest in 1972 would

In 2004, PBS's "Nightly Business Report" and the Wharton School named the twenty-five most influential business leaders of the last twenty-five years. Andrew Grove of Intel was placed first because of his "unconventional thinking, imagination, and integrity." The results were examined in *Lasting Leadership—What You Can Learn From the Top 25 Business People of Our Times.* The list:

- Mary Kay Ash, Mary Kay Ash, Inc. founder
- Jeff Bezos, Amazon.com CEO
- John Bogle, Vanguard Group founder
- Richard Branson, Virgin Group CEO
- Warren Buffett, Berkshire Hathaway CEO
- James Burke, former CEO, Johnson & Johnson
- Michael Dell, Dell, CEO
- Peter Drucker, educator and author
- Bill Gates, Microsoft, chairman
- William George, former CEO, Medtronic
- Louis Gerstner, former CEO, IBM
- Alan Greenspan, Federal Reserve chairman
- Andrew Grove, Intel chairman
- Lee Iacocca, former CEO, Chrysler
- Steve Jobs, Apple CEO

- Herb Kelleher, former Southwest Airlines chairman
- Peter Lynch, former Fidelity Magellan fund manager
- Charles Schwab, Charles Schwab Corp. founder
- Frederick Smith, FedEx CEO
- George Soros, founder and chairman of The Open Society Institute
- Ted Turner, CNN founder
- Sam Walton, Wal-Mart founder
- Jack Welch, former CEO, GE
- Oprah Winfrey, Harpo group of companies chairman
- Muhammad Yunus, Grameen Bank founder

have returned 26% a year through 2002, in which time Southwest never laid anyone off. Kelleher has been unconventional, once arm-wrestling a rival CEO for the right to use a slogan.

> "I always felt that our people came first. Some of the business schools regarded that as a conundrum. They would say: Which comes first, your people, your customers, or your shareholders? And I would say, it's not a conundrum. Your people come first, and if you treat them right, they'll treat the customers right, and the customers will come back, and that'll make the shareholders happy."

Kelleher said the traditional pyramidal structure of a business organization should be inverted.

"Down here, at the bottom, you've got people at headquarters. Up there, at the top, you've got people who are out in the field on the front lines. They are the ones who make things happen."

Because CEOs and chairmen are the center of attention, they have to be careful how they are perceived. British executive Sir John Harvey-Jones of ICI is wary of giving off unintended signals,

"One of the unexpected problems I have found in being chairman . . . is the fact that so many people judged the position of the company by one's own apparent mood, even to whether one smiles or not."

All leaders need to be *visible* to be seen and to be seen to be effective. That doesn't just mean having your picture on the front of the company newsletter.

"For me, the cafeteria is an excellent place to repeat that tried-and-true practice of Management 101: Management by Walking Around." —Robert E. Eckert, CEO, *Mattel*

In *A Passion for Excellence*, management guru Tom Peters writes about McDonald's founder Ray Kroc sawing the backs off managers' chairs to make the point that they should be out front with customers rather than sitting at a desk. If this sounds like a theatrical gesture, that's okay with Peters.

"All business *is* show business. All leadership *is* show business. All management *is* show business. That doesn't mean

One of the best-selling business books of recent years is Jim Collins' *Good to Great*. Collins's research picked out "good-to-great" companies which were characterized by what he terms "Level 5 leaders." A Level 5 leader is someone "who blends extreme personal humility with intense professional will." These are leaders with great resolve who are devoted to the company and are not concerned with self-promotion. In addition to business leaders, Collins cites Abraham Lincoln as a Level 5 president.

**"Those who mistook Mr. Lincoln's shy nature, and awkward manner as signs of weakness found themselves terribly mistaken, to the scale of 250,000 Confederate and 360,000 Union lives, including Lincoln's own."**

Level 5 business leaders are quiet and modest and stay out of the limelight.

**"George Cain, Alan Wurtzel, David Maxwell, Colman Muckler, Darwin Smith, Jim Herring, Lyle Everingham, Joe Cullman, Fred Allen, Cork Walgreen, Carl Reichardt— how many of these extraordinary executives had you heard of?"**

> **tap dancing; it means shaping values, symbolizing atten-
> tion—and it is the opposite of 'administration' and, espe-
> cially, 'professional management.' "**

We'll later look at the *showmanship* of General George S.
Patton. Business leaders will use their personal *charisma*,
when they have it, in their work.

> **"People like Iacocca of Chrysler, Steve Jobs, the founder of
> Apple and Mary Kay Ash of Mary Kay Cosmetics have many
> of the attributes that we have seen in political and religious
> charismatic leaders. They are invariably visionary, are viewed
> as exceptional by others, and are regarded with considerable
> devotion and awe."** —Alan Bryman, *Charisma and Leadership in
> Organizations*

In the ultra-dynamic twenty-first century business environment, *adaptability* may be the key leadership characteristic.
The *Flight of the Buffalo* details how to change.

> **"To change my leadership behavior took lots of conscientious
> work. First, I changed my mental picture of my leadership job.
> I stopped being the decision maker and micro-manager. I
> stopped deciding production schedules and fixing sales prob-
> lems. Instead, I insisted that others handle those situations.
> I changed my leadership job to providing new resources and
> developing people."**

Adaptability means altering behavior to fit new conditions. Too-
rigid adherence to one style, no matter how successful it's been
in one environment, is a recipe for long-term disappointment.

In 1978, after his long career had ended at Ford, Lee Iacocca was brought in to try to save the ailing Chrysler motor company. Iacocca's rescue is the stuff of business legend. Iacocca persuaded the federal government to lend the company $1.2 billion. Under Iacocca, Chrysler lost $1.7 billion in 1980, but by 1983, the company was making $500 million and had repaid the loans.

Part of the rescue package was deep cuts. Iacocca would be asking others to make sacrifices, so he wanted to take the lead.

> **"I began by reducing my own salary to $1.00 a year. Leadership means setting an example. When you find yourself in a position of leadership, people follow your every move. I don't mean that they invade your privacy, although there's some of that, too. But when the leader talks, people listen. And when the leader acts, people watch. So you have to be careful about everything you say and everything you do.**
>
> **"I didn't take $1.00 a year to be a martyr. I took it because I had to go into the pits."**

Robert C. Stempel, chief executive of General Motors, did the same.

> **"Stempel confronted economic adversity and the need to retrench by cutting executive compensation first and substantially, followed by extensive cutbacks in the salaried and plant employee work forces. As Stempel put it, 'The commander doesn't eat until the troops are fed.' The simple expression of sensitivity to feelings of fairness won him wide support in General Motors before decisions and actions of great unpleasantness."**

Helped by new products like the K-Car and minivans, Chrysler gradually turned around, but in Iacocca's last full year, 1991, the company lost $795 million. Much ink has been spilled subsequently on Lee Iacocca's style, how he was adept and skilled at saving Chrysler, but less effective in running the company after it was resuscitated.

> "It seems clear that the old, paternalistic concept of leadership, with the leader as the strong father figure, needs to be replaced. In today's world, a model of leadership in which leaders guide the organization through enlisting cooperation and consultation with others, rather than making unilateral decisions, may be more appropriate. Lee Iacocca, who embodied the old ideal of the charismatic, paternalistic CEO, was widely viewed as a great leader until his much more accessible and consultative successor, Bob Eaton, got dramatically better results at Chrysler. While Iacocca was effective in leading the company through the immediate crisis, his style of leadership was not the best one for rebuilding the company and preventing a similar crisis in the future."

A business leader renowned for his adaptability is John Chambers. Chambers became CEO of Cisco Systems in 1995 and led the company in a period of tremendous growth: revenue in 2000 was nine times larger than in 1995. Chambers was riding high. In March of 2000, *Fortune* asked, "Is he the best CEO in the world?" But Cisco then suffered an almighty slump in the internet and telecommunications bust of 2001 and Chambers had to lay off 8,500 workers. Chambers stayed the course and saw the company through three leaner years. Rosabeth Moss Kanter of Harvard Business School said, "His leadership is remarkable because it is sustained in the bust, not just the boom."

Chambers said that he was planning for the upturn years before they happened.

**"The time you make the changes is before anyone else sees it. There are a lot of advantages to being near a herd, because a herd has 1,000 eyes. But if you're not moving well in advance of the herd, you're in line with the herd's achievements."**

Chambers' hopefulness rubbed off on his workers. As Mona Hudak, a Cisco manager, told *USA Today*, "We're extremely optimistic that John Chambers will see to the success of all of us."

The most celebrated, and imitated, individual business leader of recent times is GE's Jack Welch. After working for GE for twenty years, Welch became chairman and CEO in 1981. Welch stayed another twenty-one years and GE's market value went from $12 billion to $280 billion. Along the way, Welch was a public and accessible figure who was a force of nature, always in motion: changing, innovating, selling, buying, and dealing. Such was his dominance that commentators reached way back to look for the seeds of Welch's success.

**"Jack Welch says he got his first taste of leadership from the scrappy, aggressive kids in the neighborhood as they played endless games and sports in an abandoned gravel pit near his home. He gained experience organizing games, choosing**

teams, looking for a competitor's vulnerability, and going for the score. Running a business is much like playing a game, except that the score is kept in dollars—in GE's case, billions of dollars. The winner is the company that ends up with the most assets and highest earnings."

Welch, who grew up in Salem, Massachusetts, says in his autobiography that if he has any leadership style, he owes it to his mother. She gave her son self-confidence, a key ingredient in effective leadership.

"Confidence gives you courage and extends your reach. It lets you take greater risks and achieve far more than you ever thought possible. Building self-confidence in others is a huge part of leadership."

In his book, Welch is constantly talking about getting the right people around him. Welch personally interacted with 18,000 executives at the company's Crotonville facility, brainstorming with them, looking for ideas.

"The year before Welch took over, GE was voted the best company in America by Fortune 500 executives. Welch's predecessor, Reg Jones, was voted top CEO in the same survey. The wisdom inside GE was that if the company was winning all these awards, there must be a good reason for it. If GE didn't have the answers, then no one did. Welch changed all of that. He was the first to admit that he had not cornered the market on good ideas, once declaring that if the company had to rely on him for all its ideas, GE would 'sink in an hour.' "
—Jeffrey A. Krames, *The Jack Welch Lexicon of Leadership*

"Above all, good leaders are open. They go up, down, and around their organization to reach people. They don't stick to the established channels. They're informal. They're straight with people. They make a religion out of being accessible. They never get bored telling their story." —Jack Welch

"Before at GE, we generally used to tell people what to do. And they did exactly what they were told to do, and not one other thing. Now we are constantly amazed by how much people will do when they are not told what to do by management." —Jack Welch

Among Welch's keys is rigorous "differentiation" among employees. Just as baseball teams look after winning pitchers and productive hitters, companies should reward good executives while relentlessly weeding out those deemed ineffective. At GE, employees were sifted into A, B, and C players. The A's have what Welch terms the four E's of GE leadership: *energy*; the ability to *energize* others; the *edge* to make tough decisions; and the ability to *execute*, all connected by passion. Seventy percent of the company are B's and the rest, C's, have to go. Welch was so vigorous in cutting jobs in the early years, he was dubbed "Neutron Jack," after the neutron bomb of the time, a device that took out people but left buildings standing.

"Removing people will always be the hardest decision a leader faces. Anyone who 'enjoys doing it,' shouldn't be on the payroll, and neither should anyone who 'can't do it.' "

We already discussed Jack Welch's original vision for GE in 1981. Others came along the way—his commitment to be

No. 1 or No. 2 in each business they were involved in, or "fix, sell, or close," it. "Boundaryless" behavior, and four major initiatives in the 1990s: Globalization, Service, the quality program Six Sigma, e-business. Each was pursued relentlessly across the company.

> "An initiative is long lasting, and it changes the fundamental nature of the organization. Regardless of the source, I became the cheerleader. I followed up on all of them with a passion and a mania that often veered toward the lunatic fringe."

Welch stamped his personality on the company in operating managers meetings each January; "Session C" human resources reviews of executives; Crotonville coaching sessions and board meetings; and company celebrations, of which Welch was very fond. Such a forceful and dynamic man must have left few people without a very strong impression.

> "Management professor and Welch biographer Noel Tichy contends that 'opinions of Welch range from "Jack Welch is the greatest CEO GE ever had" to "Jack Welch is an asshole." The two views are quite compatible. Leadership made it necessary to be an asshole at times. All the great leaders, from Martin Luther King to Gandhi, could become assholes at the drop of a hat.' "

# MILITARY LEADERS

"Military genius is a gift from God, but the most essential quality of a general-in-chief is the strength of character and resolution to win at all costs."
—Napoleon Bonaparte

"There never has been a great and distinguished commander of mean intelligence."
—Karl Von Clausewitz

Nowhere are lines of authority more strictly defined than in the military. Every member of the armed forces is part of a rigid hierarchy, with the commander in chief at the top and today's recruit at the bottom. Everyone has a rank within the hierarchy and knows exactly where they stand. Rank is reinforced by codes of behavior, with juniors saluting seniors and addressing them accordingly. Discipline is paramount and orders are supposed to be carried out unhesitatingly.

If leadership is more than simply the exercise of power or authority, then isn't it impossible to have leadership, in the richer sense of the word, in the military? This isn't leadership, it's power. The reality is that anyone in a position of power, a colonel, a general, a police chief, a CEO, or a football coach, can issue an order or direction, but that doesn't make them a leader. The mutually reinforcing relationships of leaders and followers that we have discussed have to be established before there can be genuine leadership. In the military, it is only the *style* that differs, not the content. Field Manual 22-100, *Army Leadership*, has the following definition:

> **"Leadership is influencing people—by providing purpose, direction, and motivation—while operating to accomplish the mission and improving the organization."**

As the trade edition of the manual points out, this says nothing about issuing orders commandingly. The manual has three words on the cover: *Be, Know, Do*; a marvelously succinct leadership credo.

If the underlying leadership principles are very similar to civilian life, the personal stakes are different. Rules of leadership change in wartime. In combat, where leadership is at its most raw and basic, absolute trust is the essential component because decisions mean the difference between life and death. "Effectiveness" in business means productivity or profits; in wartime it means survival. The vision of leaders tends to be collapsed for the majority of soldiers, sailors, marines, and air force personnel. There are larger strategic issues at high command, but for most service people, the future consists of doing what you have to do *that minute* to survive and fight. Anyone who helps you achieve that is a leader, and they usually show it by their personal example.

As we noted, there is no substitute in leadership training for experience. But the armed forces cannot afford to wait for leadership to develop on its own. As *The Air Force Officer's Guide* notes,

> "To carry out its role in support of national objectives, the armed forces have a unique requirement to maintain a young and dynamic officer corps that is capable of developing and managing a large combat-ready force and of assuming wartime leadership."

The military tries to teach leadership at all levels, preparing its men and women for anticipated and unanticipated contingencies. No branch of the services views individuals as a blank slate they can imprint their design upon. The Marines may look at 250 people before they find a suitable candidate. Many of the individuals they take have decided not to go to college; some are from troubled homes and many have minor violations against their name. In *The Extraordinary Leader*, John Zenger and Joseph Folkman look at the Marines as a case study for excellence in leadership preparation, beginning with the meticulous recruiting.

> "All the usual predictors of success are not generally present in this group of recruits. Yet many of them are transformed into effective leaders after a two- to three-year period of time, and go on to display remarkable leadership skills as their careers continue."

In an article in *Inc.* magazine and a subsequent book, David H. Freedman looked at the Marines' success at training leaders. Selecting the right recruits is key. The Marines will rotate their best people through personnel jobs to maintain the highest standards. Some of the hardest jobs to get in the Marines are those that orchestrate the careers of other Marines. Two of any leader's most important jobs are gathering good people around him- or herself and then keeping them. Most organizations would be well served looking at the Marines' attitude to personnel decisions both in recruiting from outside and in developing careers in-service.

In the Marines, a few officer candidates come from the Naval Academy, most from college. They go to Officer Candidate School (OCS) at Quantico which acts, Freedman says, as a ten-week, seven-day-a-week, 24-hour-a-day interview designed to weed out the unsuitable. What the program is looking for is leadership. As for what that leadership looks like, Colonel John Lehockey, commander of OCS says, "It has no exact definition. It's our job to recognize it." OCS is mentally and physically exhausting. Those who survive its tests and exercises, including the famous Crucible obstacle course, go on to take The Basic School—TBS—which is a six-month course of officer training.

*The Extraordinary Leader* outlines the basics of the Marines training program. An experienced non-commissioned officer is paired with a new lieutenant who will provide instant feedback. Teamwork is drilled into every officer trainee. Intricately planned missions will be changed at the last second and roles switched: the patrol leader will become the medic, for example. Everyone on the team will have to know everyone else's job for the mission to succeed. Marines operate by the Rule of Three: three-people teams, with three alternatives to any problem. And they look for a "70-per cent solution" when a quick decision has to be made. In those cases it's better to arrive at and make a partly thought-through solution than not take any action at all.

David Freedman's *Inc.* piece discusses the importance of case studies in Marines officer training. In addition to planning and executing missions and technical training, a great deal of time is spent looking at actual engagements. In the Marines they're called "Sea stories." Marine Colonel Robert E. Lee tells of how he was given an order in Vietnam in 1975 to take twelve Marines and secure a merchant ship from deserting South Vietnamese soldiers. He wasn't told how; just to get it done. Lee took a skill that he had been taught, how to take a building, and transferred it to this situation he hadn't encountered before. Lee visualized the ship as a building and had his men take control one floor at a time, starting from the top deck.

Lee's story illustrates that in war you have to expect the unexpected. Decision making has to devolve to those people actually on the ground. But what decision to make? How does a leader lead? As Freedman asks,

> "How do you teach generic leadership? There are no rules, no checklists, no set processes that apply to any but the most rote of situations, says Lee. Instead, the Basic School tries to hone decision making the way a chess master does: through exposure to as many scenarios as possible, so that the brain learns to recognize patterns it can apply to entirely new situations. That's how Lee solved his ship-securing problem, and that, claims Lee, is how all good managers solve the toughest challenges. Sea stories are the very best way to get those scenarios across, he says."

So at Basic School, 300 hours are spent with instructors telling stories like these, essential building blocks for leadership.

Another text that uses the Marines as an exemplar for good leadership training is *Semper Fi: Business Leadership the Marine Corps Way* (Dan Carrison and Rod Walsh). The authors describe how leadership is gradually instilled in a recruit.

> "A recruit going through basic training learns how to lead by degrees. His first command may be as menial as taking responsibility for picking up the cigarette butts on the barrack grounds. The next step along the path to leadership might be marching first a squad of twelve across the parade grounds, later a platoon of fifty, then a company of two hundred. To the recruit, leadership is only a stripe away, visible and achievable. The desire to lead is created through a course of progressive resistance, where every additional burden is incremental, until the mature Marine is prepared to take on the ultimate leadership challenge—a combat command."

The Academy is reminding cadets of everything they don't know and it's clear that they don't know a lot. Recruits begin by learning followership—self-discipline, stress, and time management. Then, they go on to learn leadership.

The armed forces recognize that they have to attract individuals who want to serve but also want to be recognized as individuals. By concentrating on teaching leadership they can plausibly claim to focus on individual development. *Be-Know-Do* is adapted from the official Army leadership manual:

> "In a new world that is more diverse, localized, and challenging, leadership has to be everyone's job. There is no alternative. The Army has long understood that there is no

Can we extrapolate leadership lessons from the military and apply them to the rest of society? Numerous books try to do that, especially for the world of business. While it won't be possible to behave in your company as if you are a Navy SEAL or a marine, reading widely across a range of these books might shake loose some ideas from all these military analogies. Some examples:

> **"No soldier will ever be inspired to advance into a hail of bullets by orders phoned in on the radio from the safety of a remote command post; he is inspired to follow the officer in front of him.**
>
> **"Business managers must recognize the identical principle: it is much more effective to get your personnel to follow you than to push them forward from behind a desk."** —Dan Carrison and Rod Walsh

In *Take Command! Leadership Lessons from the Civil War*, Tom Wheeler writes of the crucial role played at Gettysburg by lower ranks—a native American fighter; the youngest brigade commander in the Union army; a college professor; and a regiment of 262 Minnesotans that lost 80% of its number to plug a gap and gain five crucial minutes.

> **"The lessons of Gettysburg are equally applicable today in the marketplace battle. Companies like 3M Corpor-**

ation, Southwest Airlines, and Nortel Networks have
built their success by pushing leadership down the corporate hierarchy.

"Individuals determine victory." —From *Be-Know-Do*

"Strategy is key to leadership. But using military terms
willy-nilly to describe business is a fallacy. One might just
as well do the same with the technical terms used in medicine or in battle." —Major-General William A. Cohen

substitute for principled leadership. The Army's slogan—*An
Army of One*—was designed with that in mind."

Service manuals offer lists of traits and leadership principles
for their trainees. They are similar to the lists in many management books and are useful as personal checklists, an inven-
tory you can take of your own performance. The lists aren't
exhaustive by any means, and are highly subjective. The air
force list has six traits and ten principles, while the army gives
nineteen traits and eleven principles, and the marines fourteen
traits and eleven principles. The air force's leadership traits
are:

- Integrity
- Loyalty
- Commitment

- Energy
- Decisiveness
- Selflessness

*Fundamentals of Marine Corps Leadership* lists fourteen leadership traits:

- Integrity
- Knowledge
- Courage
- Decisiveness
- Dependability
- Initiative
- Tact
- Justice
- Enthusiasm
- Bearing
- Endurance
- Unselfishness
- Loyalty
- Judgment

And the eleven leadership principles:

- Be Technically and Tactically Proficient
- Know Yourself and Seek Self-Improvement
- Know Your Marines and Look Out for Their Welfare
- Keep Your Personnel Informed
- Set the Example
- Ensure that the Task is Understood, Supervised, and Accomplished

- Train Your People as a Team
- Make Sound and Timely Decisions
- Develop a Sense of Responsibility Among Subordinates
- Employ Your Command in Accordance With Its Capabilities
- Seek Responsibility and Take Responsibility for Your Actions and the Actions of Your Unit.

At the highest levels, leaders of quite different characters and style have made significant impacts. (See the chapter on generals Patton and Eisenhower.) General George C. Marshall was a five-star general at the end of World War II. Marshall was in charge of the vast corporation that was the army. In 1939, when Marshall was chief of staff, the army had 174,000 soldiers; by 1945, it had 8.2 million people in uniform. Marshall was a reformer who reorganized this giant entity. He was a bold promoter of men like Dwight Eisenhower, Omar Bradley, Mark Clark, and Joe Stilwell. According to *Be-Know-Do*, "For generals who could not adjust to the sweeping changes in the Army, he made career shifts as well: he retired them."

> "There are as many different styles of command as there are commanders. A MacArthur or a Patton conveyed an aura of indomitable will. A [Vinegar Joe] Stillwell or an [Air Force General] Ira Eaker led by personal example; their troops knew they shared the privations and the dangers. Omar Bradley and Dwight Eisenhower managed to convey their personal concerns for the men in their armies, inspiring affection. Marshall exerted command over all these men and more by dint of mastery of the complexities of world war." —Ed Cray

Like Patton and Douglas MacArthur, Ulysses S. Grant is another example of a leader of indomitable will. Grant's command in the Civil War was characterized by his fierce determination, by what Josiah Bunting describes as "imposing his will on the armies."

> "In every battle and campaign in which Grant commanded there seems to have been some defining moment in which he, however unconsciously, communicated his determination not to back off. Such quiet demonstrations of will reassure wavering men; they stir them, not to action but to determination. Thucydides is reported to have said that 'of all manifestations of power, restraint impresses me most.' Quiet obduracy in a leader is equally formidable."

In May 1864, Grant's march to Richmond got bogged down in the wilderness. It was Grant's habit to sit in camp whittling wood and smoking cigars. An officer wondered aloud what General Robert E. Lee was planning. Grant told him not to worry about Lee,

> "Ulysses S. Grant was teaching his army a new concept— the courage of their convictions . . .
>
> "That evening, to a reporter on his way to Washington, Grant said, 'If you see the President, tell him that whatever happens, there will be no turning back.' "

Historian James L. Stokesbury says, "Probably no American soldier has ever epitomized the art of leadership more fully than Robert E. Lee."

"One day when it was all winding down to its sad finish, Lee lamented what might become of his country, and one of his aides interrupted, 'General, for the last two years, these men have had no country; you are their country, and what they have fought for."

"To my way of thinking no great battle commander in all history ever reached the heights he might have reached if he did not feel this love for his men, and a profound respect for them, and the jobs they had to do." —Matthew Ridgway (1895-1993)

If no one leadership style seems more effective than any other for senior command positions, personal attachment and trust might be what works best in combat situations. This is the clearest demonstration of the effectiveness of leading by example. Today, no one expects generals to ride out in the lead helicopter, but neither do they expect them to behave like many commanders in the First World War, surely the nadir of effective military leadership. (See "Bad Leadership.") John Keegan describes how World War I differed in this respect from earlier and later conflicts.

"On earlier battlefields, that disparity had been small, if at all apparent. Wellington, indeed, was arguably at greater risk on the field of Waterloo than many of his subordinates, and at Agincourt [King] Henry [V] . . . deliberately courted risk throughout the battle. Hindenburg, Haig, Joffre, on the other hand, never smelt powder; Haig, for motives which he was adept at rationalizing, would not even visit his wounded. Their chateau-generalship (a style which, to be fair, they

In his autobiography, Norman Schwarzkopf writes about his experience as a colonel in Vietnam in 1970. Schwarzkopf would talk to men who were at the end of leave before going back into combat. When prompted, the men would complain to Schwarzkopf about having to wear helmets and flak jackets in the tropical heat.

> "They hated the minefields. They hated the heat. They hated the helmets and flak jackets. Most of the time they hated *me*. But I never made the mistake of confusing their comfort with their welfare. I'd say, 'Look guys, I ain't here to win a popularity contest. My primary concern is keeping you alive. If on the day you leave for the United States your last thought of me is, 'I hate that son of a bitch,' that's fine. Actually, I'll be happy if that happens. Because an alternative is for you to go home in a metal casket, and then you won't be thinking anything at all. That's why I make you put on helmets and flak jackets.'"

inherited rather than created) caused deep if unexpressed offence to the generation of officers who, subalterns in 1914, were senior commanders by 1940 . . ."

As we mentioned in the context of leaders and followers, the most important people, in this case the *only* important people, are the members of your unit and the most important individual is the leader of that unit, who must set an example to be effective. For Stephen Ambrose, Captain Meriwether Lewis epitomized the effective military leader.

> **"How he led is no mystery. His techniques were time-honored. He knew his men. He saw to it that they had dry socks, enough food, sufficient clothing. He pushed them to but never beyond the breaking point. He got out of them more than they knew they had to give. His concern for them was that of a father for his son. He was the head of the family."** —Stephen Ambrose

> **"The months in the desert had reinforced my longstanding conviction that sergeants really were the backbone of the Army. The average trooper depends on NCOs for leadership by personal example."** —Tommy Franks

The army also uses case studies from history to teach leadership. One subject is Dick Winters, who at the time of D-Day was a First Lieutenant of Easy Company, 506th Parachute Infantry Regiment, 101st Airborne Division. Winters was at the heart of Stephen Ambrose's book *Band of Brothers* and the subsequent HBO television series. On D-Day, Winters's job was to help secure Causeway #2 which linked to Utah Beach. Winters led twelve men in an exemplary attack on four 105mm guns guarded by 50 men that were pounding the beach. Winters lost six men (four dead and two wounded), but the causeway was opened.

Charles F. Brower, IV, head of the Department of Behavioral Sciences and Leadership at West Point, and Gregory J. Dardis, Associate Professor, wrote about Dick Winters and why he was part of their Leadership in Combat Seminar (PL470). Dick Winters was, "The paragon of the combat leader—physically fit, brave, technically competent, genuinely interested in the welfare of his men, friendly yet distant." Soldiers like Winters were tactically and technically competent and they also cared for their men's emotional and physical needs. The men knew leaders like this would not be wasteful of their lives.

> **"These leadership attributes helped soldiers overcome the real enemy—their fear—and perform their soldierly duties in combat."**

Long after the war, Robert "Burr" Smith, who had been a Sergeant in Easy Company, wrote to Winters,

> **"You were blessed (some would say rewarded) with the uniform respect and admiration of 120 soldiers, essentially civilians in uniform, who would have followed you to certain death."**

Brower and Dardis wrote of the impact of leaders like Winters.

> **"The force of example and the enthusiasm of a few leaders like Dick Winters often affected the combat performance of their units in extraordinarily disproportionate ways."**

The trials of combat forge an intense unity of purpose in units where effective leadership is displayed. Amid the chaos and peril, each man knows everyone else has his back.

"Trust is the lifeblood of the SEAL community. SEALs pack each other's parachutes, monitor each other's dive equipment, cover each other when under fire, and give each other blood transfusions. You could be the fastest sprinter in the world, but if you leave your buddy behind, you're out. SEALs have never left a buddy behind in combat, not even a buddy's corpse." —Jeff and Jon Cannon

Combat leaders apply everything they have learned, but more than their expertise, it is their steadfast example and demeanor that will make them effective. The case study of Omaha Beach in Part III demonstrates that the direct circumstances of war, the directive "follow me," can be enough to establish leadership. There is underlying trust—you must have faith in the person that they know what they're doing—but the key is the example.

A reporter followed Captain Read Omohundro of Bravo Company of the First Battalion, Eighth Marines during the assault on the city of Falluja in Iraq in November 2004. It was close and deadly urban warfare.

"Time and again through the week, Captain Omohundro kept his men from folding, if not by his resolute manner then by his calmness under fire. In the first 16 hours of battle, when the combat was continuous and the threat of death ever present, Captain Omohundro never flinched, moving his men through the warrens and back alleys of Falluja with an uncanny sense of space and time, sensing the enemy, sensing the location of his men, even in the darkness, entirely self-possessed."

When Captain Omohundro said to his men, "Damn it, get moving," the men, "looking relieved that they had been given direction amid the anarchy, were only too happy to oblige." Later, Captain Omohundro admitted that he had felt the strain of battle.

> " 'It's not like I don't feel it,' Captain Omohundro said. 'But if I were to show it, the whole thing would come apart.' "

Experiences in combat stay with people their whole lives. George H.W. Bush flew planes off aircraft carriers in the Pacific during the Second World War. In *The Greatest Generation*, Tom Brokaw reports President Bush describe an incident that includes a relatively small example of leadership, perhaps, but an exemplar of decisiveness and imperturbability.

> "He remembers vividly standing on the carrier deck when another plane made a bad landing. As the pilot tried to take off again, the plane veered out of control and its propeller cut a crew member in half. As Bush stood there, stunned, staring at a severed leg, a salty chief petty officer, 'rallied the shocked sailors.' 'Goddamnit, get back to work. Swab the deck, clear the deck, get ready for the next plane.' More than fifty years later that navy chief stands out in the mind of President Bush as a man who, under great adversity, took charge, rallied the men, got the job done—did his duty."

# SPORTS LEADERS

◎ ◎ ◎

"To me, the players got the wins, and I got the losses. Caring for one another and building relationships should be the most important goal, no matter what vocation you are in."
—Dean Smith

"A team that has eleven leaders on the field, all taking it upon themselves to get the job done, is a team that's tough to beat."
—Mia Hamm

Sports offer excellent leadership opportunities. For kids, well-coached sports can teach the importance of teamwork and how different individual contributions are needed for group success. For adults, coaching sports provides you a chance to lead in the community and make a difference. Provided that winning is not your sole focus, you can pass on a host of positive lessons through youth sports.

In the pros, on the other hand, winning certainly is the priority. Vince Lombardi is associated with this saying, "Winning isn't everything; it's the only thing," that neatly sums up the attitude of big-time sports. That obsession with winning is why so many leadership lessons are taken from sports and why so many winning coaches and players write books on leadership and management. Sports leaders are winners, and we want to see how that translates to the world the rest of us inhabit.

Every game and series that is played has potential metaphorical significance. It's not just sports fans who know about a great comeback (Red Sox vs. Yankees, 2004); a great play at the last moment (Doug Flutie's "Hail Mary" pass caught by Gerard Phelan for Boston College against Maryland in 1984); and great moments and sequences immortalized in portentous-sounding phrases like "The Drive," "The Catch," and "The Immaculate Reception." Games follow a narrative arc with a beginning, a middle, and an end. They often include arresting storylines and the chance for an unpredictable finish or an unforgettable performance. Out of these, reputations for leaders and leadership are made.

Coaches, of course, can't hit a single ball, catch one pass, or sink any shots. It's in preparing and motivating the team between games, and in setting an example for their players, that coaches earn their money.

**"A leader's most powerful ally is his or her own example. Leaders don't just talk about doing something; they do it. Swen Nater, a former player at UCLA, told me once, 'Coach, you walked the walk.' He meant that I led by example."** — John Wooden

Football coaches famously spend hours breaking down game film and preparing their players for the next opponent, snatching a few hours' sleep on a cot in the office. Constantly repeated drills and practices reinforce skills and are a key part of *preparedness*. Long-time Miami Dolphins head coach Don Shula teamed up with leadership expert Ken Blanchard to write a book. It includes Shula's notion of "overlearning" that explains the purpose of relentless practice:

> **"Overlearning means that players are so prepared for a game that they have the skills and confidence needed to make the big play. More than anything else, overlearning—constant practice, constant attention to getting the details right every time—produces hunger to be in the middle of the action. When players have absolutely no doubt about what they're supposed to do, or how to do it, they thrive on pressure. If the heat's on, they want it coming their way."**

The second leadership piece for effective coaches is *motivation*. The teams of Duke University basketball coach Mike Krzyzewski have won three national titles. Coach K also has written a leadership book, in which he discusses motivation:

> **"I once heard a high school coach tell a kid that it was not his job to motivate players, that they should show up motivated. Well, I just shook my head. I could not disagree more with a statement like that. I believe the main job of a coach is to motivate. The main job of a leader is to inspire."**

Dean Smith, the North Carolina basketball coach who worked ten miles along the road from his great rival Mike Krzyzewski, compiled an 879-254 record in 36 seasons, winning two national championships along the way. All his teams

The sustained success of the Bill Belichick's New England Patriots teams means he is looked at as a paradigm of the successful coach. He runs his team using excellent management and leadership skills. Belichick is a good recruiter and judge of talent who surrounds himself with talented deputies. He is an able motivator and a team-first manager who won't hesitate to unload players who don't buy into his system. A story in the *Boston Globe* described "Bill Belichick, CEO."

"Belichick's all-business approach spills over into the way his players act on and off the field. The Patriots don't taunt opponents, and they don't gloat. They talk about the things Belichick does—concentrating on details, executing the game plan, cutting down on mistakes, taking one game at a time. It sounds boring, but to Peter L. Slavin, the approach makes sense.

" 'A lot of teams rely on emotional highs to succeed,' said Slavin, the president of Massachusetts General Hospital, who has a business degree from Harvard to go along with his medical degree. 'Emotional highs work for a game or two, but not for a season,' said Slavin. What does work is Belichick's single-minded focus. 'What he has is a sustainable solution,' said Slavin."

were meticulously prepared and executed the coach's on-court philosophy embodied in this mission statement:

> **"If you asked me to define my coaching and leadership style, I'd describe myself as an open-minded dictator. My basketball philosophy boils down to six words: Play hard; play together; play smart."**

Off the court, Dean Smith provided his students with guidance and leadership. He looked after the best interests of the young men on the team, advising stars like Michael Jordan and James Worthy to turn pro when there was nothing more they could achieve at college and could maximize their earnings potential. At the same time, Smith's teams had very high graduation rates and students went on to successful careers that Smith would follow proudly. Smith spoke out about civil rights and he would take his students to meet death row inmates at the state prison in Raleigh, something he says his religious faith prompted him to do. Smith believes coaches and players develop a special bond:

> **"I don't know of any other relationship that compares to that between a coach and a player, which has its own peculiar emotional sphere, separate even from the parental one. The sharing of work toward a common goal, the mutual shouldering of emotions that go with winning and the disappointments of losing can't be found in any other walk of life."**

Teams need leaders on the field to motivate and inspire during the game when the coach is marooned on the sidelines. Players establish a reputation as leaders off the field as well.

Yankees manager Joe Torre describes Derek Jeter's quick assumption of the role of leader.

> **"Derek Jeter turned twenty-five during the 1999 season, but he already had the leadership qualities of someone a lot more experienced. At his young age, players already look up to him, and it's not because he's such a good player. It's because he handles being so good so remarkably well."**

Jeter is always the first player at the top of the dugout steps congratulating a teammate for a big hit. By diving into the stands to make a catch, by hitting well in key situations, by taking an extra base, Jeter is a terrific leader by example.

There's no huddle in baseball, so players have to find ways of picking up their teammates during play. Florida Marlins reliever Chad Fox spoke about the leadership style—leading with a hard stare—of his All-Star catcher Ivan "Pudge" Rodriguez who helped the Marlins to the World Series in 2003.

> **"He's definitely our leader, on and off the field. Sometimes it's not even vocal. He can do it with his intense body language. Just the way he looks at you inspires you.**
>
> **"Sometimes on the mound, I'll start questioning myself. I'll look at Pudge, and he'll just give me a stare that says, 'Let's go. Be aggressive.' If he believes in me, it helps me believe in myself."**

The great leaders understand that they have to put the team first in order for them to win. Bill Russell, captain of the Boston Celtics, realized that he had to subordinate individual goals to the needs of the team.

"As a result, I became the kind of leader who understood that doing the most for my team would best guarantee success. To get there, I had to get past a lot of things that really weren't really vital to winning but that made me feel good—like taking shots. I can't emphasize this enough."

Players lead in different ways. Brandi Chastain talks about two teammates on her championship-winning U.S. National soccer team.

"There isn't necessarily one type of captain who's best to lead the National Team, a 3 v. 3 team, or any team. There are many successful models. Most people think that leaders have to be people you recognize as soon as they enter a room. Julie [Foudy] is definitely that kind of person. But Joy Fawcett, another National Team leader, doesn't fit the stereotypical mold and is nonetheless an effective leader. She works very hard every day and goes about getting better. She is very soft spoken, but she always finds a way to get the job done and to get people to respect her and emulate her."

Brett Favre, quarterback of the Green Bay Packers, also leads by example. Favre has described sitting in the locker room at halftime of a game in which his team was trailing by ten points. During the interval, as players talked among themselves, "I just listened because I knew what we needed to do," Favre said later. "And the talk wasn't going to get it done." Favre just went out and did it, leading one of his regular fourth-quarter comebacks with the Packers winning the game on a last-second field goal. Mike Sherman, Packers coach, said of Favre, "To be able to rely on his leadership and abilities at those times gives us an opportunity to win a game like this." Favre leads by doing and the players respond because they have faith that he will win.

The greatest winner was Michael Jordan. His transcendent ability and extraordinary competitiveness forced his teammates to improve their play. Los Angeles Lakers great Magic Johnson was also a marvelous player, but a great motivator too, as David Halberstam recounts,

> "[Magic] Johnson was a natural leader on the court, and he played the right position for it, point guard. In the shrewd assessment of Mark Heisler of the *Los Angeles Times*, who had covered both men for a long time, Jordan was by contrast not a natural leader, he was a natural *doer*. His game did not evolve naturally from sharing the ball and making other players better. One of the few men who knew them both very well, James Worthy, once said that if anything, Johnson was more intense than Jordan: 'Michael is more intense within himself, Magic is intense for everybody.' "

According to their coach, Phil Jackson, on Jordan's Chicago Bulls teams, other players played more vocal leadership roles.

> "Michael didn't really want to be a team leader, but his inspirational play thrust him into that capacity. Scottie [Pippen] (and Bill Cartwright) were the unsung team leaders—talking privately to the players, helping them accept their roles . . . It was Scottie who helped his teammates find their comfort zones within the team's framework by constantly acknowledging their contributions."

Jordan and Magic Johnson are examples of rare individual players who can carry a team to victory by a combination of their supreme talent and unbreakable determination. Leaders like this step forward at key moments and take charge. Boston Celtic Larry Bird was another such player.

> "During the final seconds of an especially tense game, Boston Celtics coach K.C. Jones called a time-out. As he gathered the players at courtside, he diagrammed a play, only to have [Larry] Bird say, 'Get the ball out to me and get everyone out of my way.'
>
> "Jones responded, 'I'm the coach and I'll call the plays!' Then he turned to the other players and said, "Get the ball to Larry and get out of his way.' It just shows that when the real leader speaks, people listen."

Even when we realize we're not going to play centerfield for the Yankees or score goals for the USA like Mia Hamm, sports provide lessons we can carry through life. It's here we might first find our feet as a leader. Dwight Eisenhower, for one, used sports this way. "It was in sports that he first discovered his talents as a leader and an organizer," writes Stephen Ambrose. He put together afternoon games and helped organize the Abilene High School Athletic Association, of which he was elected president his senior year of high school.

Eisenhower wanted to win but he also played fair. In a football game the Abilene team's opponents had a black player at center. No one but the young Eisenhower, who usu-

Sports writers, coaches, and players frequently use military analogies when talking about their games. Some of the analogies are crass, the rest simply inappropriate. But there are many meaningful links between sports and the military. Pat Tillman was a safety with the Arizona Cardinals who turned down a $3.6 million contract to join the Army Rangers after the September 11 attacks. On patrol in Afghanistan in April, 2004, Tillman was killed by friendly fire. Tillman's college coach at Arizona State, Dirk Koetter talked about his former player,

> **"We do our leadership meetings two days a week. When I ask our players to give examples of almost any characteristic, no matter what the lesson is, Pat Tillman's name always comes up. He is off the charts in that respect."**

In a story on the ESPN web site, Adrian Wojnarowski wrote about First Lieutenant Alex Moore, who played football for Army and who went on to serve and be wounded in Iraq. After losing heavily to Navy in the biggest game of the season, Moore said. "As a leader, I can't lose anymore now. At this time next year, I'll be a platoon leader and I cannot be on the losing side then." Moore took charge of a platoon of 75 men and prepared like he had prepared for football, studying all night, immersing himself in details, asking more experienced men for help. Losing to Navy helped drive him forward.

**"Whenever I wanted to sleep there, I'd hear that Navy fight song again in my mind, and I'd be up, pushing harder. Football taught me to be aggressive, and out there with bullets flying, you've got to make the right decision right away. And you learn that in football. You learn that poise. No matter what, you've got to be the first one through the door, and I tried to do that on the offensive line there. Looking back, I should've done more to lead. I wish I had done more, but I also know: Football was the best leadership tool that I ever had at the Academy."**

ally played end, would line up across from him. Eisenhower made a point of shaking the center's hand before and after the game, showing up his teammates in the process. Dean Smith writes about how his father integrated the high school team he coached in Kansas in 1934 and about the courage of Paul Terry, the black tenth grader who played with the team despite being abused and refused service in restaurants and being banned from the state tournament because of his race.

Many athletes, like tennis great Arthur Ashe, have chosen to use their status and high profile to act as leaders in the community. Ashe said he felt a responsibility. "If God hadn't put me on earth mainly to stroke tennis balls, he certainly hadn't put me here to be greedy," Ashe wrote. "I wanted to make a difference, however small in the world." Ashe became an activist in many areas: campaigning against apartheid in South Africa, for health care, and for AIDS awareness, among other causes. Another good example is basketball's David Robinson, who was instrumental in founding a school, the Carver Academy, in San Antonio. Robinson and his wife donated $9 million to the school.

Other athletes have served as social pioneers. Eddie Robinson was head football coach at Grambling State University in Louisiana from 1941 to 1997, a period spanning Pearl Harbor and the entire Cold War. It was also a period that saw tremendous upheavals in race relations in the United States. In 1955, Robinson's team won its first black college national championship, and in December of that year, Rosa Parks was arrested. In his autobiography, Robinson wrote about the state of football then, and how he wanted to change it.

**"In 1956 there were no black head coaches at the big white colleges or in the NFL and no black quarterbacks at either level. If we could make a big enough impact with football at Grambling, if our plans worked and our goals were met, then the national stage would provide us the opportunity to smash the stereotypes that blacks couldn't be leaders, be they athletes, civil rights activists, corporate leaders, or politicians. That was something that I wanted to achieve very badly. I wanted to help show the way, to tear down those brick walls so blacks could coach at the big, predominately white, schools."**

Robinson also wrote about the problems black players have encountered playing quarterback. Black players have traditionally been discouraged from playing the position because white coaches said they lacked the necessary leadership skills. Countless players were forced to switch positions. Mike Howell played well as a quarterback for Eddie Robinson at Grambling in 1964 but tried out for the NFL as defensive back, and played seven seasons there for the Cleveland Browns.

The first black quarterback in the NFL was Willie Thrower, who played one game for the Chicago Bears in 1953. Marlin Briscoe started as quarterback for Denver in 1968 and later played as a wide receiver. The first African American to start the season as quarterback was Joe Gilliam of the Pittsburgh Steelers in 1972. Fittingly, Grambling graduate Doug Williams was the first black quarterback to win a Super Bowl, in 1988. The fallacies surrounding the idea of "the black quarterback" should be buried finally under the stats put up by players like Donovan McNabb, Steve McNair, and Byron Leftwich. On April 21, 2001, Michael Vick was the first black quarterback taken number one in the draft.

In 1947, Branch Rickey, the General Manager of the Brooklyn Dodgers, put Jackie Robinson on the team and Robinson went on to single-handedly take on and defeat decades-old Jim Crow restrictions in baseball that year. (Also in 1947, three months after Robinson's debut, Larry Doby of the Cleveland Indians became the first black player in the American League.) Robinson and his fellow pioneers endured player revolts, constant threats, abuse, beanings and spike-up slides, and being habitually refused service in restaurants and hotels. Larry Doby recalled that some of his own teammates refused to shake his hand when he joined the team. Jackie Robinson and Larry Doby broke new ground with extraordinary courage and stoicism. Robinson's biographer Arnold Rampersad has written:

> **"Over a period of six months, from his first stumbling steps to the victories that closed the season, he had revolutionized the image of Black American in the eyes of many whites. Starting out as a token he had utterly complicated their sense of black people, how they thought and felt, their dignity and courage in the face of adversity. No Black American man had ever shone so brightly for so long as the epitome not only of stoic endurance but also of intelligence, bravery, physical power, and grit."**

Robinson found some allies among his fellow players. In 1947, slugger Hank Greenberg was playing for the Pittsburgh Pirates. As a Jewish player, Greenberg had heard slurs and now Jackie Robinson was hearing them too. Different taunts perhaps, but with the same malevolent intent. In a game in Pittsburgh, Robinson was hearing it as usual from sections of the crowd. Robinson got on base and took a big lead. Robinson slid back into first hard where he met Greenberg, the Pirates first baseman. Greenberg gave him a hand up.

> **" 'Stick in there," Jack remembered Greenberg telling him. 'You're doing fine. Keep your chin up.' 'Class tells.' Jack commented to a reporter. 'It sticks out all over Mr. Greenberg.' "**

Leadership can be found in seemingly small gestures like this. Popular Dodger Pee Wee Reese, who became Robinson's best friend on the team, made another. Reese made what was for the time a stunning act of solidarity with his teammate. Where and when it happened is in doubt; it might have been in a game in Cincinnati, it might have been Boston. Opposing players were abusing Reese vilely for playing with Robinson. Knowing the words were meant for him, Robinson had a "hopeless, dead feeling," that Reese sensed. So Reese walked over and stood next to Robinson and by some accounts put his hand on his teammate's shoulder, all the while staring at the hecklers. It was a deep expression of respect and a fine piece of leadership toward a man in the midst of making one of the great sustained leadership statements of all time.

# POLITICAL LEADERS

◎ ◎ ◎

**"The hardest part of leadership is compromise."**
—Tip O'Neill

Politics fits James McGregor Burns's models of transactional and transformational leadership very neatly. Political power is vested in the followers—the citizens ("we the people"). Politicians at all levels from the dog catcher to the president make campaign promises (from tax cuts and health care reform to more school crossings) when they vie for our votes, which they need in order to exercise power on our behalf. This is transactional leadership—"the exchange of valued things." In this case, votes are exchanged for redeemed policy promises.

Politicians make promises that are part of the vision they are trying to sell. A vision of the future is a key component of any campaign. What makes politics unusual is that people choose between competing visions. Presidential candidates offer campaign promises, and because it is the scope of their job, they'll be expected to tell voters how they want to remake the world. At its higher levels, vision-making is in the realms of transformational leadership, where leader and follower, in Burns's words, "raise one another to higher levels of motivation and morality."

But these aspects of political leadership only tell half the story. Politicians have to show leadership in two separate and specialized areas to be effective; first they have to get elected, then they have to serve. What is effective leadership in one realm may not work in another. For example, a candidate may have to horse trade with special interest groups for votes and then not be able to deliver once in office. Also, a vision that wins votes may not help you govern. Jimmy Carter won election on an anti-Washington platform that didn't serve him well when he reached office.

President Carter's years in office illustrate many of the paradoxes of presidential leadership. Carter is perceived as having been weak in the face of the taking of the hostages in Iran and the energy crisis. Carter's attempt to make human rights a priority in American foreign policy was seen as unpragmatic, and he has received infinitely more credit for his work in this area since he left office. Lofty visions, whatever they may be, tend to fall by the wayside in global politics.

President Carter did succeed in one very controversial measure: turning over the Panama Canal and having Congress approve the deal. It was an unpopular decision in this country, and President Carter continued to hear about it long after he left office. President Carter commented some years later:

> "It was more difficult to get the Panama Canal Treaties ratified by two-thirds of the Senate of the United States than it was for me to get elected president in the first place. It was a very deep and bitter political battle, and many people still haven't gotten over it."

Political leaders will rarely vote against their own best interests, meaning the wishes of the majority of their followers. One major exception was the U.S. Senate's vote for the unpopular Panama Canal Treaties. As Carter describes:

> "It was the most courageous thing that the U.S. Senate ever did in its existence. They knew that it was politically unpopular, but they knew that it was right and needed. Of the twenty senators who voted for the Canal Treaties in 1978, who were up for re-election the next year, only seven of them came back. Thirteen of them didn't come back. And the attrition rate in 1980 was almost as bad. But it was the right thing to do—a sign of maybe an all-too-rare demonstration of political courage."

The transactional nature of leadership in Congress extends beyond the relationship between leader (congressman and woman) and voter. Elections are infrequent, even if electioneering is constant. Politicians face sustained pressure from special interests, lobbyists, and pressure groups, all of which are working to influence voting behavior in exchange for their influence over the people whose views they represent.

Congressmen also face their own party leaders who want to present a united front for or against their party's program.

Tip O'Neill, long-time House Speaker, wrote about achieving compromise to reach a majority decision. He did it by appealing to conscience, patriotism, and party and personal loyalty. O'Neill knew all the congressional districts and how safe everyone was in their districts. Although he said he'd never ask anyone to fall on their sword for him, he knew just how hard to push.

> **"One time I had to ask my pal, Joe Moakley, for a particularly tough vote in the Rules Committee. He said, 'Jeez, Tip, that's a hard one.'**
>
> **'Hey, Josie,' I said, 'I don't need you on the easy ones.'**
>
> **"He voted with me."**

Presidents and presidential candidates articulate visions that seem to come from a place far removed from the horse trading for votes and influence that characterizes so much of politics. Ronald Reagan often quoted the Gospel of Matthew, 5:14–16, "You are the light of the world, a city set on a hill cannot be hid" as his vision of America. Puritan settler John Winthrop, the first governor of Massachusetts used the passage in a sermon in 1630 which talked of a "shining city upon a hill" and it was this phrase which became linked with Reagan. Justice Sandra Day O'Connor read from it at President Reagan's funeral in 2004 and it was a centerpiece of Reagan's farewell address in 1989.

> **"I've spoken of the shining city all my political life, but I don't know if I ever quite communicated what I saw when I said it.**

But in my mind it was a tall proud city built on rocks stronger than oceans, wind-swept, God-blessed, and teeming with people of all kinds living in harmony and peace, a city with free ports that hummed with commerce and creativity, and if there had to be city walls, the walls had doors and the doors were open to anyone with the will and the heart to get here. That's how I saw it, and see it still." —Ronald Reagan

"The public perception of Reagan's leadership abilities rested in part on his enduring identification with the values of mythic America, a country of the mind in which presidents are necessarily strong leaders." —Lou Cannon

President Reagan was not alone in using Winthrop's sermon. According to the web site Sourcewatch.org, "Politicians as diverse in their ideology as John Adams, Abraham Lincoln, John F. Kennedy, Michael Dukakis, Walter Mondale, and Bill Clinton have all borrowed Winthrop's vision, each of them giving it his own spin."

In his acceptance speech at the Democratic convention in 1992, Bill Clinton ended by invoking the "place called Hope," a metaphorical destination, and also the name of the town where he was born.

"Somewhere at this very moment a child is being born in America. Let it be our cause to give that child a happy home, a healthy family, and a hopeful future. Let it be our cause to see that that child has a chance to live to the fullest of her God-given capacities.

"Let it be our cause to see that child grow up strong and secure, braced by her challenges but never struggling alone, with family and friends and a faith that in America, no one is left out; no one is left behind.

"Let it be our cause that when this child is able, she gives something back to her children, her community, and her country. Let it be our cause that we give this child a country that is coming together, not coming apart, a country of boundless hopes and endless dreams, a country that once again lifts its people and inspires the world. Let that be our cause, our commitment, and our New Covenant.

"My fellow Americans, I end tonight where it all began for me—I still believe in a place called Hope. God bless you, and God Bless America."

Few, if any, politicians have matched Lincoln as an orator. The 272 words of the Gettysburg Address and the 703 words of his second inaugural address have become national touchstones.

> "Leaders teach. Lincoln, in his second inaugural address, provided an extraordinary example of the leader as teacher. Teaching and leading are distinguishable occupations, but every great leader is clearly teaching—and every great teacher is leading." —John Gardner

The speech, given on March 4, 1865, talked about the Civil War and God's part in continuing the war so long. Lincoln did not predict, as he had done before, how long the war would last. As Lincoln's biographer David Herbert Donald put it, he included, "one of the most terrible statements ever made by an American public official."

"Yet, if God wills that it continue, until all the wealth piled by the bond-man's two hundred and fifty years of unrequited toil shall be sunk, and until every drop of blood drawn with the lash, shall be paid by another drawn with the sword, as was said three thousand years ago, so still it must be said, 'the judgments of the Lord, are true and righteous altogether.' "

Lincoln spoke of the nation's debt to those who had fought, died and suffered, and ended:

"With malice toward none; with charity for all; with firmness in the right, as God gives us to see the right, let us strive on to finish the work we are in; to bind up the nation's wounds; . . . to do all which may achieve and cherish a just, and a lasting peace, among ourselves and with all nations."

Such visionary statements, including FDR's inaugural address linked to the New Deal which has already been mentioned, are designed to *motivate* and *inspire*. Often, the visions are vague, even abstract. The vision is distinct from, and complementary to, the program the politician hopes to implement. This differs from a company vision, which encapsulates the program in a few words and is the measuring stick for success.

Political leaders go into office with a program to implement, but events may overtake them. Even in calm times, the president's power is contingent on factors like Congress, as well as economic and geopolitical forces that are beyond his control. Bob Woodward writes about this with regard to Bill Clinton. Sitting in the Oval Office with aides in 1994,

"Clinton was asked what he thought of his role in the economy. Was he the commander in chief of the economy, as the public seemed to think?

"Clinton paused some time before answering. 'More like a captain of a ship,' he said, grasping for the metaphor of a very old ship with oars. 'That is, I can steer it, but a storm can still come up and sink it. And the people that are supposed to be rowing can refuse to row.' "

The greatest challenge a president can face is war. Professor Eliot A. Cohen analyzed four politicians at war for his book, *Supreme Command*. The four were Lincoln, Georges Clemenceau (French Prime Minister at the end of World War I), Winston Churchill, and David Ben-Gurion, father of the state of Israel. He talked to Brian Lamb on *Booknotes* about them. Cohen cited examples of the ruthlessness of these leaders in war. Lincoln was in many ways a gentle man—he wrote pained letters of condolence to relatives of soldiers who had been killed. But at the Battle of Fredericksburg, when General Ambrose Burnside sent soldiers to attack an open position and suffered 10–12,000 casualties, Lincoln said,

"If we just had a general who was willing to do this every day for a week of days at the end of this, the Army of the Potomac would still be a mighty host, the rebel army would be shattered, the insurrection would be over and [the Union] restored. The war won't be over until we find a general who understands that arithmetic."

Cohen also mentions Churchill, who in June 1940 ordered the Royal Navy to sink the French fleet in Algeria to prevent it falling into the hands of the Germans. One thousand three hundred French sailors died in the action. They were men who had fought alongside the British. Churchill said it was a necessary tragedy. Eliot Cohen says,

**"One of the things that all four of these leaders had, which seemed to be a tremendous requirement of good political leadership is [what Lincoln's assistant secretary of war] Charles Dana says about Abraham Lincoln: 'He had no illusions.' That's one reason why I think all four of these people were also melancholy: They were without illusions."**

Every few years, groups of academics come together to rank the presidents. As we'll discuss in relation to President Eisenhower, reputations rise and fall over the years. The Federalist Society and the *Wall Street Journal* asked 132 professors of history, law, and political science to rate the chief executives. Seventy-eight responded. The results are detailed in the book *Political Leadership*. The academics rated three presidents as "Great": Washington, Lincoln, and FDR; followed by the "near-greats": Jefferson, Theodore Roosevelt, Jackson, Truman, Reagan, Eisenhower, Polk, and Wilson. After the "above average," the "average," and the "below average," came the "failures": Andrew Johnson, Franklin Pierce, Warren Harding, and James Buchanan.

The complicated legacies a president can leave are demonstrated by Lyndon Johnson, rated "above average" at 17th. Domestically, LBJ ushered in the Great Society programs: Medicare, Medicaid, education reform, public funding for the arts, and, most notably, civil rights legislation: the Civil Rights Act (1964), the Voting Rights Act (1965), and fair housing regulations (1968). Yet it was Johnson who took the country deeper and deeper into the war in Vietnam.

The poll shows how subjective opinions of the effectiveness of leaders can be. Bill Clinton (average, #24) was placed both much higher and much lower by some voters. There was agreement, however, on the most-overrated president: 43 of 78 voted for Kennedy. Second was Ronald Reagan with 23 votes. Yet Reagan was voted the most *under*rated too, joining LBJ and Eisenhower in the top ten in both categories.

President Kennedy remains beloved by many people. His biographer Robert Dallek says that part of the reason is that Kennedy was martyred. Also, television captured his "Youthful appearance, good looks, charm, wit, and rhetorical idealism and hope," contributing to his ongoing appeal.

> **"The public's faith in Kennedy's sincerity is an additional element in his continuing hold on the country. In an era of public cynicism about politicians as poseurs who are stage-managed and often insincere, Kennedy's remembered forthrightness strengthens his current appeal."**

Dallek speculates that Kennedy's bad health and womanizing, plus his dealings with mobster Sam Giancana, mean Kennedy may not have made it through a second term.

Presidential biographers look for elements of the man's character that helped him, or forced him, to lead. Robert Caro has written three volumes on the life of LBJ and he portrays a man who was a relentless force.

> **"Even as a boy, of course, he could not endure being only one of a group—in a companion's phrase, 'could not stand, just could not *stand* not being the leader,' not only of boys his own age but of older boys. 'If he couldn't lead, he didn't care much about playing.'"**

Ronald Steel wrote of Johnson's ability to persuade people.

> **"He had a formidable intellect and a remarkable ability to induce others to do his bidding. As president he managed, for example, to persuade the vain Arthur Goldberg to resign a lifetime seat on the Supreme Court in order to serve as his delegate to the United Nations. He could, it was said, persuade almost anyone to do almost anything."**

David Maraniss found Bill Clinton's empathy persuasive.

> **"Clinton's ability to empathize with others, his desire to become a peacemaker and bring diverse groups together, always struck me as the better part of his character. It was, to me, the first necessary ingredient of any good leader, and something that most American politicians seemed to lack."**

Lou Cannon is Ronald Reagan's premier biographer. Early in his first presidency, Reagan showed he could get things done, persuading Congress to pass his Budget and tax measures in 1981. He also made a big impression by firing 13,000 members of the Professional Air Traffic Controllers Organization

(PATCO) who walked out in August. Reagan said he was sorry to do it:

> "Sorry or not, Reagan's action sent a resonant signal of leadership that would be long remembered. 'It struck me as singular,' said Donald Rumsfeld, White House chief of staff under President Ford and no Reagan admirer. 'You had a president who was new to the office and not taken seriously by a lot of people. It showed a decisiveness and an ease with his instincts. . . .' Reagan did not fully realize the importance of his decision at the time, but would later say that his action in the strike was 'an important juncture for our new administration. I think it convinced people who might have thought otherwise that I meant what I said.' " —Lou Cannon

When leadership expert Peter Drucker was interviewed by Forbes.com in 2004, he spoke colorfully about Harry Truman's iron-clad trustworthiness.

> "Charismatic leadership by itself certainly is greatly overstated. Look, one of the most effective American presidents of the last 100 years was Harry Truman. He didn't have an ounce of charisma. Truman was as bland as a dead mackerel. Everybody who worked for him worshiped him because he was absolutely trustworthy. If Truman said no, it was no, and if he said yes, it was yes. And he didn't say no to one person and yes to the next one on the same issue."

Why is it important to pore over the character of our leaders, even to the extent of ranking the presidents? Political leaders are nothing without followers. Although each politician who is elected to office represents everyone in his or her particular constituency, they are put there by voters who have made a choice. Good followership is informed citizenship. Politicians cannot lead without us. Their noblest achievements, as well as their most disastrous blunders, are all made on our behalf.

# REVOLUTIONARY LEADERS

© © ©

"The successful revolutionary is a statesman, the unsuccessful one is a criminal." —Erich Fromm

The great revolutions of history demonstrate a significant truth for leaders: it's much easier to tear something down than it is to build its replacement. It's relatively easy for revolutionary leaders to provide a vision to attract followers when the government they are fighting is repressive or corrupt. Revolutions often start with just a few individuals united in their opposition to a regime. The notion of succeeding and actually replacing the government seems like a pipe dream. Turning that dream into a mechanism for effectively running a country has proved beyond the capabilities of many revolutionary leaders.

History is full of cautionary tales. In 1917, Russia had one revolution, which deposed the Tsarist government, and one coup, in which Lenin and the Bolsheviks took advantage of the weakness of the Provisional Government to seize power. The Bolshevik party in 1917 was small but extremely well-disciplined. The party went on to consolidate its own authority rather than that of the "soviets"—the workers' committees—in whose name it had acted in seizing power.

The Bolsheviks, like many revolutionaries of the late nineteenth and early twentieth centuries, were self-proclaimed Communist parties who paid great attention to the writings of Karl Marx, notably, *The Communist Manifesto*, which Marx wrote with Friedrich Engels. *The Communist Manifesto* can be seen as a visionary document in that it describes one particular future, although it lacked details about getting there.

Marx and Engels's work was published in 1848. In it, they stated that "The history of all hitherto existing society is the history of class struggles." The Paris Uprising of 1848 marked the first great battle between the classes, namely the "proletariat" and the "bourgeoisie." The proletariat, for Marx and Engels, was the enlightened members of the working class who would seize the assets' power from the ownership class. In a period of "socialism," landed property would be abolished, along with inheritances. Income tax would be established and credit and the means of production would be centralized in the state.

Communist doctrine shows how difficult it is for leaders to follow an abstract historical plan and how revolutionary intentions can be so quickly overwritten with much the same tyranny that prevailed before. A communist society, by its nature, should be without political leaders, if decisions are made by all. Of course, the Soviet Union became a society dominated by its leaders. The first Soviet leader was Lenin, who died in 1924. In the words of historian Sheila Fitzpatrick, he:

> ". . . had been transformed by death into the Leader, endowed with almost godlike qualities, beyond error or reproach, his body embalmed and reverently placed in the Lenin Mausoleum for the inspiration of the people. The posthumous Lenin cult had destroyed the old Bolshevik myth of a leaderless party."

At the time of the revolution, Bolsheviks spoke of avoiding the example of the French Revolution that deposed the King in 1789 only to have Napoleon Bonaparte crown himself emperor in 1804. While the French Republic did embody some of the revolutionary principle of "liberty, equality, and fraternity," it succumbed to the brilliant military leader and dictator, Napoleon. The French, having deposed the king, faced the same dilemmas as the Russians. Having taken power, what to do with it? In *Citizens*, historian Simon Schama articulated the choice,

> "Revolutionary France could not be, at the same time, a rejuvenated great European power and a confederation of forty thousand elected communes. At some point its leaders would have to decide whether it should approximate more the model of imperial Britain, where constitutional devolution was stringently restricted in the interests of the power of the central state, or republican America, where the national government was supposed, in theory, to be no more than the agent of consenting provincial electors."

Politically, the American Revolution took a quite different turn. The vision laid down in the Constitution established the principle of "we the people."

> "By asserting that all sovereignty rested with the people, the Federalists were not saying, as theorists had for ages, that all governmental power was merely derived from the people. Instead, they were saying that sovereignty remained always with the people and that government was only a temporary and limited agency of the people—out to the various government officials, so to speak, on a short-term, always recallable loan." —Gordon S. Wood

In George Washington, the American Revolution had a leader who shied away from personal power. Unlike Napoleon, he did not owe his leader's authority to glory found on the battlefield.

> "Washington's ultimate success as the American commander in chief . . . never stemmed from his military abilities. He was never a traditional military hero. He had no smashing, stunning victories, and his tactical and strategic maneuvers were never the sort that awed men. Instead, it was his character and political talent and judgment that mattered most. His stoicism, dignity, and perseverance in the face of seemingly impossible odds came to symbolize the entire Revolutionary cause. As the war went on year after year, his stature only grew, and by 1779 Americans were celebrating his birthday as well as the Fourth of July."
> —Gordon S. Wood

Jon Lee Anderson, in his biography of Che Guevara, points out some distinctions between the characters of Che and Cuban leader Fidel Castro. Castro, Anderson writes, "probably always thought of himself as Cuba's future leader." If Castro was part of anything, whether it was a poetry competition or a basketball team, he wanted to win. He wanted to lead any group he was involved in. "For Guevara," on the other hand, "politics were a mechanism for social change, and it was social change, not power itself, that impelled him." But as Anderson says, "Both wanted to carry out revolutions."

**"As a soldier and statesman in the formative years of the American republic, George Washington provided leadership in a time of bitter conflict by embodying the basic values espoused by his countrymen: patriotism, honesty, integrity, and the democratic process."** —Steven I. Davis

Washington was initially reluctant to be the new republic's first President. He'd promised he would retire and was worried about becoming too famous. The historian of the revolution Gordon S. Wood has written,

**"Washington's excessive coyness, his extreme reluctance after 1783 to get involved in public affairs, and his anxiety**

over his reputation for virtue were all part of his strenuous effort to live up to the classical ideal of the republican leader. It shows, as nothing else so effectively can, the extent to which these enlightened values affected the actions of the revolutionary leaders."

"The greatest act of his life," Wood writes, was to resign as commander in chief of the American forces after the British recognized American independence and return to his farm at Mount Vernon.

**"His retirement had a profound effect everywhere in the Western world. It was extraordinary, it was unprecedented in modern times—a victorious general surrendering his arms and returning to his farm."**

Nelson Mandela spent twenty-seven years in prison in South Africa, a victim of the apartheid regime his African National Congress fought to overthrow. Mandela was finally released in 1990, and he was elected president of South Africa in the country's first free elections.

A lawyer, Mandela joined the ANC in 1944, and originally followed the non-violent path of another great lawyer-turned-leader, Mohandas Gandhi. After the Sharpeville massacre of demonstrators in 1960, Mandela changed his stance and advocated force. He wrote in his autobiography,

**"In India, Gandhi had been dealing with a foreign power that ultimately was more realistic and far-sighted. That was not the case with the Afrikaners in South Africa. Non-violent passive resistance is effective as long as your opposition adheres**

**to the same rules as you do. But if peaceful protest is met with violence, its efficacy is at an end."**

Mandela also wrote about his motivation, and the drive that sustained him through his long years in jail. He joined the ANC, he said,

**"It was [this] desire for the freedom of my people to live their lives with dignity and self-respect that animated my life, that transformed a frightened young man into a bold one, that drove a law-abiding attorney to become a criminal, that turned a family-loving husband into a man without a home, that forced a life-loving man to live like a monk. I am no more virtuous or self-sacrificing than the next man, but I found that I could not even enjoy the poor and hunted freedoms I was allowed when I knew my people were not free."**
—Nelson Mandela

**"The good leader, the authentic leader has to have credibility. Nelson Mandela is not the most riveting orator, and yet thousands hang on to every word as he addresses huge crowds who flock to hear him. Why? It is because they perceive that he is a great man who has credibility."** —Desmond Tutu

Few leaders deserve to be called "great," and fewer still among the leaders of violent revolutions, who have often tended toward tyranny. Many leaders have had visions which had revolutionary implications—Martin Luther King, Gandhi, Jesus. They might have been considered in our last chapter, or in this one, or in the next, for their work also has political and spiritual dimensions in varying degrees.

# SPIRITUAL LEADERS

> "You have to decide in life whether you want to influence people or impress them. You can impress people from a distance but you can only influence them up close. We desperately need authentic leaders today, who are real and vulnerable. Our greatest life messages actually come out of our weaknesses, not our strengths."
>
> —Rick Warren

What are the responsibilities of spiritual and religious leaders? In a free society, individuals can follow any spiritual path they choose, or none. Individuals might find inspiration in personal reading and contemplation, or they might turn to organized religion in the form of a particular church, temple, or mosque. If the latter, the leaders of the various denominations and beliefs that exist will make varying demands of them. But while believers might be bound strongly to their individual faith, they may be less committed to the worldly leaders who preside over the institutions.

Religious leaders and followers have debated for centuries

over the role of the organization in organized religion. The Reformation came about because of what were perceived to be church abuses as well as the individual desire to interpret faith. The debate in the Christian church has never relented. As Southern Baptist authority Reggie McNeal has written.

> **"The single most challenging cultural shift facing many spiritual leaders involves the huge reorientation away from the church that has accelerated since the late 1980s. . . . Simply put, Jesus is hot, the church is not. Organized religious effort holds less and less appeal."**

Of course, the Catholic church retained its representative on earth, the Pope, the Archbishop of Rome. Over the centuries, successive popes have spoken out against what they see as deviations from good church practice in the realms of personal behavior and moral values. Pope John Paul II frequently spoke out against the rise of corporate power and violence, and on issues like abortion, divorce, the death penalty, and stem cell research.

In the pope's own writings, he stressed his pastoral role, as described in the Bible. "The shepherd is for the sheep, not the sheep for the shepherd," he has written. "He is bound so closely to them, if he is a real shepherd, that he is ready to lay down his life for the sheep. (John 10:11.)"

> **"Together with the preaching of the word, administration of the sacraments is a bishop's primary duty, to which all his other responsibilities are subordinate. His whole life and activity must be directed toward this goal."**

*Theocracies* are societies ruled by religious leaders. Some Muslim states currently apply Islamic Sharia law. When strictly enforced, Sharia law regulates all activity into one of five categories: obligatory, recommended, permitted, disliked, or forbidden. Sharia law originates in the Koran; the Hadis which are the sayings of the prophet Mohammed, and fatwas which are rulings by Islamic scholars. "Sharia," which means "path to water," was applied comprehensively in Iran after the 1979 revolution, and is used in Saudi Arabia. It is applied selectively in countries like Pakistan, as well as in some parts of other countries like Nigeria and Sudan.

While Pope John Paul II and his predecessors made pronouncements about social issues, some Catholics have advocated that the church go further into the realm of politics than popes have traditionally been willing to go. While the Second Vatican Council (1962–65) made changes to the liturgy and defined the church in the modern world, for some Catholics, notably "Liberation theologians" like the Peruvian Gustavo Gutierrez, the church stopped short of advocating real change. In 1968, at a Conference of the Latin American Church in Medellín, Colombia, leaders spoke more openly of "liberation." As Gustavo Gutierrez has written,

"Vatican II talks about a church in the world and describes the relationship in a way which tends to neutralize the conflicts; Medellín demonstrates that the world in which the Latin American church ought to be present is in full revolution. Vatican II sketches a general outline for church renewal; Medellín provides guidelines for a transformation of the church in terms of its presence on a continent of misery and injustice."

The Vatican and Latin American church leaders have clashed on methodology ever since.

Religions make very different demands of their followers. A few churches require that members pay a tithe, contributing a tenth of their earnings to church funds. Many young members of the Church of the Latter-day Saints participate in missions—two years for men, eighteen months for women. Currently, 56,000 Mormon missionaries are proselytizing in 330 missions around the world.

The Bible serves as a key source of guidance for many people. Within can be found countless pointers on leaders and leadership. Lorin Woolfe of American Management writes,

"The Leaders of the Bible were confronted with large but inspiring tasks, and they realized that the need for courage was proportional to the size and importance of the tasks. Therefore, the calls for leaders to have courage are many and frequent."

"Be strong and courageous, because you will lead these people to inherit the land I swore to their forefathers." — Joshua 1:16

The Bible serves as such a rich guide because of Jesus's status as a role model to millions of Christians. The lessons are easily drawn because his life was offered as an example.

> **"A leader's main job is, frankly, to get people to move. Jesus' job was to get people to move—from a state of sin to a state of grace, from a world of bondage to a world of freedom, from a state of tears to one of everlasting joy. This was no easy task, because Jesus quickly encountered the fact that a body in motion stays in motion, while a body at rest TENDS TO STAY AT REST."** —Laurie Beth Jones, *Jesus in Blue Jeans*

Laurie Beth Jones, author of a number of leadership books centered on Christ, goes on to say that Abraham and Moses were examples of men who moved. In our lives, change is the only constant.

The popular leadership theory of the servant-leader has its roots in a spiritual journey. "Servant-leadership" was the idea of Robert K. Greenleaf (1904–1990), who wrote an essay called "The Servant as Leader" in 1970. Greenleaf read Herman Hesse's novel *Journey to the East*, which was originally published in 1932. A band of men, including a servant, Leo, makes a mythical journey. When Leo disappears, the men come apart, and it is apparent that Leo, the servant, has been the real leader.

> **"The servant-leader *is* servants first—as Leo was portrayed. It begins with the natural feeling that one wants to serve.**

**Then conscious choice brings one to aspire to lead. That person is sharply different from one who is *leader* first, perhaps because of the need to assuage an unusual power drive, or to acquire material possessions. For such, it will be a later choice to serve—after leadership is established. The leader-first and the servant-first are two extreme types. Between them there are shadings and blends that are part of the infinite variety of human nature."** —Robert K. Greenleaf

Robert K. Greenleaf worked in business, at AT&T; and in academia, with posts at the Harvard Business School and MIT, among others. The Greenleaf Center for Servant-Leadership, in Indianapolis, founded in 1964, continues to spread his message about emphasizing service, as well as promoting the community and the sharing of power.

The type of leader mentoring that focuses on service first often has a spiritual element. The Promise Keepers, for instance, talk about being in a "war." "The battle is for personal integrity, for our families, our cities, and for cultures all around the world." They describe themselves as a different kind of warrior: "We fight this battle as 'servant-leaders.' "

**"True greatness, true leadership, is found in giving yourself in service to others, not in coaxing or inducing others to serve you. True service is never without cost. Often it comes with a painful baptism of suffering. But the true spiritual leader is focused on the service he and she can render to God and other people, not as the residuals and perks of high office or holy title. We must aim to put more into life than we take out."**— J. Oswald Sanders

"Spiritual leaders help others live out their callings in their families, their personal mission expressions, their church life. Those called to be spiritual leaders feel connected to the big picture of God's movement, his kingdom agenda." —Reggie McNeal

"As spiritual leaders, we are called to serve those that have been entrusted to us. Leadership in God's kingdom is always about a downward rising. We are also called to clothe ourselves with Humility. We are to relate to one another in such a way that the other is always valued above ourselves. Imagine a world where everyone competed to outserve the other." —Erwin Raphael McManus

These leaders, including Erwin McManus, the lead pastor of the Mosaic Church in Los Angeles, are driven forward by their faith, concerned to make a difference in their spiritual communities.

The best-selling hardcover book of all time in the United States is Rick Warren's *The Purpose-Driven Life* which, at the time of this writing, has sold more than twenty-one million copies since its publication in 2002. Sales rose again in March 2005 after it was learned that Ashley Smith had read from the book to Brian Nichols who was holding Smith hostage after allegedly killing four people in escaping from an Atlanta courtroom. It seems that Smith's reading from *The Purpose-Driven Life* helped persuade Nichols to let her go free.

The phenomenal success of Warren's description of a forty-day spiritual journey shows that spiritual leaders have a vast audience in the United States. Warren's book includes the kind of Bible-based exemplars that are familiar in the literature:

> "The Bible is filled with examples of how God uses a long process to develop character, especially in leaders. He took eighty years to prepare Moses, including forty in the Wilderness. For 14,600 days Moses kept waiting and wondering, "Is it time yet?" But God kept saying, "Not yet."

Warren's key notion of purpose has been lived out in his personal ministry. He is the founder and head of the Saddleback Community Church in Lake Forest, California. Saddleback itself has 15,000 members and its leaders have helped set up sixty churches. Warren's mantra is "Don't make it grow, make it healthy." Saddleback didn't have its own building until it had more than 10,000 members. The road to health is through purpose. Warren says churches need strategy to "grow warmer through fellowship, deeper through discipleship, stronger through worship, broader through ministry, and larger through evangelism."

> "At Saddleback we've built the church on purpose, not personality. If I were to die right now, we'd lose maybe 10% of the 'fringe' people who come to hear me, but that would still leave 90% of the other people to attend each week. No church is perfect but you can be healthy without being perfect."

The Buddhist leader, the 14th Dalai Lama, has been exiled from his native Tibet since uprisings were crushed by occupying Chinese forces in 1959. At the age of two, the boy born as Lhamo Dhondrub was recognized as the reincarnation of

In February 2005, *Time* magazine named its twenty-five "most influential evangelicals in America." The first was Rick Warren, whose *Purpose-Driven Life* is, at twenty million copies, the best-selling hardcover book in American history. Among the twenty-five is Luis A. Cortés, Jr., whom President George W. Bush met with when running for office in 2000. Cortés's Nueva Esperanza (New Hope) organization builds affordable homes, offers small business assistance, and job training. Cortés said to *Time*, "Part of integrating is understanding power. Our people have power, but they have never used it." Bill Hybels of the Willow Creek Community Church in the Chicago suburbs leads a network of 10,500 churches and trains more than 100,000 pastors each year. T.D. Jakes has made religious movies, written books, owns a record label and hosts "Mega Fest," which draws families to Atlanta by the tens of thousands. Evangelicals and their leaders come from multiple denominations and thousands of churches but share commitments, "to the divinity and saving power of Jesus, to personal religious conversion, to the Bible's authority and to the spreading of the Gospel," *Time* says.

the previous thirteen Dalai Lamas. At fifteen, he was made leader of Tibet at the same time that China invaded the country and at nineteen he was negotiating with Mao Tse-tung over the future of Tibet. Since 1959, the Dalai Lama has led his community from exile in Dharamsala in India.

The Dalai Lama is a national leader without a country. He has worked tirelessly to promote the cause of Tibetan independence throughout the world. In an interview, the Dalai Lama said he would stand down as leader of an independent Tibet so as to promote democracy. But he sees no dissonance between his spiritual and political roles.

> **"My involvement in the Tibetan freedom struggle has been part of my spiritual practice, because the issues of the survival of the Buddha Teaching and the freedom of Tibet are very much related."**

Buddhists are against any form of violence. The senior Buddhist authority Thich Nhat Hanh, who protested the war in his native Vietnam, has written,

> **"In the *Kakacupama Sutta* (*Example of the Saw*), the Buddha says, 'Even if robbers cut your limbs off with a saw, if anger arises in you, you are not a follower of my teachings. To be a disciple of the Buddha, your heart must bear no hatred, you must utter no unkind words, you must remain compassionate, with no hostility or ill-will.' As a young monk, I memorized these words and even put them to music."**

Thich Nhat Hanh has also been exiled from his country, and has dedicated his life to peace.

"We need to create communities of deep looking, deep sharing, and real harmony. We need to be able to make the best kinds of decisions together. We need peace, within and without."

Spiritual leaders lead with faith, both their own, and that of the followers who choose to accept their word. In the Burns model, this is transformational leadership, the joint pursuit of real change. In 1989, the Dalai Lama was awarded the Nobel Peace Prize, and in his lecture gave a plea for individuals to step forward and assume leading roles in the world community.

"Responsibility does not only lie with the leaders of our countries or with those who have been appointed or elected to do a particular job. It lies with each one of us individually. Peace, for example, starts with each one of us. When we have inner peace, we can be at peace with those around us. When our community is in a state of peace, it can share that peace with neighboring communities, and so on. When we feel love and kindness towards others, it not only makes others feel loved and cared for, but it helps us also to develop inner happiness and peace."

# INTELLECTUAL LEADERS

◎ ◎ ◎

"He that studies and writes on the improvements
in the arts and sciences labours to benefit generations yet
unborn. For it is improbable that his Contemporaries
will pay any attention to him."
—Oliver Evans (1755–1819)

In *Leading Minds*, Harvard professor Howard Gardner describes how an individual can lead with the power of his intellect rather than his personality. Gardner writes of Albert Einstein alongside Winston Churchill, one of the archetypal figures we think of when we discuss leadership. For Gardner, there is a difference between them.

"I see both Churchill and Einstein as leaders—as individuals who significantly influence the thoughts, behaviors and/or feelings of others. Churchill exerted his influence in a direct way, through the stories he communicated to various audiences; hence, I term him a *direct* leader. Einstein exerted his

> influence in an *indirect* way through the ideas he developed
> and the ways that those ideas were captured in some kind of
> a theory or treatise; hence, he qualifies as an *indirect* leader."

Albert Einstein's contributions to the pool of human knowledge were enormous and profound. A few individuals have revolutionized the way we look at the world: Einstein, Copernicus and Galileo, Newton, Freud. These men were intellectual leaders. As Gardner notes, their ideas became theories which became movements. The ideas were visions that attracted legions of followers. Even if the individual's influence was exerted *indirectly*, it had a dramatic effect. But the effectiveness of ideas may also depend on the success of more conventional leadership skills.

Sigmund Freud's theories of psychoanalysis were like a religion to the converted. Freud was a leader not only because of his ideas but also because of the rigorousness with which he propagated and protected them. Beginning in Freud's native Vienna, psychoanalysis spread, partly through the works of the International Psychoanalytic Association, founded in 1910. By 1920, there were movements in western Europe, Russia, India, and two schools in the United States. Freud (1856–1939) demanded loyalty of his acolytes, and his movement was characterized by bitter academic and personal disputes and the excommunication of figures like Carl Jung and Alfred Adler, significant theorists in their own right. Howard Gardner writes of Freud:

> "Without doubt, Freud's personal leadership capacities contributed to the success of the movement. Indeed, it is at least conceivable that the name of Freud is much better known than his one-time colleague Jung and his one-time, rival Janet,

**less because of the intrinsic superiority of his ideas than because of the brilliance and relentlessness of his campaign on behalf of their acceptance."**

According to Freud, Adler told him, "Do you believe that it is such a great pleasure for me to stand in your shadow my whole life?" Freud disdainfully rejected Adler's ideas and said it would be easy to "refute" Jung's misconceptions. When Freud wrote the history of his movement, he unapologetically and unashamedly placed himself at the center. Fair enough: "For psychoanalysis is my creation."

**"Even today when I am no longer the only psychoanalyst, I feel myself justified in assuming that nobody knows better than I what psychoanalysis is . . . "**

Freud pursued his single-minded leadership while he pioneered his way into one unexplored area of human endeavor. Howard Gardner believes Freud could have led us other places too.

**"While it is difficult to imagine Picasso as other than a painter or Einstein as other than a theoretical physicist, Freud could conceivably have been a significant biologist (in the Darwinian tradition), lawyer or jurist, or religious leader, and certainly a contributor to many areas of scholarship. Perhaps he did hit on the best domain for his own gifts, but it was certainly not the only conceivable one."**

To return to Einstein, the great physicist frequently used the platform his scientific pre-eminence afforded him to try to make his mark on the wider world. Einstein was like a reli-

Einstein may be mentioned in connection with another idea, that of *quiet* leadership. In *Leading Quietly*, Joseph Badaracco writes that some leaders display the virtues of restraint, modesty, and tenacity. They move patiently and carefully.

> **"These are accessible virtues. They are familiar, natural, sensible ways of thinking and activity. As a result, almost anyone can practice and cultivate the simple virtues of quiet leadership. They aren't reserved for special people or extraordinary events."**

Quiet leadership lends itself well to the world of ideas, where you have a better chance of leading by being persuasive than you do by being stridently aggressive.

gious leader who understood acutely the implications of his teachings. Einstein had lifted a curtain and revealed a previously obscured world, and he wanted to help us assimilate the implications of his revelations.

Stephen Hawking, another scientific giant, has written that "Einstein's life was . . . to use his own words, 'divided between politics and equations.' " During the First World War when he was a professor in Berlin, Einstein demonstrated against the conflict. After the war, he worked for international reconciliation. Once Hitler came to power, Einstein left Europe and when he saw that the Nazis might develop an H-bomb, he urged the United States to beat them to it. But once he had seen the destructive power they possessed, Einstein campaigned against nuclear weapons. His other great cause was Zionism and in 1952 Einstein was offered the presidency of the young state of Israel. He declined, saying he was too naïve in politics. Einstein said,

> **"Equations are more important to me, because politics is for the present, but an equation is something for eternity."**

Einstein reminds us that ideas do not depend upon their originator for their continued effectiveness. Once they are born and released, they have a life of their own. Thus the intellectual leader can lead indirectly even when he is no longer physically present.

> **"Man has thought twice in our century, once with Einstein, then with Gandhi. Einstein's thought transformed understanding of the physical world, Gandhi's thought transformed understanding of the political world."** —Martin Luther King, Jr.

Eleanor Roosevelt was a woman who put ideas into action. Howard Gardner considers Eleanor Roosevelt and Martin Luther King, Jr. to be "leaders of nondominant groups," leaders who spoke for invisible American populations. Neither King nor Roosevelt held elective office, rather:

> **"They evolved into leaders because of the explanations—the apologias and the visions—that they had arrived at for their own lives and times, and the ways in which they were able to communicate those evolving explanations to others."**

Martin Luther King, Jr. preached and negotiated his world-view until it was seared into the American consciousness. Eleanor Roosevelt took her ideas directly to the people rather than appealing to them politically, and when she was First Lady, she took advantage of her proximity to the centres of power.

> "Speaking out on controversial issues, working behind the scenes on others, inviting socially conscious groups to meet at the White House, tirelessly lobbying for the things she believed in—Eleanor Roosevelt was crafting a shadow New Deal. She could venture where Franklin could not go, politically as well as physically. She took stands on issues when he could not, listened to petitions he had to turn away, entertained ideas that were politically dangerous." —James McGregor Burns and Susan Dunn

Eleanor Roosevelt wanted the New Deal to go further in terms of helping underprivileged Americans: unorganized workers, the marginalized and dispossessed. Roosevelt was also a constant champion of women's rights. In the depths of the Depression, the federal government fired thousands of married women and the First Lady wasn't afraid to criticize her husband's policies. She wrote a book called *It's Up to the Women* that promoted health care and the idea that women should work outside the home for the sake of their own personal and economic independence. Blanche Wiesen Cook is Roosevelt's biographer.

> "By publishing *It's Up to the Women* in November 1933, Eleanor Roosevelt sought to go beyond the established net-

**work of women activists and reach out to all women in America to join her in a crusade for change and decency. The White House had never before been used as a platform from which the First Lady expressed dissenting political ideas."**

Roosevelt wrote a daily news column, "My Day," for twenty-six years. She also spoke on the radio. In 1937, for example, she asked, "Can you imagine what would happen if the eleven million working women in the U.S. suddenly quit their jobs and just waited for the men to support them?" Because she didn't seek office, Eleanor Roosevelt never had to compromise her opinions. Joseph Lash writes that Eleanor listened to her husband make a speech in 1938. She wasn't moved, and commented, "He did not stir me but I may have been too tired or perhaps he can't."

**"That final resigned phrase said a world about her distrust of the histrionic role assumed by almost all politicians, including Franklin. She admired self-reliance, directness, and moral courage, virtues that were in short supply among the men and women who bid for the public's votes."**

In the 1960s, the National Organization for Women campaigned for equal rights for women. As the Civil Rights movement made progress in securing legislative redress for years of discrimination, women's groups pressured the government for consideration for issues like an Equal Rights Amendment and abortion law reform. A key figure in this campaign was Betty Friedan, whose book *The Feminine Mystique* was a call to arms for women who found life in the home unfulfilling.

"A great many suburban housewives step back from, or give up, volunteer activity, art, or jobs at the very point when all that is needed is a more serious commitment. The PTA leader won't run for the school board, The League of Women Voters' leader is afraid to move on into the rough mainstream of her political party. 'Women can't get a policy-making role,' she says. 'I'm not going to lick stamps.' Of course, it would require more effort for her to win a policy-making role in her party against the competition and prejudices of the men." —Betty Friedan

Daniel Horowitz is author of *Betty Friedan and the Making of* The Feminine Mystique.

"Her book awakened hundreds of thousands, if not millions, of women to what they had long felt but been unable to articulate—the way the mystique of suburban womanhood smothered aspirations for a more fulfilling life. The reception of the book gave Friedan an audience eager to hear what she had to say, ready to have her words rouse them to action. Her appearance on radio, television, and in the lecture circuit helped turn her into a speaker who played a major role in creating some of the conditions for a revival of feminism."

This is a description of classic intellectual leadership where ideas become action.

Few books have had the revolutionary impact of Charles Darwin's *On the Origin of Species*. Darwin worked on his theory of natural selection from the end of the voyage of *The*

*Beagle* in 1836 until November 1859, when his book was published. The first anonymous review in the *Athenaeum* gave a hint of the future impact of the *Origin of Species*, saying that the book was almost too dangerous to read. "If a monkey has become a man—what may now a man become?" To begin with, Darwin hoped to influence his friends and colleagues.

> "What he did not know then was the way in which it would move out from the elite audience he primarily intended to address at home and abroad to increasingly diverse section of the reading public. His words would spread through journals, newspapers, public lectures, controversial tracts, and free-thinking magazines at the same time as great cultural shifts became manifest—shifts in the status of science, in religious belief, in the impact of publishing, education and social mobility."

Another extraordinary thinker was Isaac Newton (1642–1727). Newton was born in Lincolnshire, England and probably never traveled more than 150 miles from there in his lifetime. Despite this, Newton described many of the physical laws—earthly and celestial motion—that govern our world. It was Newton who discerned that white light is made of a combination of colors. He also discovered differential calculus independently of and years before Gottfried Leibniz, who couldn't believe he had been fairly pre-empted. Newton wrote more than a million words in his life but published almost none. Newton's legacy was enormous and at his death, writes his biographer James Gleick, "Newton's story was beginning."

> "Solitude was the essential part of his genius. As a youth he assimilated or rediscovered most of the mathematics known

to humankind and then invented the calculus—the machinery by which the modern world understands change and flow—but kept this treasure to himself."

Among Newton's works were *Philosophiae Naturalis Principia Mathematica* (*Mathematical Principles of Natural Philosophy*), or the *Principia*, which was published in 1687, years after Newton wrote it. He wrote his *Opticks* in 1675, but would only agree to its publication in 1703 when Robert Hooke, Newton's arch-rival and predecessor as president of the prestigious Royal Society, was dead. In his own lifetime, Newton's findings were disseminated narrowly.

"Newton's nascent legend diffused only by word of mouth in a tiny community. . . . In Berlin, Leibniz told the Queen of Prussia that in mathematics there was all previous history, from the beginning of the world, and then there was Newton; and that Newton's was the better half. Tsar Peter of Russia traveled to England in 1698 eager to see several phenomena: ship-building, the Greenwich Observatory, the Mint, and Isaac Newton." —James Gleick

If the Tsar had waited a couple of years, he could have saved a trip, because Newton became Master of the Mint in 1700, a position that carried the very comfortable salary of £500, plus a percentage of each pound coined. Isaac Newton lived well and had an illustrious career—he was given the first state funeral a commoner was ever awarded in Great Britain—and his ideas gave him immortality.

◎ ◎ ◎

The great inventors have been some of our most important innovative leaders. Harold Evans's book *They Made America* gives the stories of men and women who pioneered in the realm of business invention. Alongside Thomas Edison, who was a prodigious inventor, and Charles Goodyear, who vulcanized rubber, is Oliver Evans, who installed the first automatic production line and who also designed a high pressure steam engine.

Current intellectual leaders that Harold Evans includes in his survey of inventors are men like Steve Jobs, whose expertise lies in marketing technical innovations like the iPod and the iMac and whose business acumen saw him move from Apple, to ownership of Pixar, and back to Apple again. Technical leadership comes from innovators like Steve Wozniak, who designed the first Apple in Jobs's bedroom and built it in Jobs's garage.

Perhaps the most powerful intellectual leader today is Microsoft's Bill Gates. Gates's domain is the realm of ideas, and he dominates his part of the business world. Harold Evans reports that Bill Gates is so wealthy that it would not be worth his time to spend three seconds picking up a $100 bill he dropped—he makes $50 a second. Gates hasn't developed any great innovations himself. The BASIC language Gates and Paul Allen adopted in 1974 was invented ten years before by two Dartmouth professors.

"*People* magazine once dubbed him the 'Edison' of software. He keeps a photo of Edison in his office, next to Einstein's and da Vinci's, but he is more like John D. Rockefeller. Microsoft's Windows operating system controls 90 percent of all personal computers; Standard Oil controlled 90 per-

**cent of the nation's oil refining capacity by 1879."** —Harold
Evans

Gates's originality lay in realizing the importance of controlling the industry's standard operating system and executing it
with Windows. Gates works with tremendous determination
and attracts loyal employees. "Company meetings have filled
Seattle stadiums with thousands of employees thundering in
unison, " 'Win-dows! Win-dows! Win-dows!' " writes Harold
Evans. The workers might be applauding a product, a philosophy, a movement, or a brand.

Today, technical breakthroughs are exploited for money,
and innovation—ideas—is a key factor in a business's com-
petitive advantage. Some intellectuals live only for their ideas.
Some may attract a following because of the power of the idea
itself, in spite of the thinker's diffidence, while a few apply the
leadership skills of a general or a CEO and promote their
ideas so they don't have to rely solely on their own merits to
be effective.

# BAD LEADERS AND
# BAD LEADERSHIP

> "In a speech I gave about assertiveness, I mentioned that using Attila the Hun as a role model for leadership was like studying Ted Bundy, the serial killer, and saying, 'Sure he killed a lot of women, but let's look at how he got those dates!' "
> —Laurie Beth Jones, *Jesus CEO*

Wess Roberts's *The Leadership Secrets of Attila the Hun* has sold more than half a million copies since it was published in 1985. Laurie Beth Jones's point about the appropriateness of studying Attila as a leader is that he was someone who, as she put it, raped and pillaged and plundered for a living. Attila was a failure as a leader, she says, because he, when he wanted something, he simply took it. He pulled up the flowers rather than planting a garden. Attila may have been an *effective* leader, who identified goals and achieved them to the satisfaction of his followers, but that doesn't make him a good leader. A cynical transaction between a tyrant and followers is not good leadership—for that there has to be a moral component. This is admittedly a gray area where subjective ethical judgments about good and bad apply.

There are as many kinds of bad leaders as there are good. What all leaders have in common are followers, without whom no leader can do anything. Leaders and followers can come together for ill as well as good. Leadership authority Robert Terry poses one of the great questions of leadership: how to disqualify the effective despot from the discussion.

> "At leadership seminars, I am often asked the 'Hitler' questions: Was Hitler a leader? Did Hitler exhibit leadership? And I frequently hear the conclusion: Hitler was authentic; he lived his beliefs. My view is contrary. Yes, Hitler was a 'leader' in that he was elected and supported by followers. However, he rarely exhibited leadership. He was a tyrant, oppressor, exploiter, and despot."

> "Leadership is not reducible to one person. *It is a set of relationships that unfold over time.* It is one thing to attend to the character of the relationships. Bosses hire employees; bosses fire employees. Followers pick their leaders; it is hard, if not impossible, to fire a follower. Work in a volunteer organization and this reality at times is overwhelming."

In *Leadership*, James McGregor Burns writes that Hitler and Stalin were despots who did not recognize their peoples' needs. Both men created cults around themselves, as dictators tend to do. At a Nazi Party rally in Nuremberg in 1934, Rudolf Hess said "Adolf Hitler is the Party. The Party is Adolf Hitler." Burns says, "Nothing transactional there." For Burns, the army, the key element in German society whose support Hitler needed, was loyal as long as he was a commanding figure.

It was in 1934, in August, that Hitler established his dictatorship. President Paul von Hindenburg died and Hitler combined his own office of Chancellor with Hindenburg's. Hitler also became head of state and Commander in Chief of the Armed Forces. He then made officers and men sign an oath of allegiance not to Germany or the constitution, but to him. In *The Rise and Fall of the Third Reich*, William Shirer describes how significant the oath was.

> "It was an oath which was to trouble the conscience of quite a few high officers when their acknowledged leader set off on a path which they felt could only lead to the nation's destruction and which they opposed. It was also a pledge which enabled an even greater number of officers to excuse themselves from any personal responsibility for the unspeakable crimes which they carried out on the orders of the Supreme Commander. . . ."

Officers were able to hide behind the fact that they had sworn an oath.

> "Later and often, by honoring their oath they dishonored themselves as human beings and trod in the mud the moral code of their corps."

The war crimes trials that followed the Second World War specifically discredited the idea that a soldier is exonerated from illegal acts if he was, in his view, obeying an order. Good

Is it okay for leaders to lie and cheat in what they perceive to be our best interests? Politicians routinely fail to give straight answers to pointed questions or they gloss over weaknesses. In many cases, the blunt truth would be worse. In pursuit of a policy goal, a leader can reasonably choose to steer the issue his way, as Roosevelt did consistently to get the United States to support Great Britain when it stood alone against Nazism from 1940.

Robert Kaplan talks about the idea of distinguishing public virtue and private virtue in cases like this. FDR got Congress to approve Lend-Lease in 1941 by what Kaplan calls, "Somewhat mischievous evasions of truth." Arthur Miller has said that means we are in debt to FDR for his lies.

> **"In his *Discourses on Livy*, Machiavelli sanctions fraud when it is necessary for the well-being of the *polis*. This is not a new or cynical idea: Sun-Tzu writes that politics and war constitute 'the art of deceit,' which if practiced wisely may lead to victory and the reduction of casualties. That this is a dangerous precept and easily misused does not strip it of positive applications."** —Robert D. Kaplan

As Kaplan says, not all leaders can be given the same leeway.

> **"Of course, the military virtue of Machiavelli and Sun-Tzu is not always appropriate to civil leadership. Generals should use deceit; judges should not."**

followership trumps bad leadership and effective followers need to deny bad leaders the support they require.

It is easy to conclude that active support was more important to the Nazi Party than passive, or tacit acceptance. In a controversial study, provocatively entitled *Hitler's Willing Executioners*, Daniel Goldhagen says that German society did put an end to at least one element of the Nazi's murderous policies: the killing of disabled people. Outcry from the church was joined by popular protest and the murder was ended, though not before more than 70,000 people were killed. But there was only one large-scale protest against the policy of eliminating Jews, which was when women in Berlin agitated against the arrest of their husbands and secured their release.

> **"The long and impressive record of Germans' dissent from *particular* Nazi policies did not by any means translate into *general* opposition to the regime itself, to the Nazi German system and its primary goals of a racially purified Germany and a militarized, resurgent Germany within Europe."**

Hitler's dictatorship crushed opposition at the same time as it elevated the stature of the *Fuhrer*. In the soviet Union, Stalin vaingloriously renamed half the country for himself. Similarly, in China, Chairman Mao established a personal and ideological cult.

Individuals may follow a bad leader for any number of reasons. The follower may buy into the leader's pathology or take material rewards from him. Personal, tribal or ethnic loyalties could come into play. The leader might provide a feeling of security. In a time of war, tyrannical leaders like Hitler and Stalin can cloak their policies behind a veil of national interest and security.

> **"Even the very worst of leaders, the demagogues and tyrants, offer us the illusion of security that insulates us from the pain of our anxiety. Indeed, we should note that authoritarian leaders commonly create a stronger sense that things are under control than do democratic leaders."**

Bad leadership also has grades and nuances. Leaders make mistakes. They might simply make a bad decision, even with the best of intentions. Or they might suffer a moral lapse. President Clinton was vilified in some quarters after the Monica Lewinsky debacle but in others, it was perceived that sexual indiscretions are a personal matter that have no bearing on a leader's qualification to lead. Was all of Richard Nixon's presidency damned by Watergate? No leader is perfect; some are less imperfect than others.

Many figures of authority lack the kinds of leadership skills we have discussed and therefore resort to coercion to get people to do their bidding. (Perhaps you know someone like this.) Good discipline is one thing; intimidation another. One-time commander-in-chief of the Air Force's Strategic Command, General George Lee Butler notes:

> **"Make no mistake; leading by fear and threat and intimidation is neither toughness nor an acceptable expedient. It is a personality disorder. It represents the worst flaws of character in a leadership position."**

Character flaws such as arrogance and pride will be exposed in a leader. Many leaders are full of themselves, having crossed the line from healthy self-confidence.

> **"[Lt. Gen.] John C.H. Lee was a martinet who had an exalted opinion of himself. He also had a strong religious fervor (Eisenhower compared him to Cromwell) that struck a wrong note with everyone. He handed out the equipment as if it were a personal gift. He hated waste; once he was walking through a mess hall, reached into the garbage barrel, pulled out a half-eaten loaf of bread, started chomping on it, and gave the cooks hell for throwing away perfectly good food. He had what [General] Bradley politely called 'an unfortunate pomposity' and was cordially hated. Officers and men gave him a nickname based on his initials, J.C.H.—Jesus Christ Himself."**

Great stories, such as the Greek myths and the plots of Shakespeare's plays, are full of leaders who overreach or fall prey to greed, arrogance, and stupidity. These stories find their contemporary versions in all walks of life, especially the corporate world.

> **"If Othello were CEO of Enron and Oedipus Rex in charge of WorldCom, they might well have made the same mistakes as Jeff Skilling and Bernie Ebbers. In tragedies both ancient and modern, leaders fall because of arrogance."** —Davis L. Dotlich and Peter C. Cairo, *Why CEOs Fail*

Personal failings give drama to leadership situations. Executive coaches David Dotlich and Peter Cairo list failings that leaders are susceptible to: melodrama, volatility, over-caution, eccentricity, and so on. Barbara Kellerman, research director of Harvard's Center for Public Leadership, has outlined types of bad leadership: incompetent; rigid; intemperate; callous; corrupt; insular; evil. She cites Juan Antonio Samaranch, former head of the International Olympic Committee.

**"He was leader and steward of a movement of high ideals, but Samaranch grew sloppy and sleazy. Among his many other mistakes, he willingly, even eagerly, engaged with bad people. Olympic awards were bestowed on malevolent dictators such as East Germany's Erich Honecker and Romania's Nicolae Ceausescu."**

Leaders can make decisions so terrible that they undermine all credibility in their leadership ability. First World War generals threw men into the treacherous no-man's land between the trenches for years in mostly futile attempts to capture a few yards of ground. British General Sir Douglas Haig has borne the brunt of blame for these self-inflicted massacres in Great Britain. In one engagement, Passchendaele, from July to August 1917 alone cost Britain 70,000 dead and 170,000 wounded. Renowned military historian John Keegan has written, "The point of Passchendaele, as the Third Battle of Ypres has come to be known, defied explanation."

In a single day on the Somme—July 1, 1916—British forces suffered 57,470 casualties (19,240 dead) in the course of capturing three square miles. British generals concocted a disastrous plan of assault. Writer Percy Crozier described the heart-breaking scene that resulted: an example of incredible,

Attila the Hun, who would impale enemies on spikes, has company for unlikely leadership role models. Joining him is popular fictional murderer, adulterer, racketeer and all-round father-of-the-year, mob boss Tony Soprano who features in a couple of books. Unlike the subject of *Leadership Soprano Style*, real leaders don't have to ask, "What do I get if I whack Carmine?"

> **"I believe that Tony provides an excellent model for getting solid performance out of people and creating strong relationships in and out of the organization."** —Deborrah Himsel

And from *Tony Soprano on Management*:

> **"When he hears that Big Pussy may be wearing a wire, Tony pays him a visit and reminds him that he has friends and options. Good leaders are tuned in; they are aware of how people are doing."** —Anthony Schneider

In due course, henchmen like "Big Pussy" and Ralphie are eliminated, or fired "with extreme prejudice" according to the book. Remember: "you don't fire—or clip—someone without good reason."

and suicidal followership resulting from criminally incompetent leadership.

> "I see rows upon rows of British soldiers lying dead, dying or wounded, in no man's land. Here and there I see an officer urging on his followers. Occasionally I can see the hands thrown up and then a body flops to the ground. . . . Again I look southward from a different angle and perceive heaped up masses of British corpses suspended in the German wire in front of the Thiepval stronghold, while live men rush forward in orderly procession to swell the weight of numbers in the spider's web."

America's involvement in the war in Vietnam can also be seen as the result of multiple failures of leadership. As soon as he became President, Lyndon Johnson aggressively expanded the U.S. role in southeast Asia. Barbara Tuchman writes:

> "Forceful and domineering, a man infatuated with himself, Johnson was affected in his conduct of Vietnam policy by three elements in his character: an ego that was insatiable and never secure; a bottomless capacity to use and impose the powers of office without inhibition; a profound aversion, once fixed upon a course of action, to any contra-indications."

Military leaders contend that having engaged in the war, politicians were too timid to commit to it fully, meaning that the forces were under-manned and lacked the resources to prevail. Colin Powell learned a lesson in Vietnam that he later applied in the first Gulf War: never take on an enemy unless and until victory is certain. Speaking of Vietnam, he wrote in his autobiography:

> **"Many of my generation, the career captains, majors, and lieutenant colonels seasoned in that war, vowed that when our turn came to call the shots, we would not quietly acquiesce in half-hearted warfare for half-baked reasons that the American people could not understand or support."**

Like the rest of us, leaders fall short of their aspirations and make mistakes. We should expect that our leaders learn from these mistakes and not repeat them. History awaits the first flawless leader.

Perhaps we place too much stock in our leaders. We certainly rely on the mass of decisions made by the leaders around us in our daily lives. But do the high-profile leaders—football coaches, CEOs, generals—deserve all the attention they receive? In an article published in *Slate* in 2002, James Surowiecki writes that Lee Iacocca was the first superstar CEO, and that CEO worship began with the publication of his book in 1984.

> **"Although it may be hard to believe after a decade and a half of CEO worship, all the available evidence suggests that most chief executives have only a negligible impact on the performance of the companies they run. There are, of course, exceptions. But corporate performance depends far more on what industry a company is in, what proprietary advantages**

**it has, and the general quality of its work force, than it does on who's at the very top.**

**"And in those cases where leadership does make a differ-ence, the successful leaders don't fit the corporate-savior model."**

So here is a note of caution: forget both the blame heaped on leaders and the credit they take. Ask: how much can leaders control the events they apparently preside over? A field goal that goes one foot over the other side of a post can turn a win-ner into a loser; a president rides booms and sits out busts that are created by unseen economic forces. Luck plays a large part in leadership good and bad. As essayist Ralph Waldo Emerson (1803–1882) reminds us, it is better not to go overboard with either praise or blame as we judge our everyday leaders.

**"We cloy of the honey of each peculiar greatness," he wrote. "Every hero becomes a bore at last."**

# PART III:

## EFFECTIVE LEADERS: WHAT CAN THEY TEACH US?

# WINSTON CHURCHILL

> "There comes a special moment in everyone's life,
> a moment for which that person was born. That special
> opportunity, when he seizes it, will fulfill his
> mission—a mission for which he is uniquely qualified. In that
> moment, he finds greatness. It is his finest hour."
>
> —Winston Churchill

The popular study of leadership would be immeasurably poorer without the career of Winston Churchill (1874–1965) to draw on. From an era of Great Men (in the sense of significant rather than illustrious), Churchill has emerged as the Greatest. Each of the leaders of the major combatants of the Second World War—Hitler, Stalin, Mussolini, FDR, and Churchill—personified his nation's struggle. Three of these men are vilified by history. Roosevelt presided over a reworking of American government and society that is being undone and he remains a politically divisive figure. Churchill's reputation as a wartime leader only grows with time so that today he is rivaled only by Lincoln as a paradigm for leadership in crisis.

Churchill's career both rewards study as an exemplar of matchless perseverance and also neatly illustrates some leadership maxims. May 1940, when Great Britain faced Nazi Germany alone, was the ultimate leadership challenge, and one which Churchill handled brilliantly. Yet five years later, Churchill's party lost the 1945 election, demonstrating the limits of even a great leader. Churchill presented the British people with extraordinary vision for the bleakest wartime adversity. But as the war came to an end, the same people rejected the man and chose a different model for a peacetime Britain.

Churchill also shows us the value of hope, the power of rhetoric, and the virtue of obstinacy. Furthermore, his timing was perfect. In his *21 Irrefutable Laws of Power*, John C. Maxwell uses Churchill to illustrate his fourth rule: "The Right Action at the Right Time Results in Success." The key point about Churchill's leadership is that the "Right Time for Churchill" happened to be the lowest point in British history.

> **"Winston Churchill was a charismatic visionary, and he was perhaps the only leader who could have saved Great Britain during the war. He was also moody, autocratic, stubborn, and sometimes dead wrong. Leading is all about the interaction of a leader with timing and context."**

Before 1940, Winston Churchill would have been thought an unlikely figure to become the leader of Britain. Although he eventually served 62 years in the House of Commons and was often in the government, he was a political maverick.

Churchill spent the 1930s in the "wilderness," an insider on the outs. It was Churchill's strenuous and often lonely opposition to Prime Minister Neville Chamberlain's policy of appeasing Hitler that put him in a position to lead when the policy failed miserably and Chamberlain resigned.

Churchill took over as Prime Minister on May 10, 1940 after Germany invaded Holland, Belgium, Luxembourg, and France. The Hitler-Stalin Pact secured Germany's eastern flank, the United States was pursuing a policy of neutrality, and sections of the British political establishment favored coming to terms with Hitler. Into this breach stepped Churchill. He exuded defiance, and in his legendary speeches, broadcast by radio to millions of Britons, Churchill brilliantly articulated that defiance. In his first speech to Parliament, on May 13, 1940, Churchill gave us one of his innumerable memorable phrases:

> "I say to the House as I said to ministers who joined this government, I have nothing to offer but blood, toil, tears, and sweat. We have before us an ordeal of the most grievous kind. We have before us many, many months of struggle and suffering."

Churchill punctuated these months with speeches. France quickly fell to the German forces leaving Britain isolated. In June, 1940, Churchill said that the Battle of France was over and the Battle of Britain was about to begin.

> "Hitler knows that he will have to break us in this island or lose the war. If we can stand up to him, all Europe may be free and the life of the world will move forward into broad, sunlit

uplands. But if we fail, then the whole world, including the United States, including all that we have known and cared for, will sink into the abyss of a new Dark Age made more sinister, and perhaps more protracted, by the lights of perverted science. Let us therefore brace ourselves to our duties and so bear ourselves that, if the British Empire and its Commonwealth last for a thousand years, men will say, 'This was their finest hour.' "

In August, when the air war was being waged, Churchill immortalized the debt Britain owed the Royal Air Force: "Never in the field of human conflict was so much owed by so many to so few." A speech given in 1941 will serve as a final example to underscore a cornerstone of Churchillian leadership: "Never give in, never give in, never, never, never, never—in nothing, great or small, large or petty—never give in except to convictions of honour and good sense."

The definitive edition of Churchill's speeches runs to eight volumes and four million words. Historian David Cannadine notes that Churchill worked hard at his oratory, studying the best Parliamentary speechmakers. He was also a tremendously gifted writer who took his time composing speeches. Churchill's first speech in the House of Commons took six weeks to write. The final version would often include stage directions and Churchill would practice for hours in front of a mirror. As Cannadine writes, the result was a performance:

"His own extraordinary character breathed through every grandiloquent sentence—a character at once simple, ardent, innocent and incapable of deception or intrigue, yet also a character larger than life, romantic, chivalrous, heroic, great-hearted and highly colored."

And as a result, his unbreakable will was projected forth:

"At best, by sheer force of eloquence, he imposed his own vision, and his personality, on men and on events." —David Cannadine

"There was really something in his saying 'Never, never, never, never give in.' The man's bulldog determination just stood out all over him. And I think that he's bound to be one of the great men of this whole country. There's no question about it. And remembered as that. His name will cover a lot of pages in history in the future." —Dwight D. Eisenhower

The tenor and tone of Churchill's speeches perfectly suited the dire predicament that Britain faced in the middle of 1940. Churchill had been using his oratorical powers in the House of Commons since 1900, but his speeches could seem over-dramatic in less perilous times. He was now, as Cannadine says, in his element.

John Keegan writes that Churchill wanted to live an epic life. "In 1940, events offered him the opportunity to make the present itself into an epic." In peacetime, being constantly in the public eye might look like grandstanding; in war, as the leader visited bombed-out neighborhoods of London, he was an inspiration. Ordinarily, Churchill's overbearing nature alienated his colleagues; wartime government, it could be argued, is better served by single-mindedness and unanimity of purpose. Perhaps Churchill's style could only work at all under the extraordinary circumstances of 1940. Three writers offer their opinions:

> "Churchill was not well-suited for any position but chief executive, and his energy, drive, and encyclopedic mind, when exercised in the many subordinate positions he held throughout his career, alienated many of his colleagues and superiors." —Steven F. Hayward, *Churchill on Leadership*

> "If Winston Churchill and Charles de Gaulle had 'listened,' the Allies would have lost the war. Leaders who listen are not usually the same leaders who inspire. In many ways they inspire because they *don't* listen. They follow their dreams." — Patricia Pitcher, *The Drama of Leadership*

> "His art of leadership included. . .a skill at questioning and challenging professional subordinates that few others have mastered. But all these skills would have availed nothing had they not rested on a courage that, even at the distance of fifty years, is nothing less than magnificent. That indomitable spirit, when coupled with his skills at higher war leadership, made him the greatest war statesman of the century." —Eliot A. Cohen, *Supreme Command*

Churchill's courage offers another lesson. In the worst of times, courage may be all you have. In a study that compares Hitler and Churchill, Andrew Roberts writes,

> "For much of the time between the completion of the evacuation from Dunkirk on 3 June 1940, and Hitler's invasion of

Davia J. Vaughan writes about Churchill's willingness to hold his own actions up to the light.

"Although he was often characterized as stubborn and arrogant, Churchill had a keen faculty for self-criticism. 'Every night,' he remarked to one of his aides, 'I try myself by Court Martial to see if I have done anything effective during the day. I don't mean just pawing the ground, anyone can go through the motions, but something really effective."

Russia fifty-five weeks later on 22 June 1941, Churchill did indeed regularly have to fake it. For all his superb oratory during that period, Churchill did not really know how Germany was going to be defeated. Faking it is sometimes a crucial part of leadership. Churchill's certainty transmitted itself to the British people, even though in 1940 it was difficult to understand how on any possible analysis the war could be won."

In another of his famous speeches in 1940, Churchill said, "We shall fight on the beaches, we shall fight on the landing grounds, we shall fight in the fields and in the streets, we shall fight in the hills; we shall never surrender. . . ." When the broadcast finished he turned to whoever was standing by the microphone and said, "And we will fight them with beer bottles, because that's about all we have to work with."

◎ ◎ ◎

The tide of the war eventually did turn. By the time Churchill faced a General Election in 1945, the war in Europe had finished. Roosevelt did not agree with Churchill's view of a post-war settlement in Europe, and domestically, Clement Attlee's reform-minded Labour Party challenged Churchill not as a national leader but as a partisan politician who lacked a clear vision for the future.

Churchill did serve as Prime Minister once more but his legacy has remained inextricably linked with his wartime achievements. The extent of Churchill's contribution to Britain's survival in 1940 is debated and his career before and after the war did have failures, some of which, like the disastrous Gallipoli campaign of the First World War, were serious. But leaders still turn to Churchill for inspiration in times of crisis.

Mayor Rudolph Giuliani was not a particularly popular mayor of New York City before the terrible events of September 11, 2001. On and after September 11th, Giuliani exerted strong leadership with his honesty and constant presence, his reassuring air and calmness. In his book on leadership, Giuliani described his own personal test.

> "Several times I closed my eyes and expected to open them and see the twin towers still standing. *This is not real. This is not real. This is not real.* Then I'd shake myself. *Damn right it's real, and I had better figure out what I'm going to do about it.*"

After that first day of trial, Giuliani tried to snatch a couple of hours' rest. The mayor went to the home of a friend where he'd been staying. It happens he'd been reading Roy Jenkins's biography of Churchill.

> **"For a while I read the chapters describing his becoming Prime Minister in 1940. I thought about the people of London enduring relentless bombing and continuing to lead their lives. I thought about how people in present-day Israel do the same. It reaffirmed a strong feeling I had that Americans would rise to this challenge. I fell asleep around 4:30. I woke less than an hour later and waited for the sun to come up: I wasn't sure it would. When first I saw it rise I was relieved. Now it was our turn to fight back."**

Although memories of 1940 have faded, there is perhaps a sense in Britain that Churchill was right, that this was their finest hour. Churchill's calculated embodiment of courage was his leadership strategy of that moment, an appeal to his people to make history. Jon Meacham describes Churchill's deliberate evocation of Shakespeare, and the gamble he was taking. Churchill was essentially bluffing, hoping against hope in the darkest hours of a long night. Success would make him his nation's savior, and Churchill would countenance nothing less.

> **"It was no coincidence that in his 'Finest Hour' broadcast [Churchill] tied the trials of the present to the collective consciousness of the world to come. *Men will still say* was a call to arms reminiscent of Shakespeare's Henry V bracing his men to fight from generation to generation: 'This story shall the good man teach his son. . . .' Be brave now, and the future**

will cherish your memory and praise your name—an impressive, if risky, means of leadership, for under stress not all of us are like Bedford and Exeter."

Dwight Eisenhower spoke at Churchill's funeral in 1965 as the spokesman for the millions of Americans who had fought alongside the British. President Eisenhower summed up Churchill's contribution as he saw it. "To those men Winston Churchill *was* Britain."

## Five Lessons:

- The right moment can bring forth the right leader.
- Never, never, never give in.
- Great oratory can be great leadership.
- Faking it might work.
- Reputation, no matter how great, might not overcome lack of vision.

# George S. Patton and
# Dwight D. Eisenhower

> "Leadership is the thing that wins battles. I have it but I'll be damned if I can define it. It probably consists of what you want to do, and then doing it, and getting mad as hell if someone tries to get in your way. Self-confidence and leadership are twin brothers."
>
> —George S. Patton

A fine study in contrasting leadership styles is offered by the intertwined careers of generals George S. Patton, Jr. and Dwight D. Eisenhower. The men first met at the end of World War I and were friends, and often rivals, for more than twenty-five years. They came from very different backgrounds: Patton from money, Eisenhower not. Patton was "Old Blood and Guts," Eisenhower relaxed and personable. Eisenhower was the ultimate "political" general while Patton was nothing if not impolitic. What brought the two men into regular contact during the Second World War was Patton's brilliance as a military leader and Eisenhower's role in deciding if Patton was worth keeping around given all the trouble he caused.

George Patton saw service with General John Pershing in 1916, chasing Pancho Villa in Mexico, and then in Europe commanding the new military invention, the tank, at the end of the First World War. Armored warfare became Patton's specialty, and between the wars Patton first commanded an armored brigade, then an armored division. Patton led the First U.S. Armored Corps in North Africa in 1942 and the American forces that invaded Sicily in 1943. After D-Day, Patton's Third Army sped through northern France and then in his most brilliant campaign relieved the American forces trapped by the German Ardennes Offensive, otherwise known as the Battle of the Bulge. After the war, Patton was military governor of Bavaria for a time, but he was frustrated by anything other than combat. In December 1945, Patton died from injuries he received in a car crash.

At the time of the United States' entry into the Second World War, Dwight Eisenhower had never held an active command. Eisenhower held a number of staff jobs in Washington before Chief of Staff George C. Marshall, recognizing Eisenhower's planning abilities, leapfrogged him straight over the rank of colonel and chose him for an increasingly important series of jobs in the European Theater. Eisenhower eventually became Supreme Allied Commander in Europe. Eisenhower was in charge of Operation Overlord, the Allied invasion of France, and oversaw the liberation of western Europe. After the War, Eisenhower was Chief of Staff and the first Supreme Commander of NATO until he was persuaded to run for President in 1952.

Eisenhower the administrator frequently had to deal with

Patton's transgressions. The most well-known case was the notorious "slapping" incident in August 1943. During the invasion of Sicily, Patton visited hospitals filled with wounded men. Geoffrey Perret describes what happened in his biography of Eisenhower:

> "Encountering a soldier without any evident injury, Patton had called the man a coward, slapped him across the face with his gloves and kicked him in the backside. A week later, visiting another evacuation hospital, he had met yet another soldier who claimed he was suffering from combat fatigue. 'It's my nerves,' said the soldier. 'I can't stand the shelling anymore.' Patton had called him 'a yellow bastard,' threatened to shoot him, waved his Colt .45 in the man's face, slapped him, walked away, then gone back and slapped him again, hard enough this time to send his helmet liner flying."

Eisenhower, who was in charge of the invasion, read a report of the incident and said, "I guess I'll have to give George Patton a jacking up." Eisenhower reprimanded Patton but decided he was too valuable to fire, even for this. Eisenhower prevailed on journalists who had been witness to the slapping to keep it quiet. "His method is deplorable," wrote Eisenhower of Patton to one of the journalists. "But the result is excellent." And when news of the incident later leaked, Eisenhower defended Patton.

Omar Bradley, who was in Sicily with Patton and who was chosen ahead of Patton to command U.S. ground forces in Normandy, later said he would have relieved Patton had the decision been his. Bradley, who was no fan of either Eisenhower or Patton, for different reasons, was one of those who was put off by Patton's profanity and showing off. After the invasion of Normandy, a momentous milestone was achieved when Patton crossed the Rhine into Germany. When Patton did so,

> " . . . he drove across a pontoon bridge, stopped in the middle, got out, and pissed in the Rhine. It was a standard performance. Churchill would do the same later. On the far bank, imitating William the Conqueror as he stepped ashore in England, Patton deliberately stumbled, knelt, and picked up a handful of German soil." — Martin Blumenson, *Patton*

In *American Generalship*, Edgar Puryear writes,

> "Showmanship is an important factor in successful leadership. It is part of feel, particularly what influences the troops favorably. Patton wore his ivory-handled pistols, a shiny helmet with oversized generals' stars, stars on his neck collar, stars on his shoulders, a formfitting jacket with brass buttons, a riding crop, whipcord riding breeches, and boots. Ike wore his jacket named the 'Ike' jacket and also riding britches, boots, a riding crop, and a smile that [Omar] Bradley said was worth several divisions."

Clearly Eisenhower's showmanship was different from Patton's. Patton, by his own admission, swaggered. Patton's nephew once asked his uncle why he did so, and why he swore and made intemperate remarks that were quoted in the press, another of Patton's foibles.

> "In any war a commander, no matter what his rank, has to send to sure death, nearly everyday, by his own orders, a

certain number of men. Some are his personal friends. All are his personal responsibility, to them as his troops, and to their families. Any man with a heart would, then, like to sit down and bawl like a baby, but he can't. So he sticks out his jaw, and swaggers and swears. As for the kind of remarks I made, why sometimes, I just, by God, get carried away by my own eloquence."

Patton's soldiers respected his success—in North Africa, in Sicily, across France, at the Battle of the Bulge—and his leading from the front. Throughout his career, Patton was in the vanguard of the charge, as he had done on a horse in 1916 in Mexico, or, later in a tank or a Jeep. Leading by example was a refrain he repeated often.

"Your primary mission as a leader is to see with your own eyes and be seen by your troops while engaged in personal reconnaissance."

"You young lieutenants have to realize that your platoon is like a piece of spaghetti. You can't push it. You've got to get out in front and pull it."

"Commanders must remember that the issuance of an order, or the devising of a plan is only about five per cent of the responsibility of command. The other ninety-five per cent is to insure by personal observation, or through the interposing of staff officers, that the order is carried out."

Patton was there, and was there to see that he won.

"No one who experienced Patton's brand of leadership was in any doubt of his sincerity. Indeed, if there was a single, defining theme in his training methods, it was to repeat—again and again—how to stay alive and win on the battlefield. 'Do as I have taught you,' he would proclaim, 'and you will stay alive.' Patton understood, as few did, that tough, realistic, training combined with strong, effective leadership, spelled the difference between success and failure."

Omar Bradley thought Patton believed that war was a crusade. Bradley witnessed Patton, before an attack in Sicily, tell his staff that if they didn't succeed, "let no one come back alive."

"The techniques of command vary, of course, with the personality of the commander. While some men prefer to lead by suggestion and example and other methods, Patton chose to drive his subordinates by bombast and by threats. These mannerisms achieved spectacular results. But they were not calculated to win affection among his officers and men." — Omar Bradley

Patton wrote his son George on D-Day [as originally typed],

"I am sure that if every leader who goes into battle will promise him self that he will come out either a conqueror or a corpse he is sure to win. There is no doubt of that. Defeat is not due to losses but to the destruction of the soul of the leaders. The 'Live to fight another day' doctrine."

Patton's inability to hold his tongue got him into repeated trouble. In April 1944, some remarks nearly got Patton fired. Speaking at a serviceman's club, Patton said it was the destiny of the British and Americans to rule the world. Eisenhower told Marshall he was ready to relieve Patton, but Marshall reminded Eisenhower that Patton had experience fighting German General Erwin Rommel who was in charge of defenses in Normandy, the site of the impending Allied landings. Eisenhower thought about it a couple of days and relented. Patton would command the Third Army. Stephen Ambrose writes,

> "Patton bragged that he was tolerated as an erratic genius because he was considered indispensable, and he was right. The very qualities that made him a great actor also made him a great commander, and Eisenhower knew it. 'You owe us some victories,' Eisenhower told Patton when the incident was closed. 'Pay off and the world will deem me a wise man.' "

> "Without a solid record of success, Patton's theatrics would have been sheer buffoonery. Dizzy Dean is reported to have said, 'If you done it, it ain't bragging.' Patton, 'done it' over and over again." —Alan Axelrod, *Patton on Leadership*

Once the war was over, though, Eisenhower had no reason to retain Patton when his public statements became still more outrageous. Eisenhower reprimanded Patton after he told a group of ex-Nazi officers in a compound that it was "madness" to intern them. While Eisenhower was thinking about what to do with him, Patton complained that Jewish Displaced Persons were responsible for the terrible conditions in the camps where they were being held. At a press conference arranged so that Patton could show he was not anti-Semitic or pro-Nazi, Patton said, "The way I see it, this Nazi thing is very

much like a Democratic and Republican election fight."
Finally Eisenhower took away the Third Army from Patton
and gave him the Fifteenth, which was charged with writing
the official history of the war.

> **"In the end, Eisenhower, decided that leadership—at least in
> his army—had a moral as well as an effectiveness dimen-
> sion."** —James O'Toole, *Leadership A to Z*

◎ ◎ ◎

Part of Eisenhower's job as Supreme Allied Commander was
mediating among the various British and American generals
under his command. Eisenhower had to negotiate a political
and diplomatic minefield. After a disastrous engagement for
the U.S. Army at Kasserine in Tunisia, British commanders
were scathing in their criticism of their American counter-
parts. American generals, notably Patton and Bradley, felt
Eisenhower was siding with the British. "I would rather be
commanded by an Arab," wrote Patton. "I think less than
nothing of Arabs." He also said, "Ike is more British than the
British and is putty in their hands."

Geoffrey Perret contrasts this Eisenhower, who as Supreme
Commander was perceived by some as a negotiator and a
compromiser—"a chairman of the board type," with his
demeanor in his other job:

> **"There was Eisenhower the commander of the U.S. Army in
> Europe. In this role, he sometime seemed almost a different
> man. Acting as the senior American general in Europe, freed
> from the quasi-political constraints of his role as supreme
> commander, he was beyond any doubts a firm, confident,**

> **hard-driving general. What he offered was strong leadership—'aggressive, outspoken and sharply definite about what he wanted,' was how one general described it.' "**

After the war, both parties courted Eisenhower, so confident were they of his chances to win office. Deciding to stand for the Republicans, Eisenhower ran for President as a non-politician and easily beat Adlai Stevenson in the 1952 election. Throughout his two terms, Eisenhower was tremendously popular; his approval ratings often reached 70% and averaged 64% over the eight years. Still, Eisenhower was criticized at the time for a lack of leadership. As Stephen Ambrose says,

> **"In contrast to FDR and Truman, Eisenhower seemed to be no leader at all, but only a chairman of the board, or even a figurehead, a Whig President in a time that demanded dramatic exercise of executive power."**

This is the same criticism leveled at Eisenhower the Supreme Commander. Eisenhower could be extremely firm and decisive, but his style was never ostentatious and there was little of that swagger. Eisenhower himself would say,

> **"In war and peace I've had no respect for the desk pounder, and have despised the loud and slick talker. If my own ideas and practices in this matter have sprung from weakness, I do not know. But they were and are deliberate or, rather, natural to me. They are not accidental."**

Presidential scholar Fred Greenstein says that Eisenhower publicly concentrated on his role as head of state and downplayed the prime ministerial functions that are the second half of the president's job. President Eisenhower preferred to appear to be above the political fray. For example, he declined to take on Senator Joe McCarthy in public, and instead got Vice President Nixon to do that, though he played an important role in the Senate censure of McCarthy in 1954.

Eisenhower was very analytical, mediating among advisers to reach decisions. This could be a recipe for inertia, for example when the United States learned that the Soviet Union had launched the *Sputnik* spacecraft, and it downplayed the potentially dominant role of the chief executive. Also, Eisenhower was terrible on TV and not good at public speaking. Eisenhower couldn't reach past the politicians and appeal directly to the people, so everything had to be done behind the scenes. Fred Greenstein describes this "hidden-hand" leadership as ". . .better suited for a national icon than a garden-variety politician." Greenstein says it probably wouldn't be possible in today's media-saturated environment for a President to lead in this fashion.

Eisenhower's unconventional style was initially lightly regarded by scholars. Arthur Schlesinger, Jr. took a survey of attitudes towards presidents in 1962 and Eisenhower ranked 20th, behind Herbert Hoover. Ike finished in the same slot in 1980. But attitudes changed and Eisenhower's reputation grew. Schlesinger took another poll in 1996 and Eisenhower came tenth; by the time of a C-SPAN survey in 2000, he had climbed to ninth.

History's verdict is very often different from the contemporary view and Eisenhower now appears as a better leader than he apparently seemed at the time. With the benefit of hindsight, Eisenhower's effectiveness is more evident. From our perspective, with the Cold War won, Eisenhower presided over of period of peace and prosperity. Eisenhower chose not to intervene in Vietnam and fought to keep a lid on defense spending. The West did not directly go to war with the Communist Bloc and everyone can be grateful for that.

> **"He showed a striking capacity to think in politically astute ways, but presented himself as a guileless folk hero. He also worked hard at carrying off his distinctive style of leadership, but left the impression that it was all effortless."** —Fred I. Greenstein

As supreme commander and president, Eisenhower was criticized for weak leadership. His unostentatious style was effective in both circumstances, although in the presidency, the weakness of his public communications and his unwillingness to engage in political horse trading made a reforming legislative agenda difficult to achieve. Eisenhower did have vision, he was decisive and ambitious, but he put a smile on with it. George Patton's all-out style was effective in the vital years of large-scale combat and then only on the battlefield itself. Taking away the battlefield from him brought Patton to a dead halt and finally forced his boss's hand.

## Five Lessons:

- Effectiveness can come at a heavy price.
- The "erratic genius" walks a fine line.
- Even the best can mess up only so many times because every boss has a limit.
- Judging leadership is highly subjective.
- Consensus leadership is a style, not a sign of weakness.

# VINCE LOMBARDI

◎ ◎ ◎

> "I think I would have been a good football player even if Julie Andrews had been my coach, but I don't know if I would have been a champion without Vince. He made us think like champions."
>
> —Jerry Kramer

> "Of course, I am his creation. I literally owe my life to that man—both on and off the field."
>
> —Bart Starr

In sports, a handful of great coaches stand above the rest. John Wooden, who led UCLA to ten national basketball championships, including seven in a row from 1967 to 1973, is one. Another is Vince Lombardi (1913–1970), whose Green Bay Packers won the first two Super Bowls. Lombardi is forever linked to professional football's championship game: since his death, National Football League teams compete for the Vince Lombardi Trophy in the Super Bowl.

Lombardi's tremendous reputation rests on his nine years as head coach in Green Bay. In sports there is an easy statistical measure of effectiveness: the win/loss record. Not only did Lombardi's teams win a very high percentage of their games—his record in Green Bay was 98-30-4—but he also won the games that mattered most. Under Lombardi, the Packers only lost one play-off game (out of ten) and he delivered five championships, in 1961, 1962, and 1965, '66 and '67. Lombardi is not just associated with winning, but with winning it all.

Brooklyn-born Lombardi played football on scholarship at Fordham and was a member of the Fordham line known as the "Seven Blocks of Granite." It took time for Lombardi to hone his leadership skills. Lombardi took some classes at law school and played semi-pro ball before starting his coaching career at St. Cecilia's High School in Englewood, New Jersey. He then coached at Fordham and at West Point under Red Blaik. In 1954, he joined the staff of the New York Giants where another assistant was Tom Landry, later head coach of the Cowboys. In 1959 Lombardi moved to Green Bay as head coach and general manager.

Lombardi's excellence as a leader and motivator was appreciated during his first season in Green Bay when he turned a squad that had gone 1-10-1 the year before into a 7-5 team. (Lombardi coached the Washington Redskins for one year in 1968 after leaving the Packers and took them to a 7-5-2 record, their first winning season in fourteen years.) Details of Lombardi's leadership are richly recorded in print. Packers guard Jerry Kramer wrote books when he was still playing and Lombardi is the subject of a superb biography, *When Pride Still Mattered* by David Maraniss.

Almost all of Lombardi's players talk in reverential terms about him, despite his demanding ways. Lombardi could be a tyrant, but the players knew he was making the team better and giving them a chance to win. A strict disciplinarian,

Lombardi was also a fair man who spoke out against any kind of prejudice. David Maraniss breaks down the motivational speeches Lombardi gave that sum up all he'd learned in football. Lombardi was so good that prominent Republicans tried unsuccessfully to recruit the coach into national politics. Lombardi's watchwords were discipline and perfection; loyalty and love.

> "A leader must identify himself with the group, must back up the group, even at the risk of displeasing his superiors. He must believe that the group wants from him a sense of approval. If this feeling prevails, production, discipline and morale will be high, and in return he can demand the cooperation to promote the goals of the company . . .
>
> The leader . . . can never close the gap between himself and the group. If he does, he is no longer what he must be. He must walk, as it were, a tightrope between the consent he must win and the control he must exert."

If the leader can manage this balancing act, extraordinary things are possible.

> "The new leadership is in sacrifice, it is in self-denial, it is in love and loyalty, it is in fearlessness, it is in humility, and it is in the perfectly disciplined will. This, gentlemen, is the distinction between great and little men.
>
> "You, as a leader, must possess the quality of mental toughness. This is a difficult quality to explain, but in my opinion this is the most important element in the character of the leader."
>
> "Mental toughness is many things. It is humility. It is simplicity. The leader always remembers that simplicity is the

sign of true greatness and meekness, the sign of true strength. Mental toughness is Spartanism, with all its qualities of self-denial, sacrifice, dedication, fearlessness, and love."

Lombardi's invocations of love are echoed in a passage from a book by John Wooden,

> "Remember, you can have respect for a person without necessarily liking that individual. Coach Amos Alonzo Stagg said, 'I loved all my players. I didn't necessarily like them all, but I did love them all.' What does that mean?
>
> "You love your children, but you may not like some of the things they do."

Coaches and players can have extremely strong feelings about each other. An admired, respected, and even loved coach can get great results. If players are indifferent to their coach—if he "loses" them—the leader can no longer hope to motivate and he'll be ineffective. Pure hatred is an even better motivator, though not a recommended leadership tool. Lombardi picked up players and came down hard on them as necessary. This style was set early in Lombardi's career. At St. Cecilia's he coached a kid called Mickey Corcoran who later taught Bill Parcells. Corcoran said Lombardi would,

> "Rip your butt out, then pat you on the butt. Knock you down, then build you up. He understood human behavior better than any person I've ever met."

> "After a loss early in the season in 1967 he addressed his senior players. 'Frankly, I'm worried,' he told them, even

though he wasn't worried at all. 'I just don't know what the hell to do,' he said, even though he knew exactly what needed to be done.

" 'He kind of put the horse on our shoulders and told us to carry it,' remembered Jerry Kramer." —Donald T. Phillips

Jerry Kramer said,

> "I loved Vince. Sure, I hated him at times during training camp and I hated him at times during the season, but I knew how much he had done for us, and I knew how much he cared about us. He is a beautiful man, and the proof is that no one whoever played for him speaks of him afterward with anything but respect and admiration and affection. His whippings, his cussings, and his driving all fade; his good qualities endure."
>
> **"He treated us all alike—like dogs."** —Henry Jordan

In the 1962 title game at Yankee Stadium, the Packers played the Giants in frigid conditions on a frozen field. Packers fullback Jimmy Taylor ran the ball thirty-one times, sustaining injuries to his head and elbow and biting his tongue. He had stitches at halftime and the players could hear his moans. David Maraniss writes,

> "He later explained his gutty performance by saying you never know until you are faced with it how much pain you can endure, and how much effort you have left, and then the coach steps in and pushes you even beyond that point. He never held it against Lombardi, though: the push made the difference."

"Those pep talks of his! I was thirty-six years old, and I thought I had a little sophistication, but when I heard those pep talks, I'd cry and go out and try to kill people. Nobody else could do that to me." —Emlen Tunnell

Vince Promoto, a veteran guard on the Redskins, talked to Tom Dowling for Dowling's book about Lombardi. Promoto distinguished between motivation by fear and empowering leadership, which can be cloaked in a guise that resembles fear.

"You see, some guys feel they're only doing what he wants them to do to keep from being yelled at. They're losers. You have to make one more step and see that it's not him that's making you play better football, but yourself. That's a feeling worth having."

Another, unnamed, player had a different view. He said he was motivated by fear. "But in the end it comes down to winning and losing, and I ask myself, is that fatherhood? Well, I have a kid and I don't want to be that kind of father." "He can get it out of you," the player conceded,

"He can win anywhere, providing he has just halfway decent ballplayers. But the trouble is, if you do win with Lombardi, you have the feeling you, the *team*, didn't do it. He did it."

Lombardi, who wasn't coaching to make friends, would probably consider this a compliment.

◎ ◎ ◎

No coach can be effective without good players. Lombardi's teams included ten Hall of Famers. John Wooden's basketball Hall of Fame entry lists his UCLA All-Americans: Walt Hazzard, Gail Goodrich, Lew Alcindor, Lucius Allen, Mike Warren, Sidney Wicks, Curtis Rowe, Henry Bibby, Bill Walton, Keith Wilkes, Richard Washington, and Dave Meyers. But sports history is littered with talented teams that underachieved, let down either by bad coaching or bad teamwork or both. Each could be mitigated by effective leadership.

A key element in the process of creating winning teams is preparation. Lombardi's boss at West Point, and his longtime mentor, Red Blaik, was one of the first coaches to exhaustively study game film to look for tendencies in opponents' play. Lombardi took that habit with him to Wisconsin. His practices were tough and punishing and dedicated to what Don Shula describes as "overlearning."

Lombardi was always working on minor variations of a few basic plays, the most famous being the sweep, with a back—Paul Hornung or Jimmy Taylor—rushing behind the blocks of guards Jerry Kramer and Fuzzy Thurston. Lombardi's Packers perfected this basic play. When they lined up, everyone in the stadium knew the Packers were running the sweep, but they ran it so well the opposition couldn't stop it.

**"Vince made us the smartest team in football. Sure, he pounded it into us. He chewed us out. He probably screamed at me more than at anybody else. He had to. For one thing, I was the kind of guy who needed to be pushed."** —Paul Hornung

Vince Lombardi's name is often connected with the statement, "Winning isn't everything; it's the only thing." Although he did post it in the locker room for a time, along with numerous other sayings, Lombardi neither coined it, nor particularly agreed with it, as David Maraniss relates. Lombardi didn't want to be perceived as someone who wanted to win at any and all costs, despite his intense will to win, and despite what he instilled in his players.

**"He taught me that you must have a flaming desire to win. It's got to dominate all your waking hours. It can't ever wane. It's got to glow in you all the time."** —Bart Starr

**"It was obvious to those around him that Vince Lombardi really loved football. He lived it twenty-four hours a day, got emotional about it, thought about its deeper meanings, preached it passionately. And in coaching, or leadership, or anything else, that kind of passion, knowledge, and dedication just naturally inspire other people."** —Donald T. Phillips

Together, Vince Lombardi and his players—men like the Hall of Famers Jim Taylor, Forrest Gregg, Bart Starr, Ray Nitschke, Herb Adderley, Willie Davis, Jim Ringo, Paul Hornung, Willie Wood, and Henry Jordan—dedicated themselves to winning. Lombardi pushed the players, but they responded because they succeeded—and vice versa. Lombardi remained down-to-earth, holding parties in the basement at his house for his players and buying players' wives gifts after championship seasons. He also had an impromptu meeting place on a golf course where he'd hand out money to worthy cases. Lombardi proves that great leaders aren't superhuman, merely very highly skilled and dedicated, leaving a lot of leeway for quirkiness such as his.

Max McGee was a player who repeatedly broke curfew to sneak out of training camp dorms. He was also repeatedly caught. One year, McGee was about to be fined $500 for his third offence. Lombardi was apoplectic, and shouted at McGee in front of the other players.

> " 'MAX!' he yelled, 'I said that'll cost you $500 and—' Vince turned purple, 'if you go out again, it'll cost you a thousand.' The room was totally silent, hushed. Lombardi stopped shaking and actually managed to grin a little. 'Max,' he said softly, 'if you can find anything worth sneaking out for, for $1000, hell, call me and I'll go with you.' "

## Five Lessons

- A leader might love his charges but that doesn't mean he has to like them.
- Meticulous preparation is a prime leadership skill.
- Motivation takes many forms.
- Even the greatest leaders need great teams to win for them.
- Great leadership breeds successful habits.

# Mohandas K. Gandhi and Dr. Martin Luther King, Jr.

◎ ◎ ◎

> **"The nonviolence of my conception is a more active
> and more real fighting than retaliation, whose very nature
> is to increase wickedness."**
>
> —Mahatma Gandhi

> **"We are all the leaders here in this struggle in Mississippi"**
>
> —Martin Luther King, Jr.

In 1893, the young Indian lawyer Mohandas K. Gandhi was taken off a whites-only, first-class train carriage in South Africa. From this moment on, Gandhi fought for the rights of Indians in South Africa and, when he returned to India years later, he led the great non-violence movement that played a major role in securing India's independence from Britain. Gandhi came to be known as Mahatma, or "great soul." In 1955, the young African-American scholar/pastor Martin Luther King, Jr. led a boycott of the bus system in Montgomery, Alabama, after Rosa Parks was arrested for refusing to give up her seat to a white rider. Dr. King's historic movement, inspired by Gandhi, was a key factor in securing legal gains for African Americans in the 1960s. Both men, spiritual and political leaders who preached non-violence, were killed for what they had achieved and stood for.

Gandhi had planned to stay only a short time in South Africa to assist on a legal case. But the incident in the train at the station at Maritzburg, capital of the Natal, together with repeated indignities he and other Indians received at the hands of white South Africans, pressed Gandhi to seek leadership. When a white passenger pointed out Gandhi and demanded he be removed, Gandhi got off the train and spent the night in a cold station rather than move to a third-class carriage. Within a week, he had organized a meeting of Indians in Pretoria and talked about white discrimination and how the Indians present, most of whom were Muslim merchants, could improve their situation.

Gandhi stayed in South Africa until 1915 and developed his concept of *Satyagraha*. This has come to represent Gandhi's idea of non-violence but it can also mean "truth-force" or "steadfastness in truth." In holding to this ideal, Gandhi's followers were accepting they might have to make tremendous sacrifices. Individually, they would have to change in order to change the world around them. It is Gandhi who exemplifies James McGregor Burns's idea of "Transforming Leadership." Burns writes about Gandhi's resistance efforts in South Africa that created *Satyagraha*, specifically the opposition he organized in 1906 when authorities decreed that Indians had to register themselves. *Satyagraha* was the tactic used, with *swaraj* as the goal, *swaraj* being "self-government and freedom."

> *"Swaraj* fused independence from racial or colonial oppression with *inward* liberation, a transformation of both society and self; indeed, the '*swaraj* of a people,' he said, was the 'sum total' of the *swaraj* of individuals." —James McGregor Burns

To this end, Gandhi's tactic was for Indians to refuse to submit to fingerprinting or to carry registration cards. This might have grave consequences, Gandhi warned. Resisters might be fined or jailed, suffer hard labor or be flogged, or have their property confiscated. They might fall ill and die in jail.

> **"In short, therefore, it is not at all impossible that we may have to endure every hardship that we may imagine, and wisdom lies in pledging ourselves on the understanding that we shall have to suffer all that and more."**

This stance, which Gandhi took back with him to India, was a force which, Burns says, "trumped the vast material—but feeble moral—resources of the British."

In India, Gandhi first organized indigo sharecroppers in the Bihar region, and followed with his campaign against the monopoly the colonial government held over salt. In 1930, he staged a march to the coast to gather the precious mineral.

> **"For twenty-four days, across two hundred miles, Gandhi led his following, which grew as he went to thousands of women, children, and men. He closely regulated the 'purity' of the march and brilliantly orchestrated press and newsreel coverage that made the campaign a worldwide success. His arrival**

at the sea was greeted with jubilation—except among Raj officials left sputtering with frustration."

This was the first major challenge to British authority and Burns writes that the colonial authorities never regained their balance. Gandhi worked tirelessly as leader of the pro-independence Congress Party. He attempted to bridge the great divides between India's Hindus and Muslims and to improve the condition of India's "Untouchables" who had no place in the country's rigid caste system. Gandhi spent more than 2,000 days in jail in his life and went on hunger strike, or fasted, numerous times. In Calcutta, for example, Gandhi fasted to prevent violence against the Muslim minority by the Hindu majority. He succeeded, leading the British Governor-General, Lord Mountbatten, to say,

"In the Punjab we have 55,000 soldiers and large scale rioting on our hands. In Bengal our forces consist of one man and there is nothing."

Gandhi was unable to quell the full-scale civil war that followed Indian independence and which led to the creation of Muslim Pakistan. Gandhi himself fell victim to violence, assassinated by a Hindu extremist in 1948. At the time of his death, Albert Einstein said,

"Gandhi had demonstrated that a powerful human following can be assembled not only through the cunning game of the usual political maneuvers and trickeries but through the cogent example of a morally superior conduct of life."

Gandhi exerted leadership through moral force and his extra-ordinary example. Non-violence was never a passive idea, for Gandhi was a man of action.

**"He had conquered India and changed the landscape of the human heart. Never again would people deride the idea of non-violence, for he had planted it firmly in men's minds, showing them how they could always prevent government from imposing themselves too harshly on the people."** — Robert Payne

Martin Luther King, Jr. was already headed towards a dual career as a preacher and academic when he took on his epic leadership role in 1955. His background included a degree in sociology from Morehouse College as well as a divinity degree from Crozer Theological Seminary, both of which he had when he started a doctorate at Boston University. While completing his dissertation he became pastor of the Dexter Avenue Baptist Church in Montgomery, Alabama.

In his history of the civil rights movement, *Parting the Waters*, Taylor Branch recounts how King asserted firm leadership over his church from the beginning, mandating fund-raising activities, establishing a high school scholarship and a nursery and requiring that every member register to vote, this last at a time when less than five percent of African Americans in Alabama were registered.

The segregated bus system had been challenged before the Rosa Parks case, but it was Parks's arrest on December 1,

1955 that galvanized the black community into action. The little-known King, who had been pastor for just over a year, was not the obvious choice to lead the action against the bus company. But at the first meeting of the Montgomery Improvement Association, which carried out the year-long bus boycott, none of the other, more experienced ministers was nominated as leader. Taylor Branch writes,

> "Idealists would say afterward that King's gifts made him the obvious choice. Realists would scoff at this, saying that King was not very well known, and that his chief asset was his lack of debts or enemies. Cynics would say that the established preachers stepped back for King only because they saw more blame and danger ahead than glory."

King's first job as leader was to address a rally in church. The meeting was packed to overflowing. As King saw the huge crowd from his car, he said to a friend, "This could turn into something big." King electrified the crowd. He said that there comes a time "when people get tired of being trampled over by the iron feet of oppression" and a wave of sound rose up.

> "The giant cloud of noise shook the building and refused to go away. One sentence had set it loose, somehow, pushing the call-and-response of the Negro church service past the din of a political rally and on to something King had never known before."

Dr. King's ability to inspire people was conjoined with the righteous cause embodied in Rosa Parks. King was by no means the only leader of the civil rights movement, but his legacy remains the greatest. The Supreme Court eventually declared the segregation of Montgomery's buses illegal and the service was desegregated in 1956. Dr. King went on to direct the Southern Christian Leadership Conference that organized sit-ins, freedom rides and rallies, and which placed him at the heart of civil rights efforts that focused on getting laws changed in Washington and then implemented on the ground. Like Gandhi, King was arrested and jailed frequently for his actions. Like Gandhi, he preached the virtues of non-violence, even as that stance came under mounting attack from other black leaders over the years.

The younger King was introduced to the ideas of Mahatma Gandhi while studying at the seminary. He initially rejected Gandhi's non-violence and was more affected by the theology of Reinhold Neibuhr, especially as espoused in *Moral Man and Immoral Society*, which he read in 1950. King later laid a great deal of credit for his own views with Gandhi, something that Taylor Branch said that King did partly for the good PR it brought.

> "The intellectual and moral satisfaction that I failed to gain from the utilitarianism of Bentham and Mill, the revolutionary methods of Marx and Lenin, the social contracts theory of Hobbes, the 'back to nature' optimism of Nietzsche, I found in the nonviolent resistance philosophy of Gandhi."

Ohio University political scientist Michael J. Nojeim has written a comparative study of Gandhi and King. He writes about Gandhi's role in King's philosophy,

"After his immersion in Gandhi's ideals and after practicing his own version of non-violent resistance in Montgomery, King changed his mind about the potential of applying Christ's non-violent love-ethic to political conflict. King saw Gandhi as the first person to ever recreate the love-ethic of Jesus into a force for positive moral, social change."

Martin Luther King, Jr. never met Gandhi, who had died before King's years of prominence. King did travel to India in 1959. He knew Gandhi's situation was different: Gandhi worked to remove the yoke of a colonial minority, while African Americans suffered legal discrimination in the name of the majority whites. Still, he was impressed that the government tried to help the Untouchables, which contrasted markedly with what he saw as a feeble effort at the time by the federal government back home.

King, like Gandhi, was a man of action, and the love that motivated King was a source of strength, as he explained at the lecture he gave on winning the Nobel Peace Prize in 1964.

"When I speak of love I am not speaking of some sentimental and weak response which is little more than emotional bosh. I am speaking of that force which all of the great religions have seen as the supreme unifying principle of life. Love is somehow the key that unlocks the door which leads to ultimate reality."

Martin Luther King, Jr.'s vision of America was contained in his now-legendary speech at the massive rally in Washington, D.C., on August 27, 1963. As Taylor Branch writes, King wandered away from his prepared text in the "I Have a Dream" sequence.

> "Critics would point out that the dream was ethereal, and people who yearned for simple justice would object that the content was too simple. Still, precious few among millions detected lightness or naïveté in the speech. On the contrary, the emotional command of his oratory gave King authority to reinterpret the core intuition of democratic justice. More than his words, the timbre of his voice projected across the racial divide and planted him as the new founding father. It was a fitting joke on the races that he achieved such statesmanship by setting aside his lofty text to let loose and jam, as he did regularly from two hundred podiums a year."

In a book on the speech and its impact, Drew D. Hansen writes that while people were impressed with the oratory, they were more struck by the size of the crowd. It was only later that the speech came to represent the highest ideals and aspirations of a movement, in the same way that the Gettysburg Address has grown immeasurably in stature over time. It was in the debate in 1983 about making a federal holiday for King that Hansen says the speech's authority was fully established. Representative Jim Wright of Texas summed up the attitude that now prevails,

> "It was twenty years ago this month that Martin Luther King stood in the shadow of the Lincoln Memorial and proclaimed his now famous phrase, 'I have a dream.' Is it not the same

**dream which this nation proclaims its allegiance in the Jeffersonian words, 'all men are created equal'?"**

Neither King nor Gandhi was perfect, of course, and it is foolish to expect any leader to be. But the two men are pivotal figures in the histories of their countries. They demonstrate how much can be achieved without any significant, formal position of leadership. Mohandas Gandhi was a lawyer in South Africa when he started leading others; Dr. King stepped beyond his role as a pastor at a Southern church in the United States. Tom Peters has written about the accomplishments of people who have what he calls, "Little/No formal Org-chart authority."

> **"In 1935, how much formal authority did Mohandas Gandhi have? (That's right, the fellow who created the largest democracy in the world.) In 1959, how much formal authority did Dr. Martin Luther King, Jr. have? And in 1985, how much authority was vested in Vaclav Havel . . . who led the liberation, just a handful of years later, of Czechoslovakia? And as late as 1988, say, how much formal authority did the man we now call P-r-e-s-i-d-e-n-t Nelson Mandela have?"**

Gandhi and King were both leaders of revolutions who had a strong spiritual element to their oratory. Above all, they were moral leaders, viewed in the same light as Mandela and Havel and other leaders who have transformed the societies that once treated them as criminals. To begin with, they held no formal position of power, yet they grew to establish their own roles of great significance in the establishment and transformation of their countries and the betterment of their people.

## Five Lessons

- Effective leaders do not need formal authority.
- Great leaders sacrifice much—sometimes, everything.
- Great leaders may be more celebrated in death than in life.
- The moral example is a powerful weapon.
- No leader is perfect.

# WOMEN CEOS

"When I came into this role, I didn't expect that the microscope would be on how I raise my children."

—Andrea Jung, *Avon CEO*

When Carleton 'Carly' Fiorina was ousted as chief executive of Hewlett-Packard in February 2005, the number of women CEOs of *Fortune* 500 companies fell from eight to seven. (However, one day after Fiorina left HP, Sara Lee promoted Brenda Barnes to CEO, restoring the eighth woman.) Fiorina's company had been much larger than the other seven: she was the first woman to head a top-twenty company and was *Fortune*'s most powerful woman in business for six straight years. Fiorina was a standard bearer as a woman leader in business and, as such, she was always judged twice: first as a leader, and then again as a woman leader.

The eight *Fortune* 500 women CEOs at the beginning of 2005 were:

- Carly Fiorina: Hewlett-Packard (company rank #11)
- Mary Sammons: Rite Aid, #128
- Anne Mulcahy: Xerox, #130
- Andrea Jung: Avon, #275
- Patricia Russo: Lucent, #243
- Marce Fuller: Mirant, #314
- Eileen Scott: Pathmark, #432
- Marion Sandler: Golden West Financial, #440

A story in *USA Today* early in 2005, for example, compared the stock performance of the companies run by the eight women against the rest of the S&P 500. The women lost to the men over the course of 2004, but had beaten them so handily in 2003 that they were still out ahead when measured over the two years. Of the eight companies, Patricia Russo's Lucent Technologies did best in 2004, gaining 32%. In the story, Russo was quoted as saying that expectations are the same for men and women. Gender has nothing to do with results.

**"But experts Judy Rosener of the University of California-Irvine Graduate School of Management, and Paulette**

Gerkovich of Catalyst, an organization that attempts to advance women in business, disagree. Over time, and with a larger sample size, companies with women as CEOs will perform better, they say.

"Some women, such as H.P.'s Carly Fiorina, have a leadership style similar to men's, Rosener says. But, in general, women are better at thinking long term and are more comfortable with the ambiguity of not needing a clear answer to every problem, says Rosener, who sees that as a strength."

So is there a distinctive women's leadership style to be discerned from these CEOs and other women leaders?

Carleton Fiorina arrived at HP in 1999 from Lucent Technologies having started her career at AT&T. In Peter Burrows' *Backfire*, one of the books published about Fiorina and HP when she was CEO, there is a story about the kind of masculine atmosphere in which she had prevailed. Early in her career at AT&T, Fiorina and some colleagues attended a lunch organized by a dissatisfied customer. As Fiorina arrived alone, she realized the venue was a strip club. As she sat down, her lunch partners snickered and one of the men tried to call a stripper over to the table. She declined.

"When the lunch ended, Fiorina got up and coolly left. 'It was her way of saying, "Nice try guys, but go screw yourselves,"' says former colleague Harry Carr, who heard the story from Fiorina."

HP had a tradition of promoting women and they make up more than a third of the company's managers. The company wanted someone to shake them up and the high profile and dynamic Fiorina seemed just the person. When she arrived at HP, Peter Burrows says Fiorina looked for, and received, more attention because she was a woman.

> **"Her supporters point out that she refused far more media opportunities than she accepted. That is undoubtedly true, but the woman who once told *Forbes* that 'Leadership is a performance' clearly sought out the limelight. 'People are excited to see a woman at the head of a big company,' so I'm going to use my image for publicity. . . ."**

Fiorina's aggressive leadership style was a change from the HP culture. HP's acquisition of Compaq in 2002 for $19 billion was a risk and involved a long fight with members of the old guard like Walter Hewlett, the son of one of the founders. Fiorina spent a lot of time away from the company when the culture had been hands on. Bucking long-term trends, she centralized the company and was a superstar CEO. This was fine as long as the company was doing well. But the merger with Compaq did not produce the expected profits. Companies like IBM were getting out of the PC business that HP was venturing into, and even their highly successful printer business suffered a downturn. The leadership qualities that Fiorina brought to the job were then perceived to be detrimental.

When the HP board acted, the consensus was that it was a gender-neutral decision. Indeed, women were prominent among the leading candidates to replace Fiorina. Stock market reaction was positive, as HP stock rose almost 7% next day. Michael Useem, professor of management at the Wharton School said,

In 2003, billionaire Oprah Winfrey became the first African American woman on *Forbes* magazine's list of the world's richest people. As talk-show host and media executive, Oprah has been a leader for more than twenty years. Among her contributions is her work on the National Child Protection Act (1992), which set up a national database of convicted child abusers. Her show constantly promotes positive values and images for men and women alike, and for years, through her book club, she has relentlessly and effectively promoted reading.

> **"The comfortably literary humanities majors of the world can yawn and declare that they don't need Oprah to tell them what to read, but the person who hasn't picked up a book since high school, who has never read for pure pleasure, knows, because of Oprah, the transforming power of books. And authors—from Wally Lamb to Jane Hamilton to Edwidge Danticat, and even big names like Toni Morrison—have reached a whole new readership."**

**"In this era where there is so much demand for results, boards are looking at results. A 'Carl' Fiorina would have been subjected to the same pressures."**

A mark against Carly Fiorina was that she was an outsider brought into HP, unlike either Anne Mulcahy or Andrea Jung, each of whom ascended to CEO from within her firm. Andrea

Jung was 41 when she became CEO of Avon in 1999. As she's remade the company, sales have risen 45%. Avon also has a woman at number two: their chief operating officer is Susan Kropf. Jung told *Newsweek* she expects there to be more women CEOs. "The next five years are going to be very different. There are so many women right now in strong No. 2 positions who are ready to take on the No. 1 job."

Sometime soon, we'll stop looking at these leaders differently for being women (and stop asking them how they're bringing up their children). In 1996, management consultant Karin Kenke wrote,

> **"Instead of treating women leaders as exceptions or anomalies who are categorized as 'women leaders,' and not just 'leaders,' we have to acknowledge that the number of women leaders will eventually reach critical mass."**

That mass is some way from being reached in government. In the United States' first two hundred years (1776–1976), men outnumbered women 1715-11 in the Senate and 9591-87 in the House. In 1992, there were only two women in the Senate. In 2005 the 109th Congress has fourteen women senators, and the House has sixty-five women members, giving a total of 79 women out of 535 members of congress, or 15%. Across the country, 1,663 or 7,382 state legislators are women, or 22.5%.

Karin Kenke contended in 1996 that following *situational* or *contextual* leadership theories would help women. Once we recognize that every leadership situation is different, we can look for the appropriate leader who fits the bill. But by looking upon leadership as a manifestation of authority, we're following a male paradigm. Sue J.M. Freeman of Smith College says that people's perceptions get in the way of equal opportunity because women are more associated with certain contexts and particular types of behavior.

> "Stereotypic notions that attribute emotional reactivity and relationship priority to women may render them lacking the aptitude supposedly required for the rational, objective decisiveness required for business leadership. Thus, people may not readily perceive women as leaders and they may continue to associate female traits as incompatible with the kinds of learning leadership requires."

Freeman writes that the best predictor of whether someone will make a good leader or not is, in fact, their intelligence. However, people's perceptions are different.

> "If we intend to dismantle the barriers to women's leadership, one of the first we should tackle is authority. Women must be seen as commanding and powerful, as the place where the buck stops, in the words of Harry Truman's famous Oval Office plaque: It's not so easy, especially when our society upholds 'the masculinity of authority and the authority of masculinity.' " —Marie C. Wilson

Of course, it's not only women who suffer from misperceptions. In *Voices of Diversity*, Renee Blank and Sandra Slipp examined attitudes to minorities in leadership positions. Among their findings,

"A Japanese-American lawyer said that if she acts assertively in her firm, she is called the Dragon Lady."

"A Japanese-American biochemist said, 'We're expected to do well in technical areas, be smarter, and take on extra assignments without complaining. Yet we're not rewarded for our achievements because we're not considered leaders.' "

"Many black managers complain about subordinates who go over their heads because the employees assume that the black managers don't have authority or power and that their decisions aren't valid and need to be checked out.' "

In early 2005, there were three African American CEOs of *Fortune* 500 companies: Ken Chenault of American Express, Richard Parsons of AOL Time Warner, and Franklin Raines of Fannie Mae. Stanley O'Neill, COO of Merrill Lynch, was *Fortune*'s most powerful black executive.

Redressing stereotypical perceptions is a huge task. Women's leadership advocates mention strategies. *Women in Power* discusses what authors Dorothy Cantor and Toni Bernay call "Creative Aggression"—taking the initiative, leading others and speaking out. Female aggression is stigmatized and shouldn't be, they say. *Women in Power* includes a checklist.

"There are five basic secrets of leadership and enabling messages every girl should receive":
1. You are loved and special.
2. You can do anything you want.

Josephine Esther Mentzer, better known as Estée Lauder (1908—2004), was the ninth child of Hungarian immigrants. Lauder once asked a woman in a beauty salon where she'd bought her blouse and the woman asked what difference would it make, she'd never be able to afford it. Lauder resolved to have whatever she wanted one day. Lauder's uncle was a struggling chemist with a formula for skin cream. She took her uncle's hand cream and sold it on the street and developed more creams and powders with him that she sold out of beauty salons and, in 1948, at Saks department store in New York. Lauder was a great innovator, giving away samples of products. In 1953, she started the practice of mailing promotional blotters soaked in a new scent. When Estée Lauder died in 2004, her company's sales were close to $5 billion.

3. You can take risks.
4. You can use and enjoy your Creative Aggression.
5. You are entitled to dreams of greatness.

Marie Wilson is founder and president of The White House Project, started in 1998 to work toward a more representative democracy. She is co-creator of Take Our Daughters to Work Day. In *Closing the Gap*, Wilson writes that women do, in fact, lead differently from men.

> "They are better communicators and listeners, more nurturing, more willing to involve others in decision making, and more likely to roll up their sleeves and work with the team."

Wilson has a mission goal for the White House project:

> "It is not enough to see one or two female faces amongst the sea of dark-suited men in power. We won't rest until the corridors of the Capitol, executive offices, statehouses, mayor's offices, governor's offices, and the White House are equally filled with women. The only way to ensure this is to pack the political pipeline with young women who will gain experience and knowledge about politics now, preparing them for future campaigns for the House, Senate, Governorship, and President."

That Carly Fiorina was not judged according to the usual stereotypes of women leaders may actually be a mark of progress. Viewed one way, Fiorina did much better than many men. She lasted as CEO for six years when the average tenure is about three. Still, her fall would not change those incorrect perceptions about women leaders. Even if they do bring different skills to the table, women aren't appreciated when they don't act as women are supposed to act. Sheila W. Wellington, professor at Stern School of Business at New York University, told the *New York Times*.

> "Carly gambled and lost. When men do that, the world says, 'At least he was bold; he tried.' The world is less forgiving of women, and having one of the most visible women in the business fail will really not help other women.

"Carly revels in risk, and has a tough, relentless style. A quieter, less abrasive, less in-your-face style might have brought her more time, more allies among employees and kinder, gentler treatment from the media."

The reporter wondered, wouldn't that be true of a man as well?

"Women still have the stereotype of nurturers and team builders, and that wasn't Carly. She was a tough boss, hard critic, stern judge, and women still don't get approbation for those traits."

## Five Lessons:

- Women leaders are judged twice.
- Our perceptions of leaders often do not match reality.
- An outsider is cut less slack than an insider in tough times.
- Businesses have cultures that resist change.
- The highest leadership positions are still tough to break into for women and minorities.

# THE SOLDIERS OF OMAHA BEACH

◎ ◎ ◎

" 'Everything. . .was done by small groups, led by the real heroes of the war. Very few were decorated, chiefly because no one was left to tell about what they did.' "

—Major Sidney Bingham

"Two kinds of people are staying on this beach. . . the dead and those who are going to die. Now let's get the hell out of here!"

—Unnamed colonel, Omaha Beach

On June 6, 1944, Allied forces attacked German-occupied Normandy in the largest sea-borne invasion in history. This was D-Day, the culmination of Operation Overlord, the planned liberation of Europe from the west. Large numbers of troops were dropped into enemy territory by parachute, but most were put ashore by landing craft at one of five beaches. The German resistance was heaviest at one particular site, code-named Omaha Beach.

The men who landed on Omaha Beach faced some of the most vicious and intense fighting of the war. Any plans for securing the beachhead had fallen apart by the time the first soldier reached the shoreline. Casualties were extremely high; officers and NCOs were killed or injured by the hundreds and small pockets of men became hopelessly trapped on the beach where they could easily be picked off. Into the leadership vacuum stepped countless soldiers who gathered men up and led them toward the German lines. On Omaha Beach there were numerous feats of extraordinary leadership under the worst conditions imaginable.

Omaha Beach was a desperately difficult target to attack and secure. It was an obvious landing point for an invasion and the Germans were prepared. The defenders had built bunkers, pillboxes, machine-gun posts, and trenches, and all were well-manned and heavily equipped. The shallow water and the beach were littered with anti-tank obstacles and mines. The shingle beach was overlooked by high sand dunes and hundred-foot-high cliffs that provided ideal defensive cover from which the Germans could concentrate heavy fire on all of the landing area. Finally, there were only a limited number of exit points off the beach.

The Allied plan of attack was ill-conceived. As Stephen Ambrose relates in *D-Day: June 6, 1944: The Climactic Battle of World War II*, the initial intelligence was wrong about the strength of the forces at Omaha and the air and naval bombardments that were supposed to soften up the defenses failed. Then, all but one unit landed off course, putting men right under the guns and disrupting the coordination of the assault. Landing craft were destroyed before they hit the beach, and most of the heavy equipment was lost. Men were holed up in boats up to four hours and were seasick and cramped before being deposited into the water. The exhausted, overloaded, soaked-through soldiers were sitting ducks.

Sergeant William B. Otlowski told a story illustrating how

split-second decisions on June 6 made the difference between life and death, and how initiative and leadership in the face of danger saved lives. Otlowski's barge got stuck yards from the beach. A German 88mm gun landed a shell to the barge's right. The sergeant realized the gunner was taking aim on the stationary target that was his boat and he told the second lieutenant in charge to unload the men.

> " 'He said, Sergeant, stay where you are!' And I said: 'To hell with you, Lieutenant. If you want to die, go ahead. OK, men, let's go.' I called my men and we jumped off into the water and swam to the beach. We picked up rifles, ammunition belts, and helmets as we scooted across the beach to where some men were up against the cliff.
>
> "As I turned around to look, the third round from the 88 hit right smack in the middle of the damn barge with that lieutenant and all the men on it."

Stephen Ambrose writes about Sergeant John Robert Slaughter, who was in the water an hour before he even reached the sand. There, Slaughter found himself in the same position as thousands of young men. On the beach, soldiers sought whatever cover they could find as fire rained down on them. If they moved at all, they were in immediate danger of being hit. If they stayed where they were, they might only be delaying the inevitable. The urgent task was to get to the shingle beneath the cliffs, a somewhat less perilous place. Slaughter mentions a colonel who played a key role.

> "Colonel Canham came by with his right arm in a sling and a .45 Colt in his left hand. He was yelling and screaming for the officers to get the men off the beach. 'Get the hell off this

damn beach and go kill some Germans.' There was an officer taking refuge from an enemy mortar barrage in a pillbox. Right in front of me, Colonel Canham screamed, 'Get your ass out of there and show some leadership.' To another lieutenant he roared, 'Get these men off their dead asses and over the wall.' "

Sergeant Felix Branham of Virginia of the 116th Infantry Regiment also saw Colonel Canham, and the Colonel's leadership under fire changed Branham's opinion of him.

"On the beach he saw the regimental commander, Colonel Charles Canham, urging men to get off the beach and inland. Canham was an exacting commander. He had trained the 116th mercilessly, and Branham hated him for it. But now, amid the maelstrom of Omaha Beach, Branham had to admit that perhaps Canham wasn't so bad after all. The colonel had been shot in the wrist, but it hardly slowed him. He walked around with his arm in a sling, shouting orders and encouragement."

This was the decisive leadership moment on Omaha Beach. Could any kind of order be established amid the prevailing chaos? There was no help available from HQ, and no man could know what was happening more than ten yards on either side of him. Somehow, the men had to be moved off the beach. Stephen Ambrose poses the question. "It was an ultimate test: could a democracy produce young men tough enough to take charge, to lead?"

The answer, of course, was yes. Again and again, men stepped forward to assert leadership. Not all were designated leaders. They were individuals who by force of their example and by exhortation saved men's lives and took the fight to the enemy. Ambrose quotes a private saying he was laying on the shingle and the men around him were under terrible fire. They needed someone to lead them forward. Another soldier, Sergeant William Lewis, remembers a lieutenant, Leo Van de Voort, who did just that. Van de Voort said,

> " 'Let's go, goddamn, there ain't no use staying here, we're all going to get killed!' The first thing he did was to run up to a gun emplacement and throw a grenade in the embrasure. He returned with five or six prisoners. So then we thought, hell, if he can do that, why can't we. That's how we got off the beach."

Another man, engineer Private Raymond Howell, was hit by shrapnel on his hand and in his helmet on the beach. He told himself, if he was going to die, he wasn't going to die where he was. "The next bunch of guys that go over that goddamn wall, I'm going with them."

Lieutenant Walter Taylor of 116th Infantry's Company B was one of the leaders. Staff Sergeant Frank Price said of Taylor,

> "He seemed to have no fear of anything, and no matter where he went, he was in the lead either of the march or of the fight. We followed him because there was nothing else to do."

Brigadier General Norman Cota of the 29th Division urged men forward from their position beneath the sea wall.

The oral history of D-Day is rich, and those from Omaha Beach tell and retell stories of sacrifice and bravery. Anthony J. DiStephano landed at 08:30 hours with the guns of 'C' Battery, 111th Field Artillery. His CO was Lieutenant-Colonel Thornton L. Mullins, who was already wounded at the beginning of the anecdote DiStephano tells below.

> "He began to put some fight back into the little knots of stunned, inert riflemen along the sea wall. Most of them had lost their weapons or dropped them in the sand. Lt.-Colonel Mullins crept along, talking to one man after another. While he was urging one small group to clean their guns and start returning fire from the bluffs, a sniper's bullet drilled through his hand. Mullins ignored the second wound as he had the first one, and started moving a pair of amphibious tanks into decent firing positions. . . . His search led him across a completely open patch of sand where a third bullet hit him in the stomach. Lt.-Colonel Mullins fell forward on his face and died."

"Cota circulated among the Rangers. 'What outfit is this?' Private Mike Rehm heard him ask.

" 'Rangers,' someone responded.

" 'Well, goddamn it, if you're Rangers, get up and lead the way.' "

Cota was one of the first to realize that the best route was up and over rather than through the bluffs as had originally been planned. A hole was blown in barbed wire at the base of the cliff. The first man through the hole was hit by machine gun fire and he died in full view of the men at the wall.

> "Cota realized he had to do something equally dramatic or the men would never move. He leaped up, dashed across the road and through the gap. Luckily he made it, and he turned around and shouted for the men to follow. Several Stonewallers [116th Regiment] did, and miraculously no one was hit. Their success convinced dozens more to try it."

The men made it to the bluff and started to climb toward the German positions through a trench.

Cota's was one of many pieces of brilliant improvisation that day, as all decision making devolved from titular leaders at HQ to the men on the spot. For instance, many landing craft were steered away from their designated spots so that men were put down away from the heaviest fire. As General Cota deduced, the idea of attacking the beach's exit points was impractical because they were too heavily defended.

Historian Adrian R. Lewis has written about the impromptu nature of this first, key effort to get men off the beach.

> "Soldiers from different companies and even different divisions organized into new and ad hoc units. Buddy systems were worked on. Brave men crossed the minefields. Many died in the attempt, their bodies marking the way through which others could pass. Soldiers crawled forward under enemy fire to blow or cut holes in the wire. Paths through the

**minefields and wire were pushed forward incrementally at great risk and high cost. Through these extraordinary efforts, soldiers reached the base of the bluff."**

Soldiers moving up the bluffs took German positions one by one, easing the rate of fire down onto the beach. Navy guns were brought in to attack the entrenched defenses from close range, and eventually troops could get off the beach via the exits as originally planned. The first day's fighting cost more than 2,000 casualties, but 35–40,000 men were landed and a toehold was established at the beachhead, which was secured.

The soldiers of Omaha Beach had shown great leadership. Officers and NCOs urged men on, and where there were no official leaders, men stepped forward and assumed command. In *Five-Star Leadership*, consultants Patrick Townsend and Joan Gebhardt write that Omaha Beach was no accident. It was made possible by the long-established leadership training and codes of the armed forces.

> **"While the accolades were all well deserved, the fact is that the heroic actions so apparent at Normandy were in the tradition of U.S. military leadership. Since the early days of the Revolutionary War, the idea of stepping into the breach, of acting in the best interests of the common cause despite the lack of specific directions has been a trademark of the American military man and woman. There has always been the 'cowboy' in the U.S. military, with the willingness to take the bull by the horns when necessary. Authority equal to responsibility, the key phrase in empowerment, is the basis of military leadership."**

## Five Lessons:

- In combat, leading and following are at their most instinctual.
- Courage + training = execution.
- When a leader steps forward, courage is contagious.
- A leader has to be brave enough for all his men.
- Inaction in a leadership moment can be fatal.

# ROSA PARKS

◎ ◎ ◎

> **"She was anchored to that seat by the accumulated indignities of days gone and the boundless aspirations of generations yet unborn."**
> —Martin Luther King, Jr.

On December 1, 1955, in a courageous display of defiance, Rosa Parks demonstrated that leadership can be found in seemingly small yet enormously powerful and significant acts. After we have discussed generals and presidents, prime ministers and war heroes, the ultimate leadership moment comes from a part-time seamstress going home from work, sitting on a bus in Montgomery, Alabama.

Rosa Parks was by no means a meek woman who found a steely resolve just that afternoon. As historian Douglas Brinkley recounts in his biography of Parks, her family had a history of disobedience and resistance to Jim Crow. Rose

McCauley's grandfather was a very light-skinned black man who'd shake hands with white people and introduce himself as "Edwards" when by convention he was supposed only to bow and scrape and use his first name. As a girl, Rosa herself pushed over a white boy on roller skates who'd tried to run her off the sidewalk in his all-white neighborhood.

Rosa McCauley dropped out of school to work in a textile factory and then left her job to take care of her mother. She married Raymond Parks, one of the founding members of the Montgomery chapter of the NAACP. Parks encouraged his wife to return to school to get her diploma and in 1941, she took a job at Maxwell Field, an air force facility. President Roosevelt had integrated the armed forces and the better conditions on the base showed Parks what was possible in the world outside.

After she joined the NAACP in 1943, Rosa Parks helped organize voter registration drives and kept chapter records and eventually became local secretary. To make money Rosa worked as a seamstress and periodically she also looked after her sick mother. Parks was a regular churchgoer as well as a mentor to local kids. As Taylor Branch has written, she "represented one of the isolated high blips on the graph of human nature, offsetting a dozen or so sociopaths."

◎ ◎ ◎

The situation in the South was coming to a head in the mid-fifties. Challenges to segregated busing had been tried already, in June 1953 in Baton Rouge, Louisiana, for example. Rosa Parks first heard Martin Luther King, Jr. speak at an NAACP meeting in Montgomery in August 1955. That August also saw the brutal murder of Emmett Till, aged fourteen, in Money, Mississippi. Till had said, "Bye, baby" to a white woman and for that he was abducted and tortured to death by the woman's husband and brother-in-law. Emmett Till had an open casket funeral, at the insistence of his mother, and Parks wept when she saw a photograph of his horrifically disfigured face. Then, in September, the suspects were found "not guilty" despite positive identifications of Till's kidnappers.

In Montgomery itself, African Americans had started to resist racist bus regulations. Local civil rights leaders were looking for a test case to take to court, and on December 1, Rosa Parks stepped forward, though inadvertently at first. After work that day, Parks did a little early Christmas shopping and got on a bus headed for home. Drivers enforced the segregation regulations differently, but each bus had a neutral zone in the middle between the white-only section at the front and the colored section in the rear. This particular day, the bus wasn't so full to begin with, so Rosa Parks sat in the middle. Eventually the bus filled up some, and there were four black people sitting in her row.

When a white woman got on and asked for a seat, the rules allowed the driver to ask black people to make way, which the driver duly did. In these circumstances, not only did one African American have to give up his or her seat for a white, but the whole row had to move, lest a white suffer the indignity of sitting in the same row as a black person. Rosa Parks saw that the driver was James Blake, locally a notorious figure who'd thrown her off a bus years before. The three people sharing Rosa Parks's row moved back. But she shifted herself next to the window, and sat and waited. Douglas Brinkley writes,

"The next ten seconds seemed like an eternity to Rosa Parks. As Blake made his way toward her, all she could think about were her forebears who, as Maya Angelou would put it, took the lash, the branding iron, and untold humiliations while only praying that their children would someday 'flesh out' the dream of equality. But unlike the poet, it was not Africa in the days of the slave trade that Parks was thinking about; it was the racist Alabama in the here and now."

This was the moment that Parks decided enough was enough.

" 'Are you going to stand up?' the driver demanded. Rosa Parks looked straight at him and said, 'No.' Flustered and not quite sure what to do, Blake retorted, 'Well, I'm going to have you arrested.' And Parks, still sitting next to the window, replied softly, 'You may do that.' "

Dignified and defiant, Parks was taken off the bus by the police and driven to City Hall where she was treated like the criminal her act technically made her. Parks wasn't allowed to have a drink of water or make a phone call but was booked and taken to jail, where she was fingerprinted and her mug shots were taken.

This was the beginning of her trial of courage. Respectable, middle-aged, church-going Parks was the perfect figure for local leaders to take to court as the test case against segregation. Rosa Parks came under pressure to let herself be the vanguard case. But Parks knew that if she went ahead, her life would change forever, not necessarily for the better. Many black people didn't want the status quo to be challenged and Parks was also urged to back off. She knew that taking the case would make her something of an outcast. Parks's husband and mother were terrified and didn't want her to proceed. Parks was quickly proved right about her job; she lost it at once. This was a huge decision for Parks and her family. Branch writes,

> "Raymond Parks came nearly undone. Having just felt primitive, helpless terror when his wife had been snatched into jail, he could not bear the thought that she would reenter the forbidden zone by choice."

Rosa Parks consented, saying, modestly, " 'If you think it will mean something to Montgomery and do some good, I'll be happy to go along with it.' "

> "The perfect client went to court on Monday, December 5, 1955, wearing a long-sleeved black dress with white cuffs and collar and a small velvet hat with pearls across the top. 'They've messed with the wrong one now,' trilled a girl in the crowd." —Gail Collins, *America's Women*

Martin Luther King, Jr. emerged as the leader of the Montgomery bus boycott, which lasted a year and ended in desegregation. In the process, King was catapulted to national attention. What was Rosa Parks' role in all that?

> "Many years later, E.D. Nixon, the black Montgomery lawyer who represented Rosa Parks, met a woman on an airplane who told him she couldn't imagine what would have happened to black people if Martin Luther King had not come to Montgomery. 'I said, "If Mrs. Parks had got up and given that

**white woman her seat, you'd never have heard of Rev. King.'"**
—Gail Collins, *America's Women*

◎ ◎ ◎

Martin Luther King, Jr. was awarded the Nobel Peace Prize in 1964. Among the award winners since then have been four women who seem as "ordinary" as Rosa Parks on face value. Betty Williams and Mairéad Corrigan were office workers in Northern Ireland until a day in August 1976 when Williams witnessed the shooting of an IRA terrorist whose runaway car knocked down and killed three children. Mairéad Corrigan was an aunt of the children, and together Williams and Corrigan founded the Northern Ireland Peace Movement that worked against the violence in the province. The women were awarded the Peace Prize in 1976. In her Nobel Lecture, Betty Williams said:

> "Because of the role of women over so many centuries in so many different cultures, they have been excluded from what have been called public affairs; for that very reason they have concentrated much more on things close to home . . . and they have kept far more in touch with the true realities . . . the realities of giving birth and love. The moment has perhaps come in human history when, for very survival, those realities must be given pride of place over the vainglorious adventures that lead to war."

The winner of the prize in 1991 was Aung San Suu Kyi, the leader of the pro-democracy movement in Burma and co-founder of National League for Democracy. Suu Kyi's father was a founder of the country who was assassinated when his daughter was two. Suu Kyi lived abroad for twenty years before returning to Burma in 1988 to take care of her sick mother. It was a time of student riots against the military junta controlling the country and Suu Kyi took up the cause of democracy for which she paid with years of house arrest and harassment.

> **"I obviously had to think about it, but my instinct was that this was not a time when anyone who cared stayed out. As my father's daughter, I felt I had a duty to get involved."**

Aung San Suu Kyi's Nobel acceptance speech in Oslo had to be given by her son, Alexander Aris, who quoted from his mother's writings,

> **"The quest for democracy in Burma is the struggle of a people to live whole, meaningful lives as free and equal members of the world community. It is part of the unceasing human endeavour to prove that the spirit of man can transcend the flaws of his nature."**

In 1997, the prize was shared by the International Campaign to Ban Landmines (ICBL) and Jody Williams, the ICBL's founding coordinator. Under Williams's leadership the ICBL grew from its foundation as a single group in 1992 to more than 1,300 groups in over eighty-five countries in five years. The ICBL succeeded in getting an international treaty banning antipersonnel landmines first accepted by 122 countries in

1997 and then made part of international law in 1999. Williams had been an aid worker in Latin America and had taught English as a Second Language.

> "Landmines have been used since the U.S. Civil War, since the Crimean War, yet we are taking them out of arsenals of the world. It is amazing. It is historic. It proves that civil society and governments do not have to see themselves as adversaries."

Leaders don't have to be people with authority and grand titles but can be secretaries, receptionists, dutiful daughters, aid workers, and seamstresses. Anyone can become a leader, and then learn the leadership skills they will need as they make their way forward. Rosa Parks is proof of that. Her leadership began at the moment when she decided to fight back. In her autobiography she has written that it has been assumed she was just tired that day.

> "People always say that I didn't give up my seat because I was tired, but that isn't true. I wasn't tired physically, or no more tired than I usually was at the end of a working day. No, the only tired I was, was tired of giving in."

# BIBLIOGRAPHY AND SOURCES

◎ ◎ ◎

## Introduction

Burns: Burns, James McGregor. *Leadership*. New York: Harper & Row, 1978.

Bennis: Bennis, Warren, and Bert Nanus. *Leaders: The Strategies for Taking Charge*. New York: Harper & Row, 1985.

Kotter: Kotter, John P. *On What Leaders Really Do*. Boston: Harvard Business School Press, 1999.

## Leadership Theories

Bennis: Bennis, Warren. *On Becoming a Leader*. New York: Basic Books, 2003.

Gardner: Gardner, John. *On Leadership*. New York: The Free Press, 1993.

Carlyle: Carlyle, Thomas. *On Heroes, Hero-Worship, and the Heroic in History*, 1840.

Carnegie: Feinster, Julie M. *In the Words of Great Business Leaders*. New York: John Wiley, 2000.

Edman: Edman, Irwin. *Human Traits and the Social Significance*. Boston: Houghton Mifflin, 1920.

"Trait theories were popular," "Leadership Theory," Charles A. Schnesheim et al in *Leadership*. Edited by A. Dale Trimpe. New York: Facts on File, 1994.

"Some researchers," Northouse, Peter. *Leadership: Theory and Practice*. Second Edition. Thousand Oaks, CA: Westview Press, 2004.

"Most of us," Gladwell, Malcolm. *Blink*. New York: Little, Brown, 2005.

"It is much like the words," Northouse, *Leadership: Theory and Practice*. 2nd ed. Thousand Oaks, CA: Westview Press, 2004.

Bennis: Bennis, Warren. *On Becoming a Leader*. New York: Basic Books, 2003.

McGregor: McGregor, Douglas. *The Human Side of Enterprise*. New York: McGraw-Hill, 1960.

"McGregor was often met," Heil, Gary, Warren Bennis, and Deborah C. Stephens. *Douglas McGregor Revisited*. New York: Wiley, 2000.

Burns: Burns, James McGregor. *Leadership*. New York: Harper & Row, 1978.

Eisenhower: *Be-Know-Do*. San Francisco: Jossey-Bass, 2004.

Powell: Powell, Colin L. *My American Journey*. New York, Random House, 1995.

Schwarzkopf: Zenger, John H, and Joseph Folkman. *The Extraordinary Leader*. New York: McGraw-Hill, 2002.

Jackson: Frady, Marshall. *Jesse*. New York: Random House, 1996.

## Leadership: Challenge and Opportunity

Kranz: Kranz, Gene. *Failure is Not an Option*. New York: Berkley Books, 2001.

Ambrose: Ambrose, Stephen E. *Undaunted Courage*. New York: Simon & Schuster, 1996.

Bennis and Nanus: Bennis, Warren, and Burt Nanus. *Leaders: The Strategies for Taking Charge*. New York: Harper & Row, 1985.

"All we had to work with," Kranz, Gene. *Failure is Not an Option*. New York: Berkley Books, 2001.

Useem: Useem, Michael. *The Leadership Moment*. New York: Times Business, 1998.

Burnett: "Flight 93: Forty Lives, One Destiny." *Pittsburgh Post-Gazette*, October 29, 2001.

Salka: Salka, John. *First In, Last Out*. New York: Portfolio, 2004.

La Guardia: Salka, John. *First In, Last Out*. New York: Portfolio, 2004.

Van Etten: cnn.com

"By his early forties," Spreitzer, Gretchen M., and Robert E. Quinn. *A Company of Leaders*.
San Francisco: Jossey-Bass, 2001.

## Vision

Bennis: Bennis, Warren. *An Invented Life*. Reading, MA: Addison Wesley, 1993.

Blanchard: Blanchard, Ken. "Turning the Leadership Pyramid Upside Down." In *The Leader of the Future*. Edited by Frances Hesselbein. San Francisco: Jossey-Bass, 1996.

Shula: Shula, Don and Ken Blanchard. *Everyone's a Coach*. New York: HarperBusiness, 1995.

Crosby: Crosby, Philip B. *The Absolutes of Leadership*. San Diego: Pfeiffer & Company, 1996.

Dilenschneider: Dilenschneider, Robert L. *A Briefing for Leaders*. New York: HarperBusiness, 1992.

De Pree: De Pree, Max. *Leading Without Power*. San Francisco: Jossey-Bass, 1997.

Friedan: Friedan, Betty. *Life So Far*. New York: Touchstone, 2001.

Weinbach: Weinbach, Lawrence. "Leading by Communicating." In *How to Run a Company*. By Carey, Dennis C., and Marie Caroline von Weichs. New York: Crown Business, 2003.

"Speed, Simplicity," Topping, Peter A. *Managerial*

*Leadership*. New York: McGraw-Hill, 2001.

Gates and Allen: Moody, F. "Mr. Software," *New York Times Magazine,* Aug 25, 1991 in Nanus, Burt. *Visionary Leadership*. San Francisco: Jossey-Bass, 1992.

"Just as no painting," Bennis, Warren. *On Becoming a Leader*. New York: Basic Books, 2003.

Dell: chiefexecutive.net.

Schultz: Schultz, Howard. *Pour Your Heart Into It*. New York: Hyperion: 1997.

Kotter: Kotter, John P. *Leading Change*. Boston: Harvard Business School Press, 1996.

Blanchard: Shula, Don and Ken Blanchard. *Everyone's a Coach*. New York: HarperBusiness, 1995.

Nanus: Nanus, Burt. *Visionary Leadership*. San Francisco: Jossey-Bass, 1992.

"Sometimes leaders," Gardner, Howard. *Leading Minds: An Anatomy of Leadership*. New York: Basic Books, 1995.

Roosevelt: First Inaugural Address, March 4, 1933.

Welch: Welch, Jack. *Jack: Straight From the Gut*. New York: Warner Books, 2001.

Nanus: Nanus, Burt. *Visionary Leadership*. San Francisco: Jossey-Bass, 1992.

Smith: *The Book of Leadership Wisdom*. Edited by Peter Krass. New York: John Wiley, 1998

Maxwell: Maxwell, John C. *Leadership 101*. Nashville: Thomas Nelson, 2002.

Burrows: Burrows, Peter. *Backfire*. New York: John Wiley, 2003.

Gerstner: Gerstner, Louis V. *Who Says Elephants Can't Dance*. New York: HarperBusiness, 2002.

Sharpnack: workingwoman.com

Kouzes and Posner: Kouzes, James M., and Barry Z. Posner. *The Leadership Challenge*. 3rd ed. San Francisco: Jossey-Bass, 2002.

## Leaders and Followers

Blank: Blank, Warren. *The Nine Natural Laws of Leadership*. New York: AMACOM, 1995.

O'Toole: O'Toole, James. *Leadership A to Z*. San Francisco: Jossey-Bass, 1999.

Burke: Burke, Lance B. *The Wisdom of Alexander the Great*. New York: AMACOM, 2004.

Clark and Clark: Clark, Kenneth E., and Miriam B. Clark. *Choosing to Lead*. Greensboro, N.C.: Center for Creative Leadership, 1996.

Peters and Austin: Peters, Tom, and Nancy Austin. *A Passion for Excellence*. New York: Random House, 1985.

Oakley and Krug: Oakley, Ed, and Doug Krug. *Enlightened Leadership*. New York: Simon & Schuster, 1993.

Topping: Topping, Peter A. *Managerial Leadership*. New York: McGraw-Hill, 2001.

Chambers: Laurie, Donald L. *The Real Work of Leaders*. Cambridge: Perseus, 2000.

Lebenthal: Zichy, Shoya. *Women and the Leadership Q*. New York: McGraw-Hill, 2000.

Zand: Zand, Dale E. *The Leadership Triad*. New York: Oxford University Press, 1997.

Bennis: Bennis, Warren. *An Invented Life*. Reading, MA: Addison Wesley, 1993.

Wills: Wills, Garry. *Certain Trumpets*. New York: Simon & Schuster, 1994.

Chaleff: Chaleff, Ira. *The Courageous Follower*. San Francisco: Berrett-Koehler Publishers, 1995.

"We have to recognize," Bennis, Warren, and Patricia Ward Biederman. *Organizing Genius*. Cambridge: Perseus, 1997.

"Nobody had to guess," Bennis, Warren, and Patricia Ward Biederman. *Organizing Genius*. Cambridge: Perseus, 1997.

"It was said," Losoncy, Lewis. *The Motivating Leader*. Englewood Cliffs, N.J.: Prentice-Hall, 1985.

Csikszentmihalyi: Csikszentmihalyi, Mihaly, "The Context of Creativity." In *The Future of Leadership*. Edited by Warren Bennis, Gretchen M. Speitzer, and Thomas G. Cummings. San Francisco: Jossey-Bass, 2001.

De Pree: De Pree, Max. *Leadership Jazz*. New York: Currency/Doubleday, 1992.

Burns: Burns, James McGregor. *Transforming Leadership*. New York: Atlantic Monthly Press, 2003.

"The Burns Paradox," Burns, James McGregor. *Transforming Leadership*. New York: Atlantic Monthly Press, 2003.

## Leaders and Managers

Calloway: Hickman, Craig R. *Mind of a Manager, Soul of a Leader*. New York: Wiley, 1990.

Center for Creative Leadership, 1996.

Philip B. Crosby *The Absolutes of Leadership*. San Diego: Pfeiffer & Company, 1996.

Hickman: Hickman, Craig R. *Mind of a Manager, Soul of a Leader*. New York: Wiley, 1990.

Kotter: Kotter, John P. *On What Leaders Really Do*. Boston: Harvard Business School Press, 1999.

*Welch*. Burr Ridge, IL: Irwin, 1994.

Hickman: Hickman, Craig R. *Mind of a Manager, Soul of a Leader*. New York: Wiley, 1990.

Plachy: "Leading vs. Managing."

In *Leadership*. Edited by A. Dale Trimpe. New York: Facts on File, 1994.

Kotter: Kotter, John P. *Leading Change*. Boston: Harvard Business School Press, 1996.

## Learning to be a Leader

Exley: *Leadership in Organizations*. Edited by John Storey. New York: Routledge, 2004.

Bennis: Bennis, Warren. *On Becoming a Leader*. New York: Basic Books, 2003.

Welch: Welch, Jack. *Jack: Straight from the Gut*. New York: Warner Books, 2001.

"The necessity for leaders," Buckingham, Marcus, *One Thing You Need to Know About Great Managing, Great Leading and Sustained Individual Success*. New York: The Free Press, 2005.

Trump: Trump, Donald. *The Art of the Deal*. New York: Random House, 1987.

Rockefeller: Feinster, Julie M. *In the Words of Great Business Leaders*. New York: John Wiley, 2000.

"Leadership is passion," Conger, Jay A. *Learning to Lead*. San Francisco: Jossey-Bass, 1992.

Bennis and Nanus: Bennis, Warren, and Bert Nanus. *Leaders: The Strategies for Taking Charge*. New York: Harper & Row, 1985.

Kouzes and Posner: Kouzes, James M., and Barry Z. Posner, "Bringing Leadership Lessons from the Past Into the Future." In *The Future of Leadership*. Edited by Warren Bennis, Gretchen M. Speitzer, and Thomas G. Cummings. San Francisco: Jossey-Bass, 2001

Goleman: Goleman, Daniel. "Leadership that Gets Results." In *Harvard Business Review of What Makes a Leader*. Harvard Business School Press, Boston: 2001.

"Leadership is learning," *Leadership in Organizations*. Edited by John Storey. New York: Routledge, 2004.

Myers: Trump, Donald J. *The Way to the Top*. New York: Crown Business 2004.

Maxwell, John C.: *The 21 Indispensable Qualities of a Leader*. Nashville: Thomas Nelson Books, 1999.

Dilenschneider: Dilenschneider, Robert L. *A Briefing for Leaders*. New York: HarperBusiness, 1992.

De Pree: De Pree, Max. *Leadership Jazz*. New York: Currency/Doubleday, 1992.

"Think of every mistake," Matusak, Lorraine R. *Finding Your Voice*. San Francisco, Jossey-Bass, 1996.

"GE doesn't have a smarter workforce," Charan, Ram, Stephen Drotter, and James Noel. *The Leadership Pipeline*. San Francisco: Jossey-Bass, 2000.

Welch: Krames, Jeffrey A. *The Jack Welch Lexicon of Leadership*. New York: McGraw-Hill, 2002.

Crotonville: Welch, Jack. *Jack: Straight from the Gut*. New York: Warner Books, 2001.

Conger: Conger, Jay A. *Learning to Lead*. San Francisco: Jossey-Bass, 1992.

Bennis and Goldsmith: Bennis, Warren, and Joan Goldsmith. *Learning to Lead*. New York: Basic Books, 2003.

O'Toole: O'Toole, James. *Leadership A to Z*. San Francisco: Jossey-Bass, 1999.

"Descriptions of Matsushita," Capodagli, Bill, and Lynn Johnson. *Leading at the Speed of Change*. New York: McGraw-Hill, 2001.

## Anyone Can be a Leader

Crosby: Crosby, Philip B. *The Absolutes of Leadership*. San Diego: Pfeiffer & Company, 1996.

Kouzes and Posner. Kouzes, James M., and Barry Z. Posner. *The Leadership Challenge*. 3rd ed. San Francisco: Jossey-Bass, 2002.

Owen: Owen, Hilarie. *In Search of Leaders*. Chichester, UK: John Wiley, 2000.

Bennis and Nanus: Bennis, Warren, and Bert Nanus. *Leaders*. New York: Harper & Row, 1985.

Cleveland: Cleveland, Harlan. *Nobody in Charge*. San Francisco: Jossey-Bass, 2002.

Riccucci, Norma in *Leaders*. Edited by Mark A. Abramson and Kevin M. Bacon. Lanham, MA: Rowan & Littlefield, 2002.

Mindell: Mindell, Arnold. *The Leader as Martial Artist*. San Francisco: HarperSanFrancisco, 1992.

Clark and Clark. Clark, Kenneth E., and Miriam B. Clark. *Choosing to Lead*. Greensboro, N.C.: Center for Creative Leadership, 1996.

"The equation of leadership," Helgesen, Sally. "Leading From the Grass Roots." In *The Leader of the Future*. Edited by Marshall Goldsmith, et al. San Francisco: Jossey-Bass, 2000.

Raelin: Raelin, Joseph A. *Creating Leaderful Organizations*. San Francisco: Berrett-Koehler Publishers, 2003.

"You know," Kuczmarski, Susan Smith, and Thomas D. Kuczmarski. *Values-Based Leadership*. Englewood Cliffs, N.J.: Prentice Hall 1995.

"I just knew," Kuczmarski, Susan Smith, and Thomas D. Kuczmarski. *Values-Based Leadership*. Englewood Cliffs, N.J.: Prentice Hall 1995.

Belasco and Stayer. Belasco, James A., and Ralph C. Stayer. *Flight of the Buffalo* New York: Warner, 1993.

Deluca: Deluca, Joel R. *Political Savvy*. Berwyn, PA: Evergreen Business Books, 1999.

*Everyone a Leader:* Bergmann, Horst, Kathleen Hurson, and Darlene Russ-Eft. *Everyone a Leader*. New York: John Wiley, 1999.

Raelin: Raelin, Joseph A. *Creating Leaderful Organizations*. San Francisco: Berrett-Koehler Publishers, 2003.

Matusak: Matusak, Lorraine R. *Finding Your Voice*. San Francisco: Jossey-Bass, 1996.

## It Starts With You

Kouzes and Posner: Kouzes, James M., and Barry Z. Posner. *The Leadership Challenge*. 3rd ed. San Francisco: Jossey-Bass, 2002.

Feiner: Feiner, Michael. *The Feiner Points of Leadership*. New York: Warner Business Books, 2004.

"Coercive leaders," Goleman, Daniel. "Leadership that Gets Results." In *Harvard Business Review of What Makes a Leader*. Boston: Harvard Business School Press, 2001.

"The research indicates," Goleman, Daniel. "Leadership that Gets Results." In *Harvard Business Review of What Makes a Leader*. Boston: Harvard Business School Press, 2001.

"The ninety percent," Feiner, Michael. *The Feiner Points of Leadership*. New York: Warner Business Books, 2004.

Bennis and Goldsmith: Bennis, Warren, and Goldsmith, Joan. *Learning to Lead*. 3rd ed. New York: Basic Books, 2003.

Harrell: Harrell, Keith. *The Attitude of Leadership*. Hoboken, N.J.: John Wiley and Sons, 2003.

Calloway: Kuczmarski, Susan Smith, and Thomas D. Kuczmarski. *Values-Based Leadership*. Englewood Cliffs: N.J.: Prentice Hall, 1995.

Krzyzewski: Krzyzewski, Mike. *Leading with the Heart*. New York: Warner Books, 2000.

Carter: Webber, Allan M. "Jimmy Carter: The Statesman as CEO." In *Leaders on Leadership*. Boston: Harvard Business Review, 1992.

Ford: Webber, Allan M. "Gerald R. Ford: The Statesman as CEO." In *Leaders on Leadership*. Boston: Harvard Business Review, 1992.

Maxwell: Maxwell, John C. *The 21 Irrefutable Laws of Leadership*. Nashville: Thomas Nelson Books, 1998.

Donnithorne: Donnithorne, Col. Larry R. *The West Point Way of Leadership*. New York: Doubleday, 1994.

Powell: Harari, Oren. *The Leadership Secrets of Colin Powell*. New York: McGraw-Hill, 2002.

Maccoby: Maccoby, Michael. "Narcissistic Leaders." In *Harvard Business Review of Leadership at the Top*. Boston: Harvard Business School Press, 2003.

"To tell capable people," Maxwell, John C. *The 21 Irrefutable Laws of Leadership*. Nashville: Thomas Nelson Books, 1998.

Bossidy: Laurie, Donald L. *The Real Work of Leaders*. Cambridge: Perseus, 2000.

Carter: Webber, Allan M. "Jimmy Carter: The Statesman as CEO." In *Leaders on Leadership*. Boston: Harvard Business Review, 1992.

Olivier: Olivier, Richard. *Inspirational Leadership: Henry V and the Muse of Fire*. London: The Industrial Society, 2001.

"I'd worked myself up," Schwarzkopf, General H. Norman. *It Doesn't Take a Hero*. New York: Bantam Books, 1992.

"I had to be," *On War and Leadership*. Edited by Owen Connelly. Princeton: Princeton University Press, 2002.

Roosevelt: Vaughan, David J. *The Pillars of Leadership*. Nashville: Cumberland House, 2000.

Amery: Sandys, Celia, and Jonathan Littman. *We Shall Not Fail*. New York: Portfolio, 2003.

Muirhead: Muirhead, Brian K., and William L. Simon. *High Velocity Leadership*. New York: HarperBusiness, 1999.

Turner: Feinster, Julie M. *In the Words of Great Business Leaders*. New York: John Wiley, 2000.

"It is commonly thought," Topping, Peter A. *Managerial Leadership*. New York: McGraw-Hill, 2001.

"One of the lessons," Topping, Peter A. *Managerial Leadership*. New York: McGraw-Hill, 2001.

Schwarzkopf: Academy of Achievement: Achievement.org June 23, 1996.

Grove: Grove, Andrew S. *Only the Paranoid Survive*. New York: Currency/Doubleday, 1996.

## Business Leaders

O'Toole: O'Toole, James. *Leadership A to Z*. San Francisco: Jossey-Bass, 1999.

Welch: Welch, Jack. *Jack: Straight from the Gut*. New York: Warner Books, 2001.

"$5.9 million," "Executive Pay: A Special Report," by Patrick McGeehan. *New York Times*, April 4, 2004.

"Leaders of this ilk," Bossidy: Bossidy, Larry, and Ram Charan. *Execution*. New York: Crown Business, 2002.

"Don't make the mistake," "Reality-Based Leadership" by Lawrence A. Bossidy, in *The Book of Leadership Wisdom*,

Edited by Peter Krass. New York: John Wiley, 1998.

Top 25 list, Reuters, November 16, 2004.

Gerstner: Gerstner, Louis V. *Who Says Elephants Can't Dance*. New York: HarperBusiness, 2002.

"3000 cards," Kuczmarski, Susan Smith, and Thomas D. Kuczmarski. *Values-Based Leadership*. Englewood Cliffs, N.J.: Prentice Hall 1995.

Southwest figures: southwest.com.

"A financial analyst," Moxley, Russ S. *Leadership and Spirit*. San Francisco: Jossey-Bass, 1999.

"I always felt," businessweek.com.

"Down here," Moxley, Russ S. *Leadership and Spirit*. San Francisco: Jossey-Bass, 1999.

Harvey-Jones: Channer, Philip, and Tina Hope. *Emotional Impact*. New York: Palgrave, 2001.

Eckert: Eckert, Robert E. "Where Leadership Starts." In *Harvard Business Review of Leadership at the Top*. Boston: Harvard Business School Press, 2003.

Peters: Peters, Tom, and Nancy Austin. *A Passion for Excellence*. New York: Random House, 1985.

"Those who mistook," Collins, Jim. *Good to Great*. New York: HarperBusiness, 2001.

"George Cain," Collins, Jim. *Good to Great*. New York: HarperBusiness, 2001.

"People like Iacocca," Bryman, Alan. *Charisma and Leadership in Organizations*. London: Sage Publications, 1992.

"To change my leadership," Belasco, James A., and Ralph C. Stayer. *Flight of the Buffalo*. New York: Warner Books, 1993.

Iacocca figures, "The Dollar-A-Year Man" by Ari Weinberg, forbes.com, May 8, 2002.

"I began by reducing," Iacocca, Lee. *Iacocca*. New York: Bantam Books, 1984.

"Stempel confronted," Gitlow, Abraham L. *Being the Boss*. Homewood, IL: Business One Irwin, 1991.

"It seems clear," Yukl, Gary, and Richard Lepsinger. *Flexible Leadership*. San Francisco: Jossey-Bass, 2004.

"His leadership," "Chambers, Cisco born again," by Kevin Maney, *USA Today*, January 21, 2004.

"The time you make," "Speaking Out: Cisco's John Chambers." *Business Week Online*, August 25, 2003.

"We're extremely optimistic," "Chambers, Cisco born again," by Kevin Maney, *USA Today*, January 21, 2004.

"Jack Welch says," Lowe, Janet. *Welch: An American Icon*. New York: John Wiley, 2001.

"Confidence gives you courage," Welch, Jack. *Jack: Straight from the Gut*. New York: Warner Books, 2001.

"The year before," Krames, Jeffrey A. *The Jack Welch Lexicon of Leadership*. New York: McGraw-Hill, 2002.

"Above all," Tichy, Noel and Ram Charan. "Speed, Simplicity, Self-Confidence." In *Leaders on Leadership*. Boston: Harvard Business Review, 1992.

"Before at GE," Slater, Robert. *Get Better or Get Beaten*: *31 Leadership Secrets from GE's Jack Welch*. Burr Ridge, IL: Irwin, 1994.

"Removing people," Welch, Jack. *Jack*: *Straight from the Gut*. New York: Warner Books, 2001.

"Management professor," Lowe, Janet. *Welch*: *An American Icon*. New York: John Wiley, 2001.

## Military Leaders

Napoleon: *On War and Leadership*. Edited by Owen Connelly. Princeton, N.J.: Princeton University Press, 2002.

Clausewitz: Clausewitz, Karl Von. *On War* in *The Book Of War*. New York: Modern Library, 2000.

"Leadership is influencing," from *Be-Know-Do*. San Francisco: Jossey-Bass, 2004.

"To carry out its role," Benton, Jeffrey C. *Air Force Officer's Guide*. 33rd ed. Mechanicsburg, PA: Stackpole Books, 2002.

"All the usual predictors," Zenger, John H, and Joseph Folkman. *The Extraordinary Leader*. New York: McGraw-Hill, 2002.

Freedman: Freedman, David H. *Corps Business*. New York: HarperBusiness, 2000.

Lehockey: Freedman, David H. "Corps Values." *Inc.* magazine, April 1988.

Zenger and Folkman: Zenger, John H, and Joseph Folkman. *The Extraordinary Leader*. New York: McGraw-Hill, 2002.

"How do you teach . . . ", Freedman, David H. *Corps Business*. New York: HarperBusiness, 2000.

"A recruit going through," Carrison, Dan, and Rod Walsh. *Semper Fi*. New York: AMACOM, 1999.

"In a new world," *Be-Know-Do*. *Leadership the Army Way*. San Francisco: Jossey-Bass, 2004.

Carrison and Walsh: Carrison, Dan, and Rod Walsh. *Semper Fi*. New York: AMACOM, 1999.

Wheeler: Wheeler, Tom. *Take Command!* New York: Currency/Doubleday, 2000.

Air force traits: Benton, Jeffrey C. *Air Force Officer's Guide*. 33rd ed.

Marine traits: Townsend, Patrick L., and Joan E. Gebhardt. *Five-Star Leadership*. New York: John Wiley, 1997.

Cohen: Cohen, William A. *The Art of the Strategist*. New

York: AMACOM Books, 2004.

"For generals who could not adjust," *Be-Know-Do*. Cray: Cray, Ed. *General of the Army*. New York: Norton, 1990.

"In every battle," Bunting, III, Josiah. *Ulysses S. Grant*. New York: Times Books, 2004.

"U.S. Grant was teaching," Wheeler, Tom. *Take Command!* New York: Currency/Doubleday, 2000.

Stokesbury: Stokesbury, James L. "Leadership is an Art" In *Military Leadership*. Edited by Robert L. Taylor and William E. Rosenbach. Boulder, CO: Westview Press, 1992.

Ridgway: *On War and Leadership*. Edited by Owen Connelly. Princeton, N.J.: Princeton University Press, 2002.

Keegan: Keegan, John. *The Face of Battle*. New York: The Viking Press, 1976.

Schwarzkopf: Schwarzkopf, General H. Norman. *It Doesn't Take a Hero*. New York: Bantam Books, 1992.

Ambrose: Ambrose, Stephen E. *Undaunted Courage*. New York: Simon & Schuster, 1996.

Franks, Tommy. *American Soldier*. New York: ReganBooks, 2004.

Brower and Dardis: Brower, IV, Charles F. and Gregory J. Dardis. "Teaching Combat Leadership at West Point," in *Leadership*: *The Warrior's Art*. Edited by Christopher D. Kolenda. Carlisle, PA: The Army Way College Foundation Press, 2001.

"You were blessed," Ambrose, Stephen. *Band of Brothers*. New York: Simon & Schuster, 2001.

"The force of example," Brower and Dardis, op. cit.

"Trust is the lifeblood," Cannon, Jeff, and Jon Cannon. *Leadership Lessons of the U.S. Navy SEALs*. New York: McGraw-Hill, 2002.

"Time and again," Filkins, Dexter. "In Falluja, Young Marines Saw the Savagery of an Urban War." *New York Times*, November 21, 2004.

"He remembers vividly," Brokaw, Tom. *The Greatest Generation*. New York: Random House, 1998.

## Sports Leaders

Smith: Smith, Dean. *A Coach's Life*. New York: Random House, 1999.

Hamm: Hamm, Mia. *Go for the Goal*. New York: HarperCollins, 1999.

Wooden: Wooden, John. *Wooden*. New York: McGraw-Hill, 1997.

Shula: Shula, Don, and Ken Blanchard. *Everyone's a Coach*. New York: HarperBusiness, 1995.

Krzyzewski: Krzyzewski, Mike. *Leading with the Heart*. New York, Warner Books, 2000.

"If you asked me to define," Smith, Dean. *The Carolina*

*Way*. New York: The Penguin Press, 2004.

"I don't know," Smith, Dean. *A Coach's Life*. New York: Random House, 1999.

"Belichik's all-business approach," Stein, Charles. "Bill Belichik, CEO." *Boston Globe*. January 28, 2004.

Torre: Torre, Joe. *Joe Torre's Ground Rules for Winners*. New York: Hyperion, 1999.

"He's definitely our leader," Kuenster, John. "Ivan Rodriguez Earned Player of the Year Honors for Leading Marlins." *Baseball Digest*. January, 2004.

Russell: Russell, Bill. *Russell Rules*. New York: New American Library, 2002.

Chastain: Chastain, Brandi. *It's Not About the Bra*. New York: HarperResource, 2004.

"I just listened," "Favre Leads Packers to Last-second Victory." AP, November 22, 2004.

"Johnson was a natural leader," Halberstam, *David. Playing for Keeps*. New York: Random House, 1999.

Jackson: Jackson, Phil. *More Than a Game*. New York: Fireside, 2002.

"During the final seconds," Maxwell, John C. *The 21 Irrefutable Laws of Leadership*. Nashville: Thomas Nelson Books, 1998.

"It was in sports," Ambrose, Stephen E. *Eisenhower.*

*Volume One: Soldier, General of the Army, President-Elect, 1890–1952*. New York Simon & Schuster, 1983.

*Lessons in Leadership from Homer to Hemingway*. Homewood, IL: Dow Jones-Irwin, 1987.

"We do our leadership meetings," ESPN.com/pattillmanfoundati-on.net

Moore: "I cannot be on the losing side," by Adrian Wojnarowski, ESPN.com, December 2, 2004.

"If God hadn't put me," Ashe, Arthur. *Days of Grace*. New York: Knopf, 1993.

Robinson: Robinson, Eddie. *Never Before, Never Again*. New York: Thomas Dunne Books, 1999.

"Over a period of six months," Rampersad: Rampersad, Arnold. *Jackie Robinson: A Biography*. New York: Knopf, 1997.

"Stick in there," Rampersad: Rampersad, Arnold. *Jackie Robinson: A Biography*. New York: Knopf, 1997.

## Political Leaders

O'Neill: O'Neill, Tip. *All Politics is Local*. New York: Times Books, 1993.

"Raise one another," Burns, James McGregor. *Leadership*. New York: Harper & Row, 1978.

"Exchange of valued things," Burns, James McGregor:

*Leadership*. New York: Harper & Row, 1978.

"It was more difficult," Academy of Achievement: Achievement.org, October 25, 1991.

"It was the most courageous thing," Academy of Achievement: Achievement. org, October 25, 1991.

O'Neill: O'Neill, Tip. *All Politics is Local*. New York: Times Books, 1993.

"I've spoken," Ronald Reagan, Farewell Address to the Nation, Oval Office, January 11, 1989.

Cannon: Cannon, Lou. *President Reagan: The Role of a Lifetime*. New York: Public Affairs, 2000.

"Politicians as diverse," Sourcewatch.org.

"Somewhere at this very moment," Bill Clinton, acceptance speech to the Democratic National Convention, New York City, July 16, 1992.

Gardner: Gardner, John. *On Leadership*. New York: The Free Press, 1993.

Lincoln: Donald, David Herbert. *Lincoln*. New York: Simon & Schuster, 1995.

"Clinton was asked," Woodward, Bob. *The Agenda*. New York: Simon & Schuster, 1994.

"If we just," Lamb, Brian: *Booknotes on American Character*. New York: PublicAffairs, 2002.

"One of the things," Lamb, Brian: *Booknotes on American Character*. New York: PublicAffairs, 2002.

Maraniss: Maraniss, David. *The Clinton Enigma*. New York: Simon & Schuster, 1998.

Presidential ratings, *Presidential Leadership*. Edited by James Taranto and Leonard Leo. New York: The Free Press, 2004.

"The public's faith," Dallek, Robert. *An Unfinished Life: John F. Kennedy, 1917–1963*. New York: Little, Brown, 2003.

Caro: Caro, Robert. *The Years of Lyndon Johnson, Volume I. The Path to Power*. New York: Alfred A. Knopf, 1982.

Steel: Steel, Ronald. *In Love With Night*. New York: Simon & Schuster, 2000.

"Sorry or not," Cannon, Lou. *President Reagan: The Role of a Lifetime*. New York: Public Affairs, 2000.

Drucker: Karlgaard, Rich. "Peter Drucker on Leadership." Forbes.com, November 19, 2004.

## Revolutionary Leaders

Fromm: Random House Webster's *Quotationary*. Edited by Leonard Roy Frank. New York: Random House Reference, 2000.

"The history of all," Marx, Karl, and Friedrich Engels. *The*

*Communist Manifesto*. New York: Signet Classics, 1998.

"An association in which," Marx, Karl, and Friedrich Engels. *The Communist Manifesto*. New York: Signet Classics, 1998.

Fitzpatrick: Fitzpatrick, Sheila. *The Russian Revolution*. 2nd ed. New York: Oxford University Press, 1994.

"Revolutionary France," Schama, Simon. *Citizens*. New York: Knopf, 1989.

"By asserting," Wood, Gordon S. *The American Revolution: A History*. New York: Modern Library, 2002.

"Washington's ultimate success," Wood, Gordon S. *The American Revolution: A History*. New York: Modern Library, 2002.

Anderson: Anderson, Jon Lee. *Che Guevara*. New York: The Grove Press, 1997.

"As a soldier and statesman," Davis, Steven I. *Leadership in Conflict*. New York: St. Martin's Press, 1996.

"Washington's excessive coyness," Wood, Gordon S. *The Radicalism of the American Revolution*. New York: Knopf, 1992.

"His retirement," Wood, Gordon S. *The Radicalism of the American Revolution*. New York: Knopf, 1992.

"In India," Mandela, Nelson. *Long Walk to Freedom*. New York: Little, Brown, 1994.

"When the hunger," Mandela, Nelson. *Long Walk to Freedom*. New York: Little, Brown, 1994.

Tutu: Boutros Boutros-Ghali et al. *Essays on Leadership*. New York: The Carnegie Corporation, 1998.

## Spiritual Leaders

Warren: pastors.com.

"The single most challenging," McNeal, Reggie. *A Work of Heart*. San Francisco: Jossey-Bass, 2000.

"The shepherd is for the sheep," Pope John Paul II. *Rise, Let Us Be On Our Way*. New York: Warner Books, 2004.

"Together with the preaching," Pope John Paul II. *Rise, Let Us Be On Our Way*. New York: Warner Books, 2004.

"Vatican II," Gutiérrez, Gustavo. *A Theology of Liberation*. Maryknoll, N.Y.: Orbis, 1973.

"The leaders of the Bible," Woolfe, Lorin. *The Bible on Leadership*. New York: AMACOM, 2002.

"A Leader's main job," Jones, Laurie Beth. *Jesus in Blue Jeans*. New York: Hyperion, 1998.

Greenleaf: Greenleaf, Robert K. *Servant Leadership*. Mahwah, N.J. Paulist Press, 2002.

"We fight this battle," www.promisekeepers.org/ambassadors.

Sanders: Sanders, J. Oswald. *Spiritual Leadership*. Chicago: Moody Publishers, 1994.

McNeal: McNeal, Reggie. *A Work of Heart*. San Francisco: Jossey-Bass, 2000.

McManus: McManus, Erwin Raphael. *Uprising*. Nashville, Thomas Nelson Books, 2003.

"The Bible is filled," Warren, Rick. *The Purpose-Driven Life*. Grand Rapids, MI: Zondervan, 2002.

"At Saddleback," pastors.com.

"The 25 Most Influential Evangelicals in America." *Time* magazine, February 7, 2005.

"My involvement," *Mother Jones*, November/December 1997.

"In the *Kakacupama Sutta*," Thich Nhat Hanh. *Heart of Buddha's Teaching*. New York: Broadway Books, 1999.

"We need to create," Thich Nhat Hanh. *Heart of Buddha's Teaching*. New York: Broadway Books, 1999.

"Responsibility does not only lie," Nobel Lecture, December 11, 1989.


### Intellectual Leaders

Evans: Evans, Harold. *They Made America*. New York: Little, Brown, 2004.

Gardner, Howard. *Leading Minds: An Anatomy of Leadership*. New York: Basic Books, 1995.

"Without doubt," Gardner, Howard. *Creating Minds*. New York: Basic Books, 2003.

"Do you believe," Freud, Sigmund. *The History of the Psychoanalytic Movement* in *The Basic Writings of Sigmund Freud*. New York: Modern Library, 1995.

"Even today," Freud, Sigmund. *The History of the Psychoanalytic Movement* in *The Basic Writings of Sigmund Freud*. New York: Modern Library, 1995.

"While it is difficult," Gardner, Howard. *Creating Minds*. New York: Basic Books, 2003.

"These are accessible virtues," Badaracco, Jr., Joseph. *Leading Quietly*. Boston: Harvard Business School Press, 2002.

"Einstein's life," Hawking, Stephen. *A Brief History of Time*. New York: Bantam Books, 1998.

"Equations are more important," Hawking, Stephen. *A Brief History of Time*. New York: Bantam Books, 1998.

King: Gardner, Howard. *Leading Minds*. New York: Basic Books, 1995.

"They evolved into leaders," Gardner, *Leading Minds*. New York: Basic Books, 1995.

Burns: Burns, James McGregor, and Susan Dunn. *The Three Roosevelts*. New York: Grove Press, 2002.

Cook: Cook, Blanche Wiesen. *Eleanor Roosevelt: Volume 2, 1933–1938*. New York: Viking, 1999.

"Can you imagine," Cook: Cook, Blanche Wiesen. *Eleanor Roosevelt: Volume 2,*

*1933–1938*. New York: Viking, 1999.

Lash: Lash, Joseph P. *Love, Eleanor*. Garden City: Doubleday, 1982.

Friedan: Friedan, Betty. *The Feminine Mystique*. New York: Norton, 1974.

Horowitz: Horowitz, Daniel. *Betty Friedan and the Making of* The Feminine Mystique. Amherst: University of Massachusetts Press, 1998.

"What he did not know," Browne, Janet. *Charles Darwin: The Power of Place*. New York: Knopf, 2002.

"Solitude," Gleick, James. *Isaac Newton*. New York: Pantheon Books, 2003.

"*People* magazine," Evans: Evans, Harold. *They Made America*. New York: Little, Brown, 2004.

## Bad Leaders and Bad Leadership

Jones: Jones, Laurie Beth. *Jesus CEO*. New York, Hyperion, 1996.

"At leadership seminars," Terry, Robert. "Leadership: Reflections and Learning." In Goldsmith, Marshall, et al. *The Many Facets of Leadership*. Upper Saddle River, N.J.: Prentice Hall, 2003.

Burns: Burns, James McGregor: *Leadership*. New York: Harper & Row, 1978.

"It was an oath," Shirer, William L. *The Rise and Fall of the Third Reich*. New York: Simon & Schuster, 1960.

"Later and often," Shirer, William L. *The Rise and Fall of the Third Reich*. New York: Simon & Schuster, 1960.

"In his *Discourses*," Kaplan, Robert D. *Warrior Politics*. New York: Random House, 2002.

"Of course," Kaplan, Robert D. *Warrior Politics*. New York: Random House, 2002.

"The long and impressive record," Goldhagen, Daniel Jonah. *Hitler's Willing Executioners*. New York: Knopf, 1996.

"Even the very worst," Jean Lipman-Blumen, "Why we Tolerate Bad Leaders," in *The Future of Leadership*. Edited by Warren Bennis, et al. San Francisco: Jossey-Bass, 2001.

"Make no mistake," Butler, General George Lee. "Some Personal Reflections on Integrity," in *The Leader's Imperative*. Edited by J. Carl Ficarotta. West Lafayette: Purdue University Press, 2001.

"John C.H. Lee," Ambrose, Stephen. *Citizen Soldiers*. New York: Simon & Schuster, 1997.

"If Othello," Dotlich, David L., and Peter C. Cairo. *Why CEOs Fail*. San Francisco: Jossey-Bass, 2003.

"He was leader," Kellerman, Barbara. *Bad Leadership*. Boston: Harvard Business School Press, 2004.

Himsel: Himsel, Deborrah. *Leadership Soprano Style.* Chicago: Dearborn Trade, 2004.

Schneider: Schneider, Anthony. *Tony Soprano on Management.* New York: Berkley, 2004.

"The point of Passchendaele," Keegan, John. "The Breaking of Armies." in *The Great War.* New York: Random House, 2003.

"I see rows upon rows," Keegan, John. "The Breaking of Armies." in *The Great War.* New York: Random House, 2003.

"Forceful and domineering," Tuchman, Barbara. *The March of Folly.* New York: Knopf, 1984.

"Many of my generation," Powell, Colin L. *My American Journey.* New York: Random House, 1995.

"Although it may be hard to believe," Surowiecki, "Blame Iacocca." *Slate,* July 24, 2002.

Emerson: Emerson, Ralph Waldo. *Essays and Lectures.* New York: Library of America, 1983.

## Winston Churchill

"There comes a special moment," Maxwell, John C. *The 21 Irrefutable Laws of Leadership.* Nashville: Thomas Nelson Books, 1998.

"The Right Action," Maxwell, John C. *The 21 Irrefutable Laws of Leadership.* Nashville: Thomas Nelson Books, 1998.

"A charismatic visionary," Pitcher, Patricia. *The Drama of Leadership.* New York: John Wiley, 1997.

"I say to the House," *Blood, Toil, Tears, and Sweat.* Edited by David Cannadine. Boston, Houghton Mifflin, 1989.

"Hitler knows," Sandys, Celia, and Jonathan Littman. *We Shall Not Fail.* New York: Portfolio, 2003.

"His own extraordinary character," *Blood, Toil, Tears, and Sweat.* Edited by David Cannadine. Boston: Houghton Mifflin, 1989.

"At best," *Blood, Toil, Tears, and Sweat.* Edited by David Cannadine. Boston: Houghton Mifflin, 1989.

Eisenhower: Eisenhower, Dwight D. *General Eisenhower on the Military Churchill.* New York: Norton, 1970.

Keegan: Keegan, John. *Winston Churchill.* New York: Viking, 2002.

"Churchill was not," Hayward, Steven F. *Churchill on Leadership.* New York: Crown, 2002.

"If Winston Churchill had listened," Pitcher, Patricia. *The Drama of Leadership.* New York: John Wiley, 1997.

"His art of leadership included," Cohen, Eliot A. *Supreme Command.* New York: The Free Press, 2002.

Roberts: Roberts, Andrew. *Hitler and Churchill*. London: Weidenfeld & Nicolson, 2003.

Vaughan: Vaughan, David J. *The Pillars of Leadership*. Nashville: Cumberland House, 2000.

"Fight them with beer bottles," Eisenhower, Dwight D. *General Eisenhower on the Military Churchill*. New York: Norton, 1970.

"Several times," Giuliani, Rudolf. *Leadership*. New York: Miramax Books, 2002.

"For a while," Giuliani, Rudolf. *Leadership*. New York: Miramax Books, 2002.

Meacham: Meacham, Jon. *Franklin and Winston*. New York: Random House, 2004.

"To these men," Eisenhower, Dwight D. *General Eisenhower on the Military Churchill*. New York: Norton, 1970.

## George S. Patton and Dwight D. Eisenhower

"Leadership is the thing," Ridge, Warren, J. *Follow Me!* New York: AMACOM, 1989.

"Encountering a soldier," Perret, Geoffrey. *Eisenhower*. New York: Random House, 1999.

"He drove across a pontoon bridge," Blumenson, Martin. *Patton: The Man Behind the Legend, 1885–1945*. New York: Morrow, 1985.

Puryear: Puryear, Jr., Edgar F. *American Generalship*. Novato, CA: Presidio, 2000.

"In any war," Axelrod, Alan. *Patton on Leadership: Strategic Lessons for Corporate Warfare*. Paramus, N.J.: Prentice Hall Press, 1999.

"Your primary mission," *On War and Leadership*. Edited by Owen Connelly. Princeton, N.J.: Princeton University Press, 2002.

"You young lieutenants," Axelrod, Alan. *Patton on Leadership*. Paramus, N.J.: Prentice Hall Press, 1999.

"Commanders must remember," Axelrod, Alan. *Patton on Leadership*. Paramus, N.J.: Prentice Hall Press, 1999.

"No one who experienced," D'Este, Carlo. *Patton: A Genius for War*. New York, HarperCollins, 1995.

"The techniques of command," Bradley, Omar N. *A Soldier's Story*. New York: Modern Library, 1999.

"I am sure," *War Letters*. Edited by Andrew Carroll. New York: Scribner, 2001.

"Patton bragged," Ambrose, Stephen. *The Supreme Commander*. New York: Doubleday, 1970.

"Without a solid record," Axelrod, Alan. *Patton on Leadership*. Paramus, N.J.: Prentice Hall Press, 1999.

"In the end," O'Toole, James. *Leadership A to Z*. San Francisco: Jossey-Bass, 1999.

"The way I see it," Perret, Geoffrey. *Eisenhower*. New York: Random House, 1999.

"I would rather be commanded," *Eisenhower: A Soldier's Life*. D'Este, Carlo. New York: Henry Holt, 2002.

"There was Eisenhower," Perret, Geoffrey. *Eisenhower*. New York: Random House, 1999.

Ambrose: Ambrose, Stephen E. *Eisenhower: Volume Two: The President*. New York: Simon & Schuster, 1984.

"In War and Peace," Ambrose, Stephen E. *Eisenhower: Volume Two: The President*. New York: Simon & Schuster, 1984.

"Better suited," Greenstein, Fred I. *The Presidential Difference*. Princeton, N.J.: Princeton University Press, 2004.

Survey figures, Pfiffner, James P. "Ranking the presidents: continuity and volatility."

"White House Studies," Winter 2003.

"He showed," Greenstein, Fred I. *The Hidden-Hand Presidency*. Baltimore: Johns Hopkins University Press, 1994.

### Vince Lombardi

Kramer: Kramer, Jerry. *Instant Replay*. Edited by Dick Schaap. New York: World Publishing, 1968.

Starr: *Lombardi: Winning is the Only Thing*. Edited by Jerry Kramer. New York: World Publishing, 1970.

"A leader must identify himself," Maraniss, David. *When Pride Still Mattered*. New York: Simon & Schuster, 1999.

"The new leadership," Maraniss, David. *When Pride Still Mattered*. New York: Simon & Schuster, 1999.

"You as a leader," Lombardi, Jr., Vince, *What it Takes to Be #1*. New York: McGraw-Hill 2001.

Wooden, John. *Wooden*. New York: McGraw-Hill, 1997.

"Rip your butt out," Maraniss, David. *When Pride Still Mattered*. New York: Simon & Schuster, 1999.

Phillips: Phillips, Donald T. *Run to Win*. New York: St. Martin's Press, 2001.

Kramer: Kramer, Jerry. *Instant Replay*. Edited by Dick Schaap. New York: World Publishing, 1968.

Jordan: sportingnews.com

"He later explained," Maraniss, David. *When Pride Still Mattered*. New York: Simon & Schuster, 1999.

Tunnell: *Lombardi: Winning is the Only Thing*. Edited by Jerry Kramer. New York: World Publishing, 1970.

Promoto: Dowling, Tom. *Coach: A Season with Lombardi*. New York: W.W. Norton, 1970.

"But in the end," Dowling, Tom. *Coach: A Season with Lombardi*. New York: W.W. Norton, 1970.

Wooden: www.hoophall.com/halloffamers/Wooden.htm.

Starr: *Lombardi*. Edited by Jerry Kramer. New York: World Publishing, 1970.

Hornung: *Lombardi*. Edited by Jerry Kramer. New York: World Publishing, 1970.

Phillips: Phillips, Donald T. *Run to Win*. New York: St. Martin's Press, 2001.

"MAX!" *Instant Replay*. Edited by Dick Schaap. New York: World Publishing, 1968.

## Mohandas K. Gandhi and Dr. Martin Luther King, Jr.

"The nonviolence," *The Essential Gandhi*. Edited by Louis Fischer. New York: Vintage Books, 2002.

King: *The Autobiography of Martin Luther King, Jr.* Edited by Clayborne Carson. New York: Warner Books, 1998.

Burns: Burns, James McGregor. *Transforming Leadership*. New York: Atlantic Monthly Press, 2003.

"In short, therefore," Payne, Robert. *The Life and Death of Mahatma Gandhi*. New York: Dutton, 1969.

"For twenty-four days," Burns, James McGregor. *Transforming Leadership*. New York: Atlantic Monthly Press, 2003.

"In the Punjab," Davis, Steven I. *Leadership in Conflict*. New York: St. Martin's Press, 1996.

Einstein: Chandra, Yogesh. *Gandhi: A Life*. New York: John Wiley, 1997.

"He had conquered," Payne, Robert. *The Life and Death of Mahatma Gandhi*. New York: Dutton, 1969.

"Idealists would say," Branch, Taylor. *Parting the Waters*. New York: Simon & Schuster, 1988.

"The giant cloud of noise," Branch, Taylor. *Parting the Waters*. New York: Simon & Schuster, 1988.

"The intellectual and moral satisfaction," King: *The Autobiography of Martin Luther King, Jr.* Edited by Clayborne Carson. New York: Warner Books, 1998.

"After his immersion," Nojeim, Michael J. *Gandhi and King: The Power of Nonviolent Resistance*. Westport, CT: Praeger, 2004.

"When I speak of love," Dr. Martin Luther King, Jr. Nobel Lecture, December 11, 1964.

"Critics would point out," Branch, Taylor. *Parting the Waters*. New York: Simon & Schuster, 1988.

"It was twenty years ago," Hansen, Drew A. *The Dream*. New York: Ecco Press, 2003.

Peters: Peters, Tom. *The Circle of Innovation*. New York: Alfred A. Knopf, 1997.

## Women CEOs

Jung: Setoodeh, Ramin. "Calling Avon's Lady." *Newsweek*, December 27–January 3, 2005.

"But experts Judy Rosener," Jones, Del. "Female CEOs struggle in '04." *USA Today*, January 4, 2005.

"When the lunch ended," Burrows, Peter. *Backfire*. New York: Wiley, 2003.

"Her supporters," Burrows, Peter. *Backfire*. New York: Wiley, 2003.

"The comfortable literary," Williams, Mary Elizabeth. "She's All Chat," *Salon.com*, May 4, 1999.

"In this era," Markoff, John. "When plus adds up to Minus." *New York Times*, February 10, 2005.

"The next five years," Setoodeh, Ramin. "Calling Avon's Lady." *Newsweek*, December 27–January 3, 2005.

"Instead of treating women," Klenke, Karin. *Women and Leadership*. New York: Springer Publishing Company, 1996.

1776–1976 figures. Cantor, Dorothy W., and Toni Bernay. *Women in Power*. Boston: Houghton Mifflin, 1992.

2005 figures: www.cawp.rutgers .edu/Facts/Officeholders/ cawpfs.html.

"Stereotypic notions," Freeman, Sue J. M. "Women at the Top," in *Women on Power*: *Leadership Redefined*. Edited by Sue J.M. Freeman, Susan C. Bourque, and Christine M. Shelton. Boston: Northeastern University Press, 2001.

Wilson: Wilson, Marie C. *Closing the Gap*. Marie C. Wilson, New York: Viking, 2004.

"A Japanese-American lawyer," Blank, Renee, and Sandra Slipp. *Voices of Diversity*. New York: AMACOM, 1994.

"A Japanese-American biochemist," Blank, Renee, and Sandra Slipp. *Voices of Diversity*. New York: AMACOM, 1994.

"Many black managers," Blank, Renee, and Sandra Slipp. *Voices of Diversity*. New York: AMACOM, 1994.

African-American CEOs: fortune.com/fortune/ blackpower.

"There are five," Cantor, Dorothy W., and Toni Bernay. *Women in Power*. Boston: Houghton Mifflin, 1992.

"They are better communicators," Wilson, Marie C. *Closing the Gap*. New York: Viking, 2004.

"It's not enough," thewhitehouseproject.org.

"Estée Lauder figures," Evans, Evans, Harold. *They Made America*. New York: Little, Brown, 2004.

"Carly gambled," Deutsch, Claudia H. "Carl Fiorina? He'd Probably be Out of Work, Too." *New York Times*, February 13, 2005.

"Women still have," Deutsch, Claudia H. "Carl Fiorina? He'd Probably be Out of Work, Too." *New York Times*, February 13, 2005.

## The Soldiers of Omaha Beach

"Two kinds of people," Balkoski, Joseph. *Beyond the Beachhead*. Mechanicsburg, PA: Stackpole Books, 1998.

Bingham: McManus, John C. *The Americans at D-Day*. New York: Forge, 2004.

Otlowski: Miller, Russell. *Nothing Less Than Victory*. New York: William Morrow, 1993.

"Colonel Canham came by," Ambrose, Stephen E. *D-Day: June 6: The Climactic Battle of World War II*. New York: Simon & Schuster, 1994.

"On the beach," McManus, John C. *The Americans at D-Day*. New York: Forge, 2004.

"It was an ultimate test," Ambrose, Stephen E. *D-Day*. New York: Simon & Schuster, 1994.

"Let's go," Ambrose, Stephen E. *D-Day: June 6, 1944*. New York: Simon & Schuster, 1994.

"He seemed to have no fear," Balkoski, Joseph. *Omaha Beach*. Mechanicsburg, PA: Stackpole Books, 2004.

"Cota circulated," McManus, John C. *The Americans at D-Day*. New York: Forge, 2004.

"Cota realized," Balkoski, Joseph. *Beyond the Beachhead*. Mechanicsburg, PA: Stackpole Books, 1998.

"He didn't know," Neillands, Robin, and Roderick de Normann, *D-Day*. Osceola, WI: Motorbooks, 1994.

"Soldiers from different companies," Lewis, Adrian R. *Omaha Beach*. Chapel Hill: University of North Carolina Press, 2001.

"While the accolades," Townsend, Patrick L., and Joan E. Gebhardt. *Five-Star Leadership*. New York: John Wiley, 1997.

## Rosa Parks

King: Brinkley, Douglas. *Rosa Parks*. New York: Viking, 2000.

"Represented one of the isolated high blips," Branch, Taylor. *Parting the Waters*. New York: Simon & Schuster, 1988.

"The next ten seconds," Brinkley, Douglas. *Rosa Parks*. New York: Viking, 2000.

"Are you going," Brinkley, Douglas. *Rosa Parks*. New York: Viking, 2000.

"Raymond Parks," Branch, Taylor. *Parting the Waters*. New York: Simon & Schuster, 1988.

"The perfect client," Collins, Gail. *America's Women*. New York: William Morrow, 2003.

"Many years later," Collins, Gail. *America's Women*. New York: William Morrow, 2003.

"Because of the role of women," Betty Williams, Nobel Lecture, December 11, 1977.

"I obviously had to think," Klenke, Karin. *Women and*

*Leadership*. New York: Springer Publishing Company, 1996.

"The quest for democracy," Aung San Suu Kyi, Nobel lecture, December 10, 1991.

"Landmines have been used," Jody Williams, Nobel lecture, December 10, 1997.

Parks, Rosa. *Rosa Parks: My Story*. New York: The Dial Press, 1992.

# NAME INDEX

⊚ ⊚ ⊚

**Adams, Abigail,** 23
Adler, Alfred, 180–81
Alexander the Great, 2, 17, 44, 80
Allen, Paul, 34, 189
Ambrose, Stephen, 22–23, 124, 139, 221, 223, 262, 263, 264–65
Amery, Leo, 93–94
Anderson, Jon Lee, 163
Aris, Alexander, 277
Ash, Mary Kay, 100, 104
Attila the Hun, 2, 191, 199
Attlee, Clement, 212
Aung San Suu Kyi, 276–77
Austin, Nancy, 46
Axelrod, Alan, 221

**Badaracco, Joseph,** 182
Barnes, Brenda, 249
Beamer, Todd, 27
Belasco, James A., 79
Belichik, Bill, 132
Bennis, Warren, 3, 11, 15, 17, 18, 23, 31, 34, 49, 50–53, 61, 64, 70, 74, 76, 88
Bernay, Toni, 256–57
Bezos, Jeff, 100
Biederman, Patricia Ward, 50–53
Bingham, Sidney, 261
Bird, Larry, 137
Blaik, Red, 233
Blake, James, 273–74
Blanchard, Ken, 32, 35, 131
Blank, Renee, 255–56
Blank, Warren, 43–44, 45
Blumenson, Martin, 218
Bogle, John, 100
Bonaparte, Napoleon, 50, 86, 111, 161
Bossidy, Larry, 2, 91–92, 98

Bradley, Omar, 120, 217–18, 220, 222
Branch, Taylor, 241, 242, 243, 244–45, 272, 275
Branham, Felix, 264
Branson, Richard, 100
Brinkley, Douglas, 271, 273–74
Briscoe, Marlin, 141
Brokaw, Tom, 127
Brower, Charles F., IV, 124–25
Bryman, Alan, 104
Buckingham, Marcus, 62
Buffett, Warren, 100
Bunting, Josiah, 121
Burke, James, 100
Burke, Lance B., 44
Burnett, Tom, 27
Burns, James McGregor, 2, 17–19, 44, 52–53, 145, 184, 238
Burnside, Ambrose, 152
Burrows, Peter, 40–41, 251, 252
Bush, George H.W., 127
Butler, George Lee, 196

**Caesar, Julius,** 13
Cairo, Peter C., 197
Calloway, Wayne, 55, 88–89
Canham, Colonel, 263–64
Cannadine, David, 208–9
Cannon, Jeff and Jon, 126
Cannon, Lou, 149, 155–56
Cantor, Dorothy, 256–57
Capodagli, Bill, 71
Carlyle, Thomas, 11–12
Carnegie, Andrew, 12, 44
Caro, Robert, 154–55
Carr, Harry, 251
Carrison, Dan, 116, 117
Carter, Jimmy, 89, 92, 146–47

Cartwright, Bill, 136
Carville, James, 51
Castro, Fidel, 163
Castro, Dr. Kenneth, 76
Chaleff, Ira, 50
Chambers, John, 47, 106–7
Charan, Ram, 68–69
Chastain, Brandi, 135
Chenault, Ken, 256
Churchill, Winston, 2, 15, 22, 86, 90,
    93–94, 152–53, 179, 205–14,
    218
Clark, Kenneth E., 45, 78
Clark, Mark, 120
Clark, Miriam B., 45, 78
Clausewitz, Karl Von, 111
Cleveland, Harlan, 75
Clinton, Bill, 149–50, 151–52, 154,
    155, 196
Cohen, Eliot A., 152–53, 210
Cohen, William A., 118
Collins, Gail, 275–76
Collins, Jim, 103
Conger, Jay, 64, 69
Cook, Blanche Wiesen, 184–85
Corcoran, Mickey, 230
Corrigan, Mairéad, 276
Cortés, Luis A., Jr., 175
Cota, Norman, 265–67
Cray, Ed, 120
Crosby, Philip B., 32, 57, 73
Crozier, Percy, 198, 200
Csikszentmihalyi, Mihaly, 52

Dalai Lama, 14th, 174, 176, 177
Dallek, Robert, 154
Dana, Charles, 153
Dardis, Gregory J., 124–25
Darwin, Charles, 186–87
Davis, Steven I., 163
de Gaulle, Charles, 18
De Pree, Max, 33, 35, 52, 67
Dell, Michael, 34, 100
Deluca, Joel, 79–80
Dilenschneider, Robert L., 32, 67

Disney, Roy, 40
Disney, Walt, 40, 51–52
DiStephano, Anthony J., 266
Doby, Larry, 141–42
Donald, David Herbert, 150
Donnithorne, Larry R., 90
Dotlich, Davis L., 197
Dowling, Tom, 232
Drotter, Stephen, 68–69
Drucker, Peter, 78, 100, 156
Dunn, Susan, 184

Eaker, Ira, 120
Eaton, Bob, 106
Eckert, Robert E., 102
Edison, Thomas, 67–68, 189
Edman, Irwin, 13
Einstein, Albert, 179–81, 181–83, 240
Eisenhower, Dwight D., 19, 120, 137,
    139, 153, 209, 214, 215
Ellington, Duke, 19
Emerson, Ralph Waldo, 202
Engels, Friedrich, 160
Evans, Harold, 189–90
Evans, Oliver, 179, 189
Exley, Charles, 61

Favre, Brett, 135–36
Fawcett, Joy, 135
Feiner, Michael, 86, 87
Fiorina, Carleton, 249, 250, 251–53,
    258–59
Fitzpatrick, Sheila, 161
Folkman, Joseph, 113
Ford, Gerald, 89
Foudy, Julie, 135
Fox, Chad, 134
Frady, Marshall, 19
Franks, Tommy, 124
Freedman, David H., 113–15
Freeman, Sue J.M., 255
Freud, Sigmund, 180–81
Friedan, Betty, 33, 185–86
Fromm, Erich, 159
Fuller, Marce, 250

Gandhi, Mohandas K., 15, 19, 30, 36, 86, 91, 110, 164, 165, 183, 237–41, 243–44, 246
Gardner, Howard, 36, 179–80, 183
Gardner, John, 11, 150
Gates, Bill, 34, 100, 189–90
Gayle, Dr. Helene, 76
Gebhardt, Joan, 268
George, William, 100
Gerkovich, Paulette, 250–51
Gerstner, Louis V., Jr., 2, 40–41, 98–99, 100
Gilliam, Joe, 141
Giuliani, Rudolph, 2, 28, 212–13
Gladwell, Malcolm, 15–16
Gleick, James, 187–88
Goldhagen, Daniel, 195
Goldsmith, Joan, 70, 88
Goleman, Daniel, 65, 87
Goodyear, Charles, 189
Gorbachev, Mikhail, 36
Grant, Ulysses S., 91, 121
Greenberg, Hank, 142
Greenleaf, Robert K., 171–72
Greenspan, Alan, 100
Greenstein, Fred, 223–24, 225
Grove, Andrew, 2, 70–71, 96, 100
Guevara, Che, 163
Gutierrez, Gustavo, 169–70

Haig, Sir Douglas, 198
Halberstam, David, 136
Hamm, Mia, 129
Hansen, Drew D., 245
Harrell, Keith, 88
Harvey-Jones, Sir John, 102
Havel, Vaclav, 246
Hawking, Stephen, 182
Hayward, Steven F., 210
Heisler, Mark, 136
Helgesen, Sally, 78
Henry V, King, 122
Hess, Rudolf, 192
Hesse, Hermann, 171–72
Hewlett, Walter, 252

Hickman, Craig R., 58, 59
Himsel, Deborrah, 199
Hitler, Adolf, 15, 50, 192–93, 195, 196, 205, 207, 210–11
Hooke, Robert, 188
Hoover, Herbert, 224
Hornung, Paul, 233
Horowitz, Daniel, 186
Howell, Mike, 141
Howell, Raymond, 265
Hudak, Mona, 107
Hybels, Bill, 175

Iacocca, Lee, 44, 100, 104, 105, 106, 201–2

Jackson, Jesse, 19
Jackson, Phil, 136
Jakes, T.D., 175
Jefferson, Thomas, 23, 49
Jenkins, Roy, 213
Jesus of Nazareth, 13, 165, 171
Jeter, Derek, 134
Joan of Arc, 13
Jobs, Steve, 44, 51, 100, 104, 189
John Paul II, Pope, 168–69
Johnson, Lyndon, 153–54, 155, 200
Johnson, Lynn, 71
Johnson, Magic, 136–37
Jones, K.C., 137
Jones, Laurie Beth, 171, 191
Jones, Reg, 108
Jordan, Henry, 231
Jordan, Michael, 133, 136–37
Jung, Andrea, 249, 250, 253–54
Jung, Carl, 180–81

Kanter, Rosabeth Moss, 107
Kaplan, Robert D., 194
Keegan, John, 122–23, 198, 209
Kelleher, Herb, 79, 98, 99, 101–2
Kellerman, Barbara, 198
Kenke, Karin, 254
Kennedy, John F., 18, 86, 90, 154

King, Martin Luther, Jr., 18, 35–36, 110, 165, 183–84, 237, 241–47, 271, 272, 275–76
Koetter, Dirk, 138
Kotter, John P., 3, 35, 58, 60
Kouzes, James M., 41, 65, 74, 85
Kramer, Jerry, 227, 228, 231
Krames, Jeffrey A., 108
Kranz, Eugene, 21–26, 29–30
Kroc, Ray, 102
Kropf, Susan, 254
Krug, Doug, 46–47
Krzyzewski, Mike, 2, 88–89, 131

LaGuardia, Fiorello, 28
Landry, Tom, 79, 228
Lao-tse, 13
Lash, Joseph, 185
Lauder, Estée, 257
Laurie, Donald L., 91–92
Lebenthal, Alexandra, 48
Lee, John C.H., 197
Lee, Robert E., 115, 121–22
Leftwich, Byron, 141
Lehockey, John, 114
Lenin, Vladimir, 160, 161
Lewis, Adrian R., 267–68
Lewis, Meriwether, 22–23, 124
Lewis, William, 265
Lincoln, Abraham, 2, 68, 103, 150–51, 153
Lombardi, Vince, 129, 227–35
Lovell, Jim, 21, 23–24
Luther, Martin, 13
Lynch, Peter, 101

Maccoby, Michael, 90
Machiavelli, Niccolo, 13, 194
Mandela, Nelson, 164–65, 246
Mao Zedong, 39, 195
Maraniss, David, 155, 228, 229, 231, 234
Marshall, George C., 120, 216, 221
Marx, Karl, 160

Matsushita, Konosuke, 70, 71
Matusak, Lorraine R., 68, 81
Maxwell, John C., 40, 66, 89–91, 91, 206
McCarthy, Joe, 224
McGee, Max, 235
McGregor, Douglas, 16–17
McManus, Erwin Raphael, 173
McNabb, Donovan, 141
McNair, Steve, 141
McNeal, Reggie, 168, 173
Meacham, Jon, 213
Miller, Arthur, 194
Mindell, Arnold, 77
Moore, Alex, 138–39
Mountbatten, Lord, 240
Muirhead, Brian, 94
Mulcahy, Anne, 250, 253
Mullins, Thornton L., 266
Mussolini, Benito, 205
Myers, John H., 66

Nanus, Burt, 3, 23, 36, 39, 64, 74, 76
Nater, Swen, 130
Nehru, Motilal, 18
Neibuhr, Reinhold, 243
Newton, Isaac, 187–88
Nichols, Brian, 173
Nixon, E.D., 275
Nixon, Richard, 89, 196, 224
Noel, James, 68–69
Nojeim, Michael J., 243–44
Northouse, Peter, 14–15, 16

Oakley, Ed, 46–47
O'Connor, Sandra Day, 148
Olivier, Richard, 92
Omohundro, Read, 126–27
O'Neill, Stanley, 256
O'Neill, Tip, 145, 148
Oppenheimer, J. Robert, 51
Otlowski, William B., 262–63
O'Toole, James, 43, 70, 97, 221
Owen, Hilarie, 74

**Parcells, Bill,** 230
Parks, Rosa, 91, 140, 237, 241–42, 271–78
Parsons, Richard, 256
Patton, George S., 2, 95, 104, 215–22, 225
Payne, Robert, 241
Perot, Ross, 90
Perret, Geoffrey, 217, 222–23
Peters, Tom, 46, 102, 104, 246
Phillips, Donald T., 231, 234
Picard, Jean-Luc (fictional character), 2
Pippen, Scottie, 136
Pitcher, Patricia, 210
Plachy, Roger J., 60
Plato, 13
Posner, Barry Z., 41, 65, 74, 85
Powell, Colin L., 19, 91, 200–201
Price, Frank, 265
Promoto, Vince, 232
Puryear, Edgar, 218

**Raelin, Joseph A.,** 78–79, 80–81
Raines, Franklin, 256
Rampersad, Arnold, 142
Reagan, Ronald, 36, 148–49, 154, 155–56
Reese, Pee Wee, 142–43
Rehm, Mike, 266
Riccucci, Norma, 76
Rickey, Branch, 141
Ridgway, Matthew, 122
Roberts, Andrew, 210–11
Roberts, Wess, 191
Robinson, David, 140
Robinson, Eddie, 140–41
Robinson, Jackie, 91, 141–43
Rockefeller, John D., 63
Rodriguez, Ivan "Pudge," 134
Rommel, Erwin, 221
Roosevelt, Eleanor, 183–85
Roosevelt, Franklin D., 15, 36–37, 39, 151, 185, 194, 205, 212

Roosevelt, Theodore, 93
Rosener, Judy, 250–51
Russell, Bill, 134–35
Russo, Patricia, 250

**Salka, John,** 28
Samaranch, Juan Antonio, 198
Sammons, Mary, 250
Sanders, J. Oswald, 172
Sandler, Marion, 250
Schama, Simon, 161
Schlesinger, Arthur, Jr., 224
Schneider, Anthony, 199
Schultz, Howard, 34
Schwab, Charles, 101
Schwarzkopf, Norman, 19, 92–93, 96, 123
Scott, Eileen, 250
Shackleton, Ernest, 2
Sharpnack, Rayona, 41
Sherman, Mike, 135–36
Shirer, William, 193
Shula, Don, 2, 32, 131, 233
Slaughter, John Robert, 263–64
Slipp, Sandra, 255–56
Smith, Ashley, 173
Smith, Dean, 2, 129, 131, 133, 139
Smith, Frederick W., 40, 101
Smith, Robert "Burr," 125
Soprano, Tony (fictional character), 2, 199
Soros, George, 90, 101
Stagg, Amos Alonzo, 230
Stalin, Joseph, 15, 195, 196, 205
Starr, Bart, 227, 234
Stayer, Ralph C., 79
Steinem, Gloria, 44
Stempel, Robert C., 105
Stevenson, Adlai, 223
Stilwell, Joe, 120
Stokesbury, James L., 121–22
Storey, John, 65–66
Sun-Tzu, 194
Surowiecki, James, 201

Taylor, Jimmy, 231
Taylor, Walter, 265
Terry, Paul, 139
Terry, Robert, 192
Thich Nhat Hanh, 176–77
Thrower, Willie, 141
Thucydides, 121
Tichy, Noel, 110
Till, Emmett, 273
Tillman, Pat, 138
Topping, Peter, 47, 95
Torre, Joe, 2, 134
Townsend, Patrick, 268
Trotman, Alex, 48
Truman, Harry, 156
Trump, Donald, 63
Tuchman, Barbara, 200
Tunnell, Emlen, 232
Turner, Ted, 95, 101
Tutu, Desmond, 165

Useem, Michael, 26, 29, 252–53

Van de Voort, Leo, 265
Van Etten, Thomas, 29
Vaughan, David J., 211
Vick, Michael, 141

Walsh, Rod, 116, 117
Walton, Sam, 98, 101

Warren, Rick, 167, 173–74, 175
Washington, George, 162–64
Weinbach, Lawrence A., 33–34
Welch, Jack, 2, 34, 38–39, 48, 59,
    62–63, 68–69, 86, 90, 97, 98, 99, 101,
    107–10
Wellington, Duke of, 122
Wellington, Sheila W., 258
Wheeler, Tom, 117–18
Williams, Betty, 276
Williams, Doug, 141
Williams, Jody, 277–78
Wills, Garry, 49–50
Wilson, Marie C., 255, 257–58
Winfrey, Oprah, 101, 253
Winters, Dick, 124–25
Winthrop, John, 148–49
Wojnarowski, Adrian, 138
Wood, Gordon S., 162, 163–64
Wooden, John, 130, 227, 230, 233
Woodward, Bob, 151–52
Woolfe, Lorin, 170
Worthy, James, 133, 136
Wozniak, Steve, 189
Wright, Jim, 245–46

Yunus, Muhammad, 101

Zand, Dale E., 48
Zenger, John, 113

# SUBJECT INDEX

◎ ◎ ◎

accountability, 88
adaptability, 48, 57, 66, 94–95, 104–9, 164–65, 212, 221–22
African American leaders, 139–43, 183–84, 237–38, 241–47, 256, 271–78
aggression, 63, 93–94, 230, 252
*Air Force Officer's Guide,* 113
ambition, 63, 155, 163
Apollo 13 mission, 21–26, 29–30
*Army Leadership* (manual), 112
arrogance, 197–98
authenticity, 88

Bible, 170–71, 174
bluffing, 210–11, 213
brainstorming, 25, 108
business leaders, 33–34, 68–69, 97–110, 201–2, 249–59

charisma, 64, 104, 106, 206
coercion, 196
commitment, 94
communication, 25, 46, 48, 67, 80, 86, 258. *See also* speeches; vision
conciliation and cooperation, 63–64, 106, 145, 148, 222–25, 254–55, 258
courage, 27–29, 93–94, 210–11, 213, 261–69, 265–68, 271–78
creative collaboration, 50–53
creativity and innovation, 19, 25–26, 51–52, 57, 101, 109, 267–68
crisis leadership, 21–30, 95, 112, 120–27, 151–53, 205–14, 215–25, 261–69

D-Day, 22, 124–25, 261–69
decisiveness, 22–23, 27, 263–69

delegation, 25, 46–48, 99, 108–9, 132
democracy, leadership and, 12, 13, 74–76, 81, 156–57, 162–64

education, leadership, 6–7, 58–59, 61–71, 73, 113–16
effectiveness, 32, 112
emotional intelligence, 87
empathy, 92, 155
empowerment, 47, 53, 76, 77–79, 232, 268
engagement, 18–19
everyday leadership, 7, 41, 64–65, 70, 73–81, 117–18, 271–78

firefighters, 27–29
followers, 6, 18–19, 43–53
   of bad leaders, 192–93, 195–96
   leaders created from, 47, 78–79, 116, 118
   religious, 170–71
   responsibilities of, 48–50, 116, 157, 180–81, 190
   responsibilities to, 44–45, 122–24, 139–43, 145–46

Great Men theory, 11–13, 44, 73–74, 86, 205

*Henry V* (Shakespeare play), 92, 213–14
hierarchical structures, 45–46, 57–58, 101–2, 111
honesty, 88
humility, 103, 162–64, 229

implementation, 37, 43
integrity, 88–89
intellectual leaders, 179–90

jobs, cutting, 109
*Journey to the East* (Hesse novel), 171–72

"Leader-Follower Paradox," 52–53,
    58–59
leaderful practice, 80–81
leaders
    bad, 4, 15, 49–50, 90, 122, 160–61,
        191–202
    demands made of, 87–88
    as followers, 50–53, 73, 75, 77, 114
    managers compared with, 55–60, 69
    qualities of, 62–65, 87–96, 162–64
    types of, 3–4
leadership. *See also specific topics*
    characteristics of, 3, 5–7, 118–22, 196–98
    leader compared with, 13, 76
    literature on, 1–3, 66
    quiet, 182
"Level 5 leaders," 103
love, 229, 230, 244
loyalty, 48–50, 57, 180–81, 190,
    192–93, 195, 229

managers, leaders compared with,
    55–60, 69
manifestoes, 39, 160–61
Marines, U.S., 91, 113–16
military leaders, 22, 111–27, 193, 198,
    200–201, 215–25, 261–69
    developing, 59, 61, 68, 268
    followers and, 45–46
    sports and, 137–39
    vision and, 34
mistakes, making, 67–68
moral components to leadership, 49–50,
    91, 191–96, 221–22, 224, 238–40,
    243–44, 246–47, 276–78
motivational leaders, 69, 85, 131–34,
    151, 228–30, 232, 233, 242–43

narcissism, 90
New England Patriots, 35, 132
Nuremberg trials, 50, 193, 195

optimism, 29, 62, 64–65

partners, 40
passion, 64, 93, 220, 234–35
perseverance, 162, 206, 208–9
persuasiveness, 155–56
political leaders, 145–57, 205–14,
    222–25, 254
political savvy, 79–80
preparedness, 131, 233
presence, 92–93
Promise Keepers, 172

realism, 91–92
relationship building, 63–64, 67, 76,
    86–87, 192
revolutionary leaders, 159–65, 237–47
role model, leader as, 94
ruthlessness, 63, 152–53

*Satyagraha* concept, 238
self-confidence, 62–63, 70, 96, 108
self-criticism, 211
September 11 terrorist attacks, 27–28,
    30
servant-leadership, 171–73
Sharia law, 169
showmanship. *See* theatrical gestures and
    symbols
*Snow White and the Seven Dwarves*
    (film), 51–52
speeches, pep talks, and oratory, 25,
    35–39, 63, 69, 92, 148–52, 206,
    207–10, 211, 229–30, 232, 242–43,
    244–45
spiritual leaders, 167–77, 237–47
sports leaders, 35, 129–43, 227–35
stereotypes and leadership, 255–59
styles of leadership, 7, 39–40, 45–46,
    85–96, 120–22, 215–25, 228–31,
    251–59

teamwork, 50–53, 114, 129, 132,
    135–37

theatrical gestures and symbols, 36, 101, 102, 104, 142–43, 218–19, 221, 238, 240, 241–42, 271–78

theories of leadership, 11–19, 52–53, 55–60, 79–81, 103, 145–46, 171–73, 254–55

timidity, 93

transactional leadership, 18, 145–48, 192

transformational leadership, 18–19, 145–46, 177, 183–85, 238–47, 271–78

trust, 25, 76, 88, 89–91, 96, 112, 122, 125–27, 156, 219–20

visibility and leading by example, 94, 98–99, 102, 104, 112, 122–27, 129–30, 134–37, 142–43, 162–65, 219–21, 231, 239–41, 243, 258–59, 263–68, 271–78

vision, 6, 31–41, 69, 85
    communicating, 35–39, 51, 59, 146, 148–52, 159–61, 206, 209, 238–39, 244–45
    forms of, 32–35
    of intellectual leaders, 180–90
    reinforcing, 39–40, 109–10
    results and, 40–41, 51–52, 112, 146–47, 160–61, 165, 228, 246

women as leaders, 33, 76, 183–86, 249–59, 271–78

# ACKNOWLEDGMENTS

◎ ◎ ◎

*Sheryl Stebbins ably leads her talented team at Random House. My thanks go to Sheryl and Jena Pincott, Laura Neilson, Beth Levy, Nora Rosansky, Tina Malaney, and Rose White. Jena cooked up the Mentor series in the first place, and I'm happy she did.*

*Again, I am grateful to my friends Bud Kliment, Adolfo Profumo, and Diane Arne for their help.*

*The staffs of the New York Public Library's Humanities and Social Sciences Library; the Science, Industry and Business Library; and the Mid-Manhattan and Morningside Heights branches were very helpful, as was everyone at the New York Society Library.*

*Kara Welsh gave me a lot of ideas and boundless encouragement. Thank you.*

*This book is for Sam, Lindsay, Madeline, Miranda, Peter, Cullen, Ava, and the next generations of leaders.*